THEOLOGY AND FORM

NICHOLAS DENYSENKO

THEOLOGY AND FORM

CONTEMPORARY ORTHODOX ARCHITECTURE IN AMERICA

UNIVERSITY OF NOTRE DAME PRESS
NOTRE DAME, INDIANA

University of Notre Dame Press
Notre Dame, Indiana 46556
undpress.nd.edu

Copyright © 2017 by the University of Notre Dame

Published in the United States of America

Library of Congress Cataloging-in-Publication Data
Names: Denysenko, Nicholas E., author.
Title: Theology and form : contemporary Orthodox architecture in America /
    Nicholas Denysenko.
Description: Notre Dame : University of Notre Dame Press, 2017. |
    Includes bibliographical references and index.
Identifiers: LCCN 2016053422 (print) | LCCN 2017000898 (ebook) |
    ISBN 9780268100124 (hardcover : alk. paper) | ISBN 0268100128
    (hardcover : alk. paper) | ISBN 9780268100148 (pdf) |
    ISBN 9780268100155 (epub)
Subjects: LCSH: Orthodox Eastern church buildings —
    United States — History — 20th century. | Architecture and society —
    United States — History — 20th century. | Church architecture —
    United States — History — 20th century. | Liturgy and architecture —
    United States — History — 20th century.
Classification: LCC NA5212 .D46 2017 (print) | LCC NA5212 (ebook) |
    DDC 246/.950973 — dc23
LC record available at https://lccn.loc.gov/2016053422

∞ *This paper meets the requirements of ANSI/NISO Z39.48-1992
(Permanence of Paper).*

To Greg Denysenko

My big brother who understands
my sense of awe and wonder

CONTENTS

LIST OF TABLES AND FIGURES

TABLES

FIGURES

ACKNOWLEDGMENTS

This project began in 2011 and I am grateful for the feedback I received from participants at the Eastern Orthodox Studies and Space, Place, and Religious Meaning groups of the American Academy of Religion, the Environment and Art seminar of the North American Academy of Religion, and colleagues at Loyola Marymount University. Special thanks to the following friends and colleagues who have vetted chapter drafts and offered valuable feedback throughout the writing and editing process: Jeanne Kilde, Richard Vosko, Adam DeVille, David Fagerberg, Dorian Llywelyn, SJ, Father Oliver Herbel, Deacon Andrei Psarev, Sister Vassa Larin, Father Michael Plekon, and Kevin Seasoltz, OSB, of blessed memory. I am particularly grateful to Gil Klein, my colleague in Theological Studies at Loyola Marymount University, who engaged me in several conversations and offered feedback and encouragement as I wrestled with the project. The book would have been impossible without the enthusiastic cooperation of numerous representatives of the parishes and communities I profiled in this study. Warm and hearty thanks to Maya Gregoret and Wanda Bahmet of St. Katherine Ukrainian Orthodox Church, along with Oleh Gregoret of blessed memory; Wayne Hajos, Susan Petry, Anastasia Borichevsky, and Father Constantine White at St. Matthew Orthodox Church, along with Charles Alexander at Broken Boxes; Father Peter Perekrestov, Vladimir Krassovsky, and Helen Sinelnikoff-Nowak of Holy Virgin Cathedral; Father Angelo Artemis of Annunciation Greek Orthodox Church; Paul Meyendorff, Father Alexander Rentel, Father John Erickson (emeritus), and Matthew Garklavs of St. Vladimir's Seminary, along with Father Alexis Vinogradov of St. Gregory the Theologian Orthodox Church in Wappingers Falls, New York; the monks and nuns of New Skete Monastery, who graciously hosted me for a four-hour discussion on various topics after Vespers on June 14, 2014, especially Brother Stavros Winner; and Father John Tomasi of Joy of All Who Sorrow Orthodox Church (JOY) mission in Culver City. Everyone mentioned here represents a living Orthodox community in America, and I am immensely grateful for the hospitality with which I have been received during every visit and interview. As always, special thanks to Tresja and Sophia for enduring the hundreds of long hours I devoted to this project.

INTRODUCTION

Most books about architecture are written by architectural historians or practicing architects. In this book, the reader will encounter references to architectural history, including classical works by Cyril Mango and Thomas Mathews, along with new scholarship by Vasileios Marinis and Nicholas Patricios.[1] The reader should note that this book will not be following the pattern established by these luminaries, as I am neither an architect nor an architectural historian. Because I am a student and scholar of liturgical studies and sacramental theology with a passion for ecclesiology, the objectives of my book do not follow the traditional patterns of architectural history.

I begin with a few experiences that motivated and inspired this study. As a child and teenager, I attended Saints Volodymyr and Ol'ha Orthodox parish in St. Paul, Minnesota, where my grandfather was the pastor. Composed largely of post–World War II immigrants from Ukraine, the parish could not afford a new structure and gathered in a historic building that had functioned as a theater and church over the course of its long history. The worship space in the building was vast and had an impressive acoustical delay, which embellished the strong immigrant voices that sang the responses to the liturgy. Saints Volodymyr and Ol'ha was one of three Ukrainian Orthodox parishes in the larger Twin Cities area, and the three parishes began the process of negotiating a union to strengthen the community and stem the imminent attrition threatening its continuing existence. The union negotiations failed, but the parish surged forward and decided to build a new structure in Arden Hills, Minnesota, renamed St. Katherine Ukrainian Orthodox Church. After several years of planning and deliberation, the new church was finally built in 1997. I was present and participated by directing the choir for the consecration of the temple.

I experienced a type of déjà vu in 2008. I began to serve as the deacon at St. Matthew Orthodox Church in Columbia, Maryland, in 2005. At the time, the parish was renting space in a community hall in Columbia, as it had for about twenty years. In 2006, the community began to construct the church, which was finally ready for occupancy in 2008. I was present for the consecration of this church just as I had been in Arden Hills in 1997, this time assisting as a deacon.

The point of this introduction is neither to set the stage for hagiographical narratives of two distinct parish communities in America nor to publicly disclose insider stories. Rather, the objective is to provide insight into my thought process on the contemporary meaning of architecture. My interaction with these new buildings was never limited to the experience of the liturgy on the interior. In fact, growing up, I spent much more time attending Ukrainian school on Saturdays and community performances, eating meals, and playing in the yard of the property than I did immersed in liturgy. Liturgy was one of many activities in which members of Saints Volodymyr and Ol'ha parish participated. When the community moved into the new facilities in Arden Hills, the arrangement of its buildings represented the realities of community activities. The parish hall is much larger than the church, and the church and hall are connected by a museum containing community artifacts and relics that communicate the historical narrative of people in the parish. The parish's new facilities granted the people the freedom and flexibility needed to engage all of their preferred activities. The architectural arrangement communicated the primary aspects of community identity and memory that the people had known all along, and the arrangement of the buildings on the property was essentially an honest expression of reality: liturgy is an important part of community life, but it is not everything.

The experience at St. Matthew was much different and, having completed my studies in liturgy and sacramental theology at The Catholic University of America in 2008, I was in a better position to reflect on my parish experience. The design and decoration of the new building was unlike anything I had seen before. The church's exterior was somewhat banal, and I learned later that this was one of the conditions of the local municipality, which placed restrictions on the exterior religious expression of buildings. In the Orthodox parishes I had visited, I noted familiar patterns: a nave, usually with seating for the assembly and some kind of iconography adorning the walls and the ceiling, often in a dome; an iconostasis with royal doors that separated the sanctuary from the nave; a place for the choir and a narthex that functioned as the entrance into the church where some liturgical offices were sung (such as betrothals and portions of Baptism). Each Orthodox parish had variations of these architectural components, but each one conformed to a general pattern. The most innovative designs I had encountered were Three Hierarchs Chapel of St. Vladimir's Seminary in Crestwood, New York, where I studied from 1997 to 2000, unique mostly because of its large skeuophylakion, which created a stronger sense of the transfer of gifts during the course of the Divine Liturgy; and St. Gregory the Theologian Orthodox Church in Wappingers Falls, New York, where I served as an intern from 1998 to 2000 during my seminary studies. The design of this church was similar to that of Three Hierarchs Chapel, which makes sense since Father Alexis Vinogradov designed both structures. St. Gregory's church has a low iconostasis that provides complete visual access to the sanctuary.

St. Matthew was unique for a number of reasons. First, the ceiling is an octagon, which defines the entire interior. The octagon tapers upward in a parabola toward a dome, so the shape is visible to all. Second, the iconostasis is very simple, with six life-sized icons but no royal or deacons' doors. Third, the nave is vast, promoting both ample visual access and a space large enough to hold many people. The community's move into the new church edifice inspired awe, wonder, joy, and the challenge of keeping up with financial commitments. The experience of worshiping in a rented space for approximately twenty years, which entailed a grueling team effort of setting up the space each week, contributed to an ethos of community participation. It did not take long for me to recognize the significant role played by laity at St. Matthew. In the final years leading up to the completion of the new edifice, a team of laypeople collaboratively painted the first icons for the new church, including the Pantocrator in the dome and the Mother of God at the high place of the sanctuary. A completely remote aspect of parish life confirmed the laity's role in building the church once the community settled into the new building.

Once the realization of sustained financial commitment became acute, the community turned to an immigrant model of fundraising by hosting a fall festival featuring ethnic foods, music, and dancing for the community. Such festivals are familiar to Orthodox communities in America, but its occurrence was somewhat ironic for a community like St. Matthew, which de-emphasized internal parish ethnicity in favor of an ecclesiology of the royal priesthood of the laity. The fall festival brought the people together in a new way, and since such local events often rely on a small handful of volunteers who do the majority of the work, the broad collaboration and contribution of laypeople at St. Matthew was confirmed by their work at the festival. One's experience of the architectural layout was shaped by the pervasive dynamic of an ecclesiology of the laity's priesthood. In reflecting on my experience at St. Matthew, it was clear to me that the horizontally oriented parish ecclesiology ultimately shaped and formed the new church's architectural design.

These two experiences challenged me when I began reading historical monographs on the theological contours of Byzantine architecture. The leading scholars of this field have richly informed academics and pastors on the dynamic symbiosis of liturgy and architecture. For the history of the Byzantine rite, this symbiosis emerges with the diary of Egeria and her descriptions of hagiopolite liturgy in the late fourth century.[2] The study of the liturgical and architectural programs of Jerusalem through the lens of the fifth-century Armenian and fifth- to eighth-century Georgian lectionaries exposes a rich liturgical life in a holy city.[3] John Baldovin's classical study of urban stational liturgy, featuring Rome, Jerusalem, and Constantinople, demonstrates the diffusion of the liturgy/architecture symbiosis in Western and Eastern urban centers of late antiquity and the early medieval period.[4] The works of Thomas Mathews, Robert Taft, and Cyril Mango trace the further development of liturgy's shaping of architecture in Byzantium. Mathews's work on Hagia Sophia and other Constantinopolitan churches is particularly influential as he meticulously pairs the shape of the buildings with the community's liturgy celebrated in them.[5] Hans-Joachim Schulz's discussion of the iconography's contribution to a paradigm shift in church architecture completes the initial picture, as the basic ritual and interior shape of the typical Byzantine church changes little after the fall of Constantinople in 1453 CE, local variants notwithstanding.[6]

To summarize: my reading of the liturgical sources and analyses of the architectural evidence demonstrated a powerful symbiosis between liturgy and architecture in Byzantine Church history. There was never a question of variation within this tradition, which I gleaned from my reading of Mango and his description of various church edifices throughout the Byzantine Commonwealth. In the scholarly community, however, the discussion focused on the relationship between liturgy and architecture, which conveniently suggested that architectural form follows liturgical function. My consultation of contemporary Catholic scholarship on liturgy and architecture yielded a similar result. Of course, such a conclusion makes sense because liturgy is what the community does when it gathers in its designated space. In my own limited experience, I learned that the contemporary descendants of the Byzantine rite modified the interior space of buildings they could afford to accommodate the liturgy they had inherited. Immigrants happily decorated the walls with icons and constructed iconostases of varying sizes and styles. During my tenure as music director at St. Mary Orthodox Cathedral in Minneapolis, we occasionally celebrated the Divine Liturgy at a local nursing home. On those monthly trips, we would bring icons of the Mother of God and Jesus and place them on music stands for a makeshift iconostasis, using a small, auxiliary table for the prothesis rite, separate and distinct from the altar. I recall a similar pattern of set-up and take-down at Christ the Savior Orthodox mission in Anoka, Minnesota.

After the monastic hegemony became complete in Byzantine liturgical history, the liturgy was somewhat reduced in its movements, with the monastery church becoming the primary model instead of the cathedral with its ambo, courtyard, and baptistery.[7] The basic tripartite church structure of narthex, nave, and sanctuary, with an iconostasis dividing the nave from the sanctuary, remained reasonably constant, and came to America with the missionaries and immigrants beginning in the late eighteenth century. So the architectural heritage of American Orthodoxy retained some semblance of symbiosis with the liturgy, but this dynamic was weakened and continued to exist largely on the account of the need to have a basic space to celebrate the liturgy in accordance with its requirements.

This basic liturgy/architecture symbiosis existed in the churches I have described here, but as the reader can see from my brief descriptions, there were other factors contributing to the architectural design besides liturgy. In the case of St. Katherine, the community built a church closely resembling the Sophia cathedral in Kyiv, a manner of expressing community identity on the exterior. Furthermore, the parish constructed a cultural center and museum that is much larger than the church to accommodate its many non-liturgical activities and rituals. St. Katherine was an exception to the axiom of form following function since the architectural program expressed multiple community identities and priorities besides the liturgy. St. Matthew's architectural design was inspired by the community's dedication to promoting a strong lay ecclesiology while providing evangelistic outreach to the local community distinct from other Orthodox communities in the area. St. Matthew's priorities were likewise inscribed on its architectural design, and while its blueprint and rationale differs significantly from that of St. Katherine, St. Matthew is also an exception to the form/function axiom.

These initial observations formed by my limited experience in the two parish communities motivated me to study the issue further. I began with a series of questions: What is the status of the architectural form/function axiom in American Orthodox structures? If parish communities inscribe their values on their architectural programs, what are those values and how do they blend with the liturgical elements of ecclesial architecture? Given the increasing theological and ecclesiological plurality in American Orthodoxy, is it possible to identify a trend in American Orthodox architecture, and if so, should one promote it? These are the questions I intend to pursue in this study.

This study profiles seven contemporary Eastern Orthodox communities in the United States, and analyzes how their space and architecture shapes their liturgical celebrations and ecclesial identities. It begins with an introductory presentation on the historical development of Orthodox architecture, primarily focusing on the post-iconoclastic synthesis emerging in the Middle Byzantine period. I discuss the reciprocal relationship between architecture and liturgy by addressing topics such as stational liturgy, the mobility of the assembly, the relationship between celebrants and assembly, placement of singers, and festal processions (such as Holy Week and Pascha) representative of the Orthodox liturgy. A theological synthesis of the dialogical relationships between architecture, liturgy, and the specific contexts of the parish communities is offered as a foundation. I then focus on the seven Orthodox communities in America that purchased or constructed their own properties. The people constituting these communities are quite diverse, as are their regions, socioeconomic contexts, and particular ecclesial identities.

PARISH PROFILES

The bulk of my analysis focuses on parishes that purchased property and built new edifices. For each parish profile, I begin by examining the historical theology and socioeconomic realities that both underpinned and modified their buildings and sacred space. Second, I present an analysis of how their property informs liturgical practice, and compare the liturgy to the prevailing Orthodox synthesis established in this introduction. Then, I conduct an analysis of their particular ecclesial identities based on their use of the sacred space. My study briefly considers the life of a mission community that rents property. An analysis of the challenges and limitations of its liturgical practices given its limited space follows. I then examine the parishes' socioeconomic contexts and reflect on their actual ecclesial identities in comparison to the prevailing Orthodox synthesis. In conclusion, I reflect on how these parish examples might contribute to the future trajectory of Orthodox architecture in America and its dialogical relationship with liturgy and ecclesial identity.

My analysis of the parish profiles demonstrates that contemporary Orthodox architecture has evolved into a multivalent symbol because of the contributions of immigrant cultural identity and the modern retrieval of Orthodox mission. My thesis proposes that contemporary Orthodox architecture has evolved beyond the form/function paradigm and shows how architecture has become a synthetic repository of immigrant cultural identity, modern liturgical theology, and mission. I focus on select Orthodox communities in America, gatherings of migrant people who established parishes while attempting to retain cultural identity and initiate missions. Some parishes in my study were established by immigrants, whereas others consist largely of converts from other Christian denominations and religions. Their unique experiences of becoming Orthodox and promoting mission contribute new and intriguing narratives that shape the contour of Orthodox worship and architecture in America. Communities were selected to represent prominent aspects of Orthodox history in America that transcend past, present, and future: a resilient immigrant community with strong connections to a native country (St. Katherine parish); a church identified with a modern saint (Holy Virgin Cathedral in San Francisco); a mission community that constructed a new edifice (St. Matthew parish); a community with an American architectural design (Annunciation parish); influential liturgical centers (St. Vladimir's Seminary and New Skete Monastery); and a mission community renting space (Joy of All Who Sorrow Orthodox Church [JOY] mission). Factors such as cultural retention, mission, the memory of a modern saint, and others contributed to the design of sacred space for each community in this study.

In this book, I carefully investigate each community's architectural structure through the lens of its history, liturgy, and identity. The limited sample size of this investigation precludes the possibility of proclaiming sweeping statements about the nature of contemporary Orthodox architecture in America, and this is intentional: the purpose of this study is to look more carefully at exactly how communities use and understand their buildings to test the hypothesis that form follows function and to articulate the multivalent meaning of Orthodox architecture in the American environment. The reader should expect to learn about immigrant identity, community memory, mission, and the perception of liturgy in contemporary American Orthodoxy. This book will establish how these community dynamics have come to be inscribed on architecture: my hope is that my initial hypotheses might break open opportunities for new research projects in each of these areas.

I expect readers to question my selection of parishes to profile in this study. Surely, a more expansive selection of parishes would yield a comprehensive analysis of Orthodox architecture in America. My selection of parishes and communities was designed to yield a sufficient sample size to explore the questions I have raised here. The study treats churches with prominent profiles (Holy Virgin Cathedral and St. Vladimir's Seminary in particular) and communities that are lesser known (St. Katherine and St. Matthew). I selected these churches because they offered prime opportunities for exploring the issues I have raised: community identity and memory, and liturgical practice. Aesthetical appeal was not a criterion for my choices, which means that this is not designed to be a book promoting pilgrimages to holy sites or touting architectural best practices. My hope is that scholars will want to join a dialogue on my hypotheses and will test them by exploring other churches in America.

In the conclusion, I attempt to synthesize my observations and deliver conclusions reflecting on the liturgy/architecture symbiosis, the future trajectory of architecture in American Orthodoxy, and the theology one can glean from this study. I organize the parishes into three architectural models: the immigrant, liturgical renewal, and American Church models. Readers should note that these models do not fit the technical types customarily presented and explained by architectural historians. Nicholas Patricios has recently provided a magisterial overview of Byzantine architectural types, including basilicas and crosses-in-square from various regions and contexts, and one should reference his comprehensive study for the details on these types.[8]

My definitions of the three models represent the multivalence of contemporary Orthodox architecture in America. Readers should anticipate reflections on how the ever-increasing phenomenon of plurality within American Orthodoxy is shaping the continued detachment of liturgy from architecture and the absence of the formation of a common architectural school. As you delve into the rest of this book, I hope you will join me in exulting in the most important conclusion: that despite its diversity and shortcomings, contemporary Orthodox architecture in America is an admirable gift of thanksgiving to God.

CHAPTER ONE

ORTHODOX ARCHITECTURE

Honoring the Past

Byzantine religious architecture has inspired awe and wonder among people, including monastics, clergy, theologians, pilgrims, historians, and liturgists. A project profiling select Orthodox architectural models in America would seem to have some organic relationship with past models. Scholars who have visited, photographed, described, and analyzed famous historical edifices have produced patterns reflecting relational layers between the buildings and the people who frequent them. Ecclesial architectural analysis often yields such relational patterns that recur with some variation across historical periods and regions. For Orthodox people in America and their buildings, it would be convenient to simply apply the prevailing hermeneutical assumptions anew since Orthodox communities in America presumably continue the architectural traditions of their native countries.

Let us begin by briefly surveying the hermeneutical assumptions potentially impacting an analysis of Orthodox America. The first assumption concerns the universality of past architectural models. First, because American Orthodoxy represents not only countries but also dozens of regions within countries that had their own unique architectural styles, it is difficult to speak of any generic Orthodox architectural style.[1] Also, it is not possible to simply reincarnate those styles in churches built within their own uniquely American socioeconomic circumstances. However, American Orthodox communities surely attempt to construct clichés of past models, though many details are certainly altered.

The second issue concerns the relationship between architecture and liturgy. The architecture/liturgy question requires serious examination, especially since their reciprocity tends to be prevalent in Orthodox history. Missionaries and immigrants retained and sustained the Byzantine liturgy in America, but the manner of its celebration often varies, depending on the local tradition of any given community. An examination of the suitability of the architectural plan for the requirements of the Byzantine liturgy is another important consideration, especially if one compares the American Orthodox context with the architectural models local American parishes consulted in building edifices.

A derivative of this architecture/liturgy paradigm also warrants examination, namely, the larger question of how architecture should shape liturgical celebration, and the opposite, how much liturgy should contribute to the architectural design of the church building as well as that of other buildings used by the community. An examination of the principles employed to design the churches presented in this study can contribute to the modification of the reciprocity between architecture and liturgy. For the remainder of this study, I refer to this issue as the symbiosis between liturgy and architecture in the American Orthodox environment.

The issue of local ecclesial identity as expressed by the people of the community is integral to a study of Orthodox architecture in America. Community memory is an emerging factor in this aspect of the analysis. An examination of how parish communities retain and sustain their history and identity significantly contributes to the ecclesial identities of Orthodox parish communities.

The following sections present select Orthodox architectural models of the past, with the purpose of establishing foundations in the areas of architectural style, the symbiosis between architecture and liturgy, and the contribution of architecture to ecclesiology. The foundations serve as pivotal points of analysis for the contemporary models featured in this study. My presentation of these three areas will not be comprehensive because extant works devoted to these subjects are available elsewhere, and this book focuses on contemporary models. The analysis instead attempts to glean principles from historical models and ascertain how they have been appropriated and modified by the select American Orthodox communities profiled in this study.

My selection of models from Orthodox history in this chapter is designed to set the stage for a comprehensive analysis of the Orthodox architectural models featured in the following chapters. Ultimately, I argue that architecture is much more than the form facilitating liturgical function, and that it expresses a community's identity, memory, mission, and ecclesiology. Seasoned readers are already aware of how the dynamics of history progressively shaped Orthodox identity from late antiquity until today. Contemporary Orthodoxy is the inheritor of multiple regional traditions expressed in liturgy, art, music, texts, and other traditions. One might describe contemporary American Orthodoxy in the same way Robert Taft describes the Byzantine rite: it is a mongrel because its current life has so many contributions from the past.[2]

In order to interpret the contemporary architectural forms in Orthodox America, one must be familiar with the salient identity markers of contemporary Orthodox America. These identity markers represent multiple episodes in the history of the Orthodox Church that remain relevant today. The primary identity markers are a rich liturgical tradition drawn primarily from the urban centers of Jerusalem and Constantinople and proclaiming a profound Christology; a monastic liturgical tradition impacted by iconoclasm and resulting in a truncated celebration of liturgy; and a complex memory of theological controversies and wars from the imperial and post-imperial Byzantine periods. Contemporary Orthodox architecture in America has also been inscribed with identity markers originating from mostly non-Orthodox sources and entities. For example, the restoration of the lay priesthood to primacy and American egalitarianism have impacted American Orthodoxy, whereas the absence of large populations and wealthy, private benefactors has resulted in the establishment of Orthodox missions that select spaces for gathering that are affordable and convenient.

A review of select models and theological trends illustrates how Orthodoxy in America has received a collection of eclectic identity markers that constitute a plurality of identities that is often expressed in architecture. Constantinople's Hagia Sophia is the first model we explore because it exemplified the ideal symbiosis of liturgy and architecture and it was the primary source of reflection for classical Orthodox Christology. Hagia Sophia's imperial legacy as the city's main church also has implications for architecture as a symbol of community memory reflecting an identity constructed in the past. This section also refers to the urban liturgy of Jerusalem to reflect on the vestiges of stational liturgy in contemporary Orthodox liturgy. The Middle Byzantine architectural model shows how the liturgical paradigm shifted on account of iconoclasm and the new monastic hegemony in liturgical celebration, especially since most Byzantine rite churches celebrate the liturgy that was truncated under monastic influence in variants of the Middle Byzantine architectural structure. I have included discussion of additional phenomena that contribute to the contemporary Orthodox architectural model in America: the appeal to the contemporary Byzantine rite to adopt principles that are similar to those employed by Catholics, where liturgical function inspires architectural form, advocated by Andriy Chirovsky; the emergence of new structures that honor new relationships between clergy and laity and facilitate the active participation of the people, noted by Jeanne Kilde; and the distinction between creating copies that recreate the past and innovations that are suitable for the present, discussed by Richard Vosko.

Contemporary Orthodox communities in America honor the heritage of a past that draws from the legacies of Hagia Sophia and the Middle Byzantine model and adjust to the realities of the present, attempting to meet the challenge of remaining faithful to Orthodoxy while being authentically American. I have structured this chapter to establish the legacies of past and present embedded in the ecclesial DNA of contemporary Orthodoxy in America to introduce readers to the primary models that shape the present scene and set the stage for a more comprehensive analysis of the models presented in the subsequent chapters.

MODELS: LESSONS FROM THE PAST

Perhaps no other church building has inspired architectural fascination as much as the famous Hagia Sophia (Church of the Holy Wisdom), which served as the cathedral of the Constantinopolitan Patriarchate until the city fell to the Ottomans in 1453 CE. Several scholars have presented Hagia Sophia's history, architectural details, contribution to Constantinople's life, and unique liturgy in detail, and I will not repeat their words here. In 1988, Rowland Mainstone produced the most comprehensive analysis of Hagia Sophia's symbiosis of architecture and liturgy, while Thomas Mathews presented a broader view of Constantinople's churches and liturgy in a 1971 study.[3] Numerous liturgical scholars draw from Juan Mateos's critical editions of liturgical manuscripts that provide precious details on Hagia Sophia's liturgy, while John Baldovin illustrated the pivotal role the cathedral played in urban Constantinopolitan stational liturgy.[4] Cyril Mango offered a magisterial historical presentation on Byzantine architecture, which includes the diffusion of Byzantine architectural styles in Greece, the Balkans, and Russia.[5] Nicholas Patricios has contributed a comprehensive and magisterial study on Byzantine architecture beginning with Christian minorities in the Roman Empire through the fall of Constantinople in the fifteenth century, arriving at seven distinct types of churches.[6] Vasileios Marinis has contributed a much-needed analysis of Middle Byzantine buildings that challenges the traditional symbiosis of architecture and liturgy and yields new information on the use of liturgical buildings.[7]

Hagia Sophia: Liturgy and Art

Justinian's reconstructed Hagia Sophia was dedicated in 537 CE, and was one of many Constantinopolitan and Byzantine church buildings adorned by domes.[8] Hagia Sophia was a marvel because of its "floating" dome between two semi-domes, though several other churches in the city were also domed, establishing a pattern for architecture throughout Justinian's vast commonwealth, reaching as far as Venice.[9] Alexander Grishin notes that Hagia Sophia became an architectural paradigm for other Orthodox communities since "many Orthodox communities throughout the empire and eastern Europe built their own versions of Hagia Sophia, but never attained the scale or the eccentric architectural boldness of the church in Constantinople."[10] Hagia Sophia's architectural plan was not alone in shaping Orthodox churches diffused throughout the commonwealth. The liturgy celebrated in Hagia Sophia was a model, establishing orders, patterns, and cycles followed by other local churches and noted by the monasteries in and near Constantinople.[11]

Historical evidence detailing Hagia Sophia's liturgy makes a significant contribution to the Byzantine liturgy Orthodox and Catholics celebrate today. Robert Taft's magisterial study on the Great Entrance informs readers about one of the two most prominent liturgical actions performed during the Byzantine liturgy: the transfer of the gifts from their area of preparation to the altar in the sanctuary.[12] Taft analyzes the entire ritual context of collecting the gifts in the small building called the skeuophylakion,[13] and how the deacons would process into the church to begin the liturgy of the Eucharist, processing through the cathedral's ambon and bringing the gifts to the bishop, who received them and placed them upon the table. Taft's meticulously detailed study demonstrates how a necessary ritual movement, which essentially consists of setting the table for the Eucharistic banquet of which liturgical participants will partake, takes on a theology of allegorical symbolism inspired by its ostentatious public performance by church officials.[14]

The visual grandeur of the Great Entrance was significantly reduced by the fusion of Hagia Sophia's cathedral rite with the much more pragmatic monastic rite. Originally an elegant procession from the skeuophylakion, over the ambon, and to the sanctuary, the Great Entrance became a simple movement beginning and ending at the sanctuary. However, the memory of the solemn entrance at Hagia Sophia at its height remains in even the most humble contemporary Eucharistic liturgy, the gifts slowly moved from the sanctuary, preceded by incense and accompanied by the singing of the Cherubikon, to be placed on the altar table for the faithful to partake of.

While Hagia Sophia's furnishings facilitated a synthesis of movement, proclamation, and prayer in harmony with the order of the Eucharistic liturgy, the experience of worship at Hagia Sophia evoked reverence and awe. Justinian is reported to have exclaimed, "Solomon, I have vanquished thee!" on the occasion of the cathedral's dedication, evidence of his own sense of awe, having arranged for the creation of a structure superior to the temples of the old covenant.[15] According to the *Russian Primary Chronicle*, the emissaries sent by Prince Vladimir to Constantinople in the tenth century are reported to have been so impressed by the liturgy that they exclaimed, "we knew not whether we were in heaven or on earth, for surely there is no such splendor or beauty anywhere upon earth."[16]

The most impressive witness to the splendor of Hagia Sophia's liturgy is the *Mystagogia* (commentary on the Divine Liturgy) authored by Maximus the Confessor sometime between 628 and 630 CE.[17] Maximus the Confessor was born in 580 CE in Constantinople and was familiar with the liturgy celebrated at the Great Church.[18] A debate on the exact liturgy Maximus knew has recently emerged with some asserting that he may have been more familiar with the hagiopolite liturgy of St. James since Maximus returned to Constantinople in the 650s.[19] Robert Taft asserts that the burden of evidence favors Maximus's familiarity with the cathedral rite of Constantinople. Maximus's chief contribution is his demonstration of the value of liturgy to his monastic community since his mystagogy reveals the cosmic mystery, the unfolding of the incarnation, where men come to union with God by the grace of the Holy Spirit.[20] Hans-Joachim Schulz states that Maximus the Confessor modified Pseudo-Dionysius's multilayered hierarchical order of descent, resulting in an interpretation of the dome as an image of heaven, which defined the iconographic order of church decoration, descending from the highest Christology literally at the top (in the dome), to the images of individual saints at the lower levels of the nave, a delicate balance of the heavenly and earthly churches gathered together for the Eucharist.[21] In summary, Maximus's *Mystagogia* became a theological prototype for interpreting Orthodox architecture.

While Maximus's theological interpretation of the building became definitive for Orthodox architecture, it is likely that he was influenced by the strong Christological trajectory of the liturgy celebrated at Hagia Sophia. A kontakion composed for the rededication of Hagia Sophia at the Christmas Vigil of 562 CE celebrates the presence of

God, in Christ, who dwells with the Christians who worship him in Hagia Sophia, which (of course) is worthy of hosting him.[22] The entire ritual context expresses a sophisticated Christology, which is understandable given Constantinople's frequent involvement in the Christological controversies of Christianity's first millennium. The hymns proclaimed the Christology of the ecumenical councils in the liturgy, and participating in a ritual context with such powerfully decorated audiovisual content could only be described as impressionable. Thus, Maximus's reference to Hagia Sophia as the context in which the assembly encounters and experiences union with God is due as much to the cathedral's solemn celebration as it is to the preestablished theological foundations one could identify in the order of the Eucharist. Maximus's effort to alert the monks to the value of participating in the cathedral liturgy reflects the impression of the presence of God made by the architectural plan and liturgical celebration and also contributes to the affixation of a permanent theological typology on the architecture of this period, exemplified by Hagia Sophia.

The historical evidence strongly suggests that participating in the liturgy of Hagia Sophia created a memorable sensory experience for the assembly. The visibility of the church and its stational liturgy that facilitated active participation contributed to its capacity to create memories. The Great Church and its medieval iconography illustrate the function and value of an institutional memory belonging to adherents of the Byzantine tradition. Amy Papalexandrou explains how the mosaic of the Virgin and Child at Hagia Sophia is an example of the way sensory experience communicates and contributes to institutional memory:

> On the one hand Christ saved through his Incarnation, made possible through the Virgin birth, as suggested in shorthand through the iconography of the image. In this sense it spoke (and speaks) to all beholders over time. On the other hand, its creation and placement in this particular place and time worked as a bold and prominent reminder of the violence of the recent past, specifically the "dark years" of Iconoclasm, during which images were destroyed and Iconophiles . . . were persecuted. As Photios proclaimed, this was a celebratory image of victory, of the salvation of the Byzantine Empire as an Orthodox (Iconophile) entity.[23]

Papalexandrou summarizes her analysis of the icon's function by defining the icon as a constant reminder of the past, present, and future, "for all beholders."[24] Papalexandrou's example begins to break open the potential for architectural and iconographic multifunctionality. Icons are not simply placed in an apse, on walls, or on an iconostasis for the purpose of function shaping form, but they also represent the historical, social, and theological contexts of their environments.

In addition to its liturgical celebration, the imperial patronage of Hagia Sophia also contributes to the synthesis of Orthodox architecture. Justinian's renowned exclamation of achievement noted above introduces his patronage of the reconstructed and majestic Hagia Sophia. But the imperial heritage of Hagia Sophia as a model is not entirely positive. Part of the heritage passed on by Justinian's edifice includes the tragedy of intra-ecclesial conflict, most notably the iconoclastic controversy, which impacted Hagia Sophia itself;[25] the brutal invasion and sacking of Constantinople by Latin Christians in 1204 CE, their occupation of the city, and their establishment of a Latin patriarchate, a memory that remains bitter to Greeks today; and the irremovable memory of imperial patronage of and participation in the liturgy of Hagia Sophia, beginning with Justinian's alleged exclamation of pride at its dedication. Allan Doig summarizes its imperial heritage:

> What does appear to have developed considerably by this time (though it may also have been true of the liturgy celebrated in the Theodosian Church) is the way the symbolic figure of the emperor has been absorbed into the ceremonial of the liturgy on those relatively rare occasions when he was present. What had been incipient with Constantine, and was now more fully developed, was the quasi-priestly status of the Emperor. Constantine's rule and the advent of a Christian Empire was seen as providential; he was chosen by God, and the ceremonial acclamations for a new Emperor became "a new David" and "a new Constantine," and though there appears not to have been an anointing even as late as the Book of Ceremonies, it records that the Patriarch prayed that God himself might "deign to anoint with the oil of gladness your faithful servant." It had been difficult for Constantine to be present at the liturgy, but by Justinian's day, the Emperor's presence, in his new Hagia Sophia, had been

structurally integrated, and to some extent by this quasi-priestly status, but to an even greater extent by the architectural and ceremonial arrangement by which his appearances and access to the chancel were very closely controlled.[26]

The emperor's participation in the liturgy symbolizes many realities of the Constantinopolitan Church in Justinian's age, such as the reciprocal relationship between church and state, the public and active participation of the emperor as an official in the Eucharistic liturgy, and the emperor's personal patronage of the edifice. Despite the fall of the Byzantine Empire, the emperor's role remains relevant today. The imperial imprint on Byzantine ecclesial identity remains vibrant in the contemporary Orthodox Church, even if no emperors are available to build new cathedrals. In this vein, the continued performance of liturgical rituals originating from the Byzantine imperial period represents another instance of Papalexandrou's explanation of the power of memory in the mosaic of Hagia Sophia. Like the mosaic and its copies, the imperially shaped liturgical rituals communicate values belonging to the Byzantine institutional memory, introducing participants and observers to the community's past and present, while perhaps hinting at the future.

SACRED SPACE: STATIONAL LITURGY IN JERUSALEM AND CONSTANTINOPLE

In assessing the past, an examination of architectural models must also include consideration of the Orthodox idea of sacred space. The presentation of Hagia Sophia above provides an initial foundation, but it does not tell the whole story. The ancient practice of urban stational liturgy and its contribution toward defining sacred space must also be considered, despite its demise in the aftermath of foreign invasions limiting the liturgical celebrations of Jerusalem and Constantinople. In this section, I briefly summarize the work of John Baldovin on stational liturgy in Jerusalem and Constantinople, and consider how principles gleaned from their respective contexts might apply to Orthodox architecture and liturgy in America today.

Stational Liturgy in Jerusalem

The stational liturgy of fourth- to fifth-century Jerusalem testifies to the redefinition of sacred space since the emperor Constantine built an ornate complex of buildings where a statue of Venus had previously stood.[27] The center of the Christian complex was Golgotha, the location of Christ's burial and resurrection, and the context was ripe for emphasizing participation in the historical location of the events surrounding Christ's salvific Pascha. Golgotha was also believed to be the center of the world, the place where Adam and Eve were buried, adding weight to the historical significance of Jerusalem as a holy place.[28] Constantine constructed a complex of buildings, with the two main churches, the Martyrium and Anastasis, not being particularly large. The architectural design was intended for a mobile assembly to move between spaces, worshiping on assigned days at different stations, including Sion, Bethlehem, Lazarium, Eleona, Imbomom, and Gethsemane, locations associated with specific sites of Christ's or others' lives in salvation history.[29] The stational liturgy reveals a sacred topography where the assembly honors the sequence of salvation history, though its liturgy does not solely emphasize history, as Baldovin and others have noted.[30]

What was the purpose of this stational liturgy? Clearly, the mobile liturgy celebrated in the sacred topography of Jerusalem illustrates the city's identity as the holy place where God saved humanity. Valuable liturgical evidence from the fourth century also identifies Jerusalem as a place where people embraced Christianity through the sacrament of Baptism. The homilies attributed to Cyril of Jerusalem (350–381 CE) and the diaries of the pilgrim Egeria, who stayed in Jerusalem from 381 to 384 CE, reveal Jerusalem to be a place of active instruction of catechumens, who participated in the city's stational liturgy on a daily basis.[31] Cyril uses the city's sacred identity to remind the neophytes of their unique contextual setting, and Egeria notes the number of pilgrims who require the bishop's mystagogical lectures to be translated into their native languages. But this evidence also reveals an apparent intent on the part of the architectural setting and liturgical celebration to provide a public witness to Christ to all inhabitants and visitors of the city.

The architectural program, firmly rooted in the inherent holiness of locations where Christ or other saints had been, extended the sacred space beyond the physical structures of the buildings to define every place through which the assembly processed as sacred. In this instance, the architecture and its accompanying liturgy implicitly identify the people of the Church, the members of the body of Christ, as bearing Christ's presence and defining the space they encounter as sacred. The evidence here demonstrates a uniquely evangelistic architectural function, where the architecture supports the public liturgy of its occupants that is purposefully evangelistic. In other words, the people share the liturgy celebrated in the core buildings of the complex with the people of the city, in order to bring them into the body of Christ. This also shows a conscious awareness of the priority of the people as the body of Christ superseding the buildings themselves, central as they were to the city's sacred topography.

Stational Liturgy in Constantinople

Constantinople's stational liturgy began to develop during the reign of Theodosius (379–395 CE), and occurred within a complex of churches outside the city walls, forming a kind of protective wall around the city.[32] The city was host to public expressions of theological strife, with the Arians using the city to chant hymns supporting their theological position, and the city itself hosting no less than two ecumenical councils.[33] Urban activity also occurred in the Hippodrome, an ancient version of the contemporary sports stadium, with a capacity of approximately 100,000 spectators, who would watch sporting events, proclamations of emperors, and other public events.[34] For the Church to assert its authority in the imperial city, it needed a mechanism to publicly demonstrate its significance. Most of the churches of the city had numerous doors and open courtyards serving as gathering places and entrances, allowing for large numbers of people to enter and exit the buildings.[35] One of the more popular stations for the processions was the Forum of Constantinople, an urban plaza near Hagia Sophia and the main thoroughfare of the city, which served as a convenient place to offer prayers for protection of the city from various calamities such as invasions, civil wars, and earthquakes.[36]

Constantinople's legacy includes its advantageous position on the sea, allowing for easy access to commerce and public events, but equally disadvantageous in terms of foreign invasion. In Church history, it hosted some of the most notorious theological controversies resulting in temporary and permanent schisms. The urban plan of the churches' layouts and their architectural structures facilitated easy access to the churches and frequent interaction with all the inhabitants of the city. In a context of ecclesiastical strife, which frequently included the participation of imperial officials, Constantinople's stational liturgy promoted the healing of divisions and unity by engaging urban constituents, drawing them to the Church, and addressing their daily concerns with prayers such as the ektene.[37] Constantinople's architectural function is similar to Jerusalem's here, in facilitating a mobile Church that prays in the public square. The public square collects the concerns of its inhabitants and is thus a place for debate, which often becomes heated. The Church's presence in the Constantinopolitan public square is thus deeply complicated because its ecclesial representatives often ended up on the wrong side of retroactive theological judgment, branded as heretics and iconoclasts who were supplanted by new occupants of the public square who stood for the truth.

But the Church's presence in the public square also serves to remind one of its position as the temple founded by prominent patrons. The stone buildings with their height, huge domes, and public visibility argued for the city's Christian grandeur.[38] But divine care for the city is entrusted to Mary, the Theotokos,[39] as evidenced by a renowned ninth- to tenth-century mosaic from the southwest exonarthex above the south door of Hagia Sophia, described by Helen Saradi:

> Constantine carries in his hands a model of the imperial capital and Justinian a model of Hagia Sophia, and each offers his model to the Mother of God. Constantinople is depicted enclosed by high walls featuring rectangular masonry and two large crosses on the door panels of the gate. Two buildings with roofs pitched in two directions rise from inside the walls. Church and city are now inextricably linked, and both are offered to the Mother of God in supplication for her protection.[40]

This example illustrates the inclusion of the important personalities in caring for Constantinople expressed by art and architecture. Hagia

Sophia is an appropriate temple for Mary and is under her care, offered to her by the fathers of the city, Constantine and Justinian. Her protection of the city occurs through a series of dialogical relationships, depending on imperial officials who are willing to entrust the city and its buildings to her. The lesson taught by Constantinopolitan topography is that the architecture and its decoration express not only the power of the Church, but also the Church's participation in the empire's challenges, which directly confront the city. These themes of Marian protection permeated deeply into Greek Orthodox consciousness largely because of the architectural facilitation of frequent ecclesial interaction with the city, so that the city itself would always be a part of the Church's life and concern. Thus, Constantinopolitan stational liturgy functions as an example of how architectural planning facilitates the Church's social interaction with the city and the extension of the Church's liturgy into the city and for the city.

PARADIGM SHIFTS: THE MIDDLE BYZANTINE CHURCH AND MONASTIC LITURGY

Despite the diffusion of Hagia Sophia's influence throughout Eastern Christianity in a process often called liturgical Byzantinization, historical events diminished the cathedral rite's prevalence, beginning with the iconoclastic controversies of the eighth and ninth centuries, through the Latin Crusade of 1204 CE, and culminating with the fall of Constantinople in 1453 CE. The aftermath of each colossal event produced a reconfiguring of ecclesial life as an adjustment to the new context. After the triumph of Orthodoxy in 843 CE, the architectural model of the Church in Byzantium endured a paradigm shift, resulting in a smaller, cross-in-square structure that included a central dome supported by columns, flanked by four barrel vaults supported by four smaller domes, with an entrance narthex on the western end and an apse protruding from the eastern end.[41] The apse often had two side rooms attached, with the south room the location for the prothesis rite and the north room a diakonikon for storage of reliquaries, vestments, and other holy objects.[42] An extensive iconographic program, one that steadily developed throughout the Middle Byzantine period, accompanied this architectural paradigm shift. Grishin notes that Christ occupied the space in the dome, with the Virgin Mary in the apse, salvation history depicting events from the life of Christ (the twelve chief feasts of the liturgical year) on the higher walls, and the hagiographical cycle of saints on the lower walls in a deliberately constructed hierarchy of the cosmos.[43]

A "New" (Nea) Church sponsored by Emperor Basil I and consecrated by Patriarch Photius in 881 CE epitomizes the new architectural and iconographic paradigm of the Middle Byzantine church.[44] Hans-Joachim Schulz explains the impact of the triumph of Orthodoxy over the iconoclasts in the harmony between architecture and iconography in the Nea's cycle of images, with Christ as Pantocrator adorning the dome and Mary occupying the apse.[45] The iconographic program serves as a hermeneutic for interpreting the architectural configuration of the church building since the apse is closer to the dome than the nave, so Mary, whose faithfulness inaugurated the economy of salvation, occupies this space.[46] Decoration of the church interior proliferated with the addition of icons on the chancel screen separating the nave and bema, and the iconostasis became a permanent fixture in Byzantine church architecture in the late Byzantine (Palaeologan) period.[47] Marinis states that images were associated with sanctuary barriers as early as the sixth century.[48] The transformation of the sanctuary barrier into a full-fledged iconostasis occurred gradually and at varying paces in a given region.[49]

Thus, the new architectural paradigm is interpreted through the hermeneutic of the emerging Christological iconographic program, and expresses a unique picture of the economy of salvation. The new paradigm was influential enough to shape changes in Hagia Sophia as well, with the renowned image of Christ Pantocrator adorning the Great Church's dome in the ninth or tenth century and replacing a gem-encrusted cross.[50]

The new independence enjoyed by monasteries in and near Constantinople also contributed to the emerging architectural model of the Middle Byzantine period. Monasteries began to occupy urban areas as cities depopulated, and monastic leaders created new strategic relationships with prestigious people in the capital, where the patrons could have access to their own family monastery.[51] Monastery churches often had a four-column plan and five domes, similar to the new church housed inside the property of the imperial palace.[52]

This program of church decoration, shaped by the new churches inside the imperial palace and the emerging monastery church, was generally copied throughout the empire and demonstrated the Church's ability to adapt to new circumstances. Grishin summarizes the new architectural paradigm of the Middle Byzantine period:

> If the early Christian basilicas sought huge enclosed spaces for large congregations, while the imperial churches of the sixth century made a statement concerning imperial power, wealth, and grandeur, the new cross-in-square churches reflected a shrinking demography, and often had as patron members of the military or civil aristocracy, and on many occasions were designated as monastic churches and also were designed to serve as the founder's tomb.[53]

In summary, Hagia Sophia contributed to the shaping of an initial Byzantine architectural model, and its furnishings reveal the order and synthesis of the cathedral Eucharistic liturgy. Taft, in reviewing how the church's furnishings contribute to the shape and meaning of the liturgy, states that "[for] the interpretation of such architectural elements and their uses, a functional approach is not only useful; it may be indispensable."[54] Ancient stational liturgy, however, expands the theological significance of Byzantine church architecture by revealing the delicate interplay between an urban architectural plan and the movement of the Church throughout the space of the city. Thus, the multivalence of sacred space in the Byzantine heritage includes more than the coordination of elements within a given property, as numerous factors contribute to the demarcation of sacred space. These factors include the sophisticated Christology expressed by architecture (typified by Maximus's mystagogy), iconography, and liturgy because these are the most prominent aspects continuing to impact the symbolism of contemporary Orthodox architecture.

Thus, the Middle Byzantine church emerged as the model during the paradigm shift, a product of urban depopulation, the aftermath of historico-theological strife (iconoclasm), and the increasing monastic influence on liturgy and architecture. The Middle Byzantine model has, of course, undergone local adaptations throughout its history, but was influential enough to impact architecture in the Byzantine common-wealth and the earliest architectural models of Rus'.[55] This smaller model became a historical repository, continuing to express the theology and ecclesiology of its more ornate antecedents by retaining liturgical movements and structures, and the Christological typology accompanying the Church's iconographic program. While the modes of expression were usually reduced since the Great Entrance and stational liturgy were simplified and the domes were generally much smaller, the ideas remained in the structures and were consequently passed on to the following generations, including contemporary Orthodox in America.

TOWARD AN ANALYTICAL MODEL: THE SYMBIOSIS OF ARCHITECTURE AND LITURGY

Liturgical historians have hypothesized the symbiosis of architecture and liturgy with detailed analyses on how architectural elements support and facilitate the requirements of liturgical celebration. Several of the monographs mentioned above cover the history of architecture and liturgy in Byzantium, most notably the magisterial works of Mathews, Mainstone, Taft, Doig, and Patricios. Taft famously states that form does indeed follow function in architecture, and my limited presentation here would appear to confirm his thesis. A question emerges in determining the degree to which the liturgy shaped the architectural plan of a given building. Does the architectural plan envision the order, flow, and movement of the liturgy, or does the liturgical ordo impose itself on a presupposed architectural plan? The implications of this question are serious if we assume that architecture and liturgy are symbiotic, and thus both represent and shape local ecclesiology. Marinis is the most recent architectural historian to address the symbiosis of architecture and liturgy, and he concludes that "an explicit interdependence of form and function dissipates."[56] His study takes a necessary step in challenging the perception that form follows function tightly. In the contemporary milieu, the perception that Orthodoxy privileges a symbiosis of architecture and liturgy prevails, and I will use this assumption as a basis for analyzing contemporary American Orthodox architectural models.

With respect to varying exterior decorations, it is likely that Grishin's description of the post-iconoclasm, Middle Byzantine model provides a type of synthesis from which principles might be articulated, while noting the existence of architectural exceptions.[57] Grishin identifies a five-domed church, with narthex on the west end and apse on the east, with the whole interior functioning as a microcosm of the Christian universe, echoing the Middle Byzantine synthesis also presented by Schulz.[58] Historical events such as the triumph of Orthodoxy over iconoclasm and the fourth Crusade impacted the shape of architecture and liturgy so that the two Eucharistic entrances were reduced in scope and magnitude, with most movement beginning and ending in the sanctuary. Such liturgical reductions apparently changed architectural planning, with a simple table of oblation within the sanctuary replacing the more ornate pastophoria and the ambon essentially rendered obsolete.[59] Here, extra-liturgical events cause turbulence in ecclesial life and force an adjustment in liturgical celebration, which also impacts the architectural plan.

When Constantinople fell in 1453 CE, the Eucharistic liturgy had developed into a complex monastic-cathedral synthesis, much reduced in movement and scale, heavily influenced by the monastic patronage it inherited when monks of the Constantinopolitan Studite and Palestinian Saba communities assumed leadership of liturgical revision in the aftermath of the iconoclastic controversies.[60] After enduring one more revision on Mount Athos, the reduced liturgy, celebrated in the smaller buildings more conducive to cenobitic monastic life, becomes the norm for Orthodoxy. Vasileios Marinis describes the architectural development in the Middle Byzantine period accordingly:

> Rather than viewing church buildings as static structures, frozen in time by the laying of last brick or tessera, I argue that Byzantine churches were material as well as open-ended social constructs and so were never finished, but they were continually in the process of becoming . . . the most fundamental way for a church to "become" re-

mained the rituals, both liturgical and nonliturgical, that developed in its spaces.[61]

Thus, sociopolitical ecclesial events tended to impact both liturgy and architecture, which appears to demonstrate that new models of liturgy and architecture emerged afterward and developed simultaneously, in all likelihood mutually influencing one another.

In the aftermath of the fall of Constantinople in 1453 CE and the invention of the printing press in the same century, the Byzantine liturgy became relatively fixed, with revisions representing fine-tuning and not radical reform. By the late nineteenth and early twentieth centuries, the perception of the Byzantine liturgy as archaic and unchanging prevailed within parish communities, and this perception contributed to a low level of symbiosis between architecture and liturgy. Émigré communities needed a basic design to accommodate the basic shape of the ritual, and even Western structures could be modified to create the distinct components of sanctuary, nave, and narthex that give shape to the essential movements of the Divine Liturgy.

The liturgy involves four chief movements, two of which are called entrances. In the first (little) entrance, the clergy exit the sanctuary via the north deacons' door and walk across the horizontal solea to the space before the royal doors, only to re-enter the sanctuary and place the Gospel book on the altar table as the people sing the introit. The second movement occurs at the Gospel reading, when the deacon exits the royal doors and proclaims the Gospel at the center of the church, or from the solea (in Slavic practice), or at an elevated ambo (in Greek practice). At the third movement, or Great Entrance, the Eucharistic gifts, prepared bread on the diskos and a chalice filled with wine and water, are taken from the prothesis (table of oblation), carried out the north door to the same spot on the solea, and placed on the altar.[62] The final major movement involves the celebrant carrying the Eucharistic gifts through the royal doors to distribute them to the people. He returns the gifts to the altar and then the table of oblation for consumption, and proceeds through the royal doors to the center of the nave to read the opisthambanos prayer, essentially the final collect of the Eucharistic assembly leading up to the people's dismissal. The basic tripartite structure of the Byzantine temple (narthex, nave, and sanctuary) thus accommodates the elementary structure and movement of liturgical celebration, resulting in a cozy relationship of architecture and liturgy that does not anticipate radical innovations on either side of the relationship.[63]

AN APPEAL FOR RESTORING LITURGY'S PRIMACY IN ITS RELATIONSHIP WITH ARCHITECTURE

The contemporary Orthodox architectural plan draws frequently, though not exclusively, from this modern symbiosis of architecture and liturgy, which conforms generally to the Middle Byzantine synthesis. An instructive attempt to articulate such principles for interpreting the contemporary symbiosis of architecture and liturgy was offered by Andriy Chirovsky in a dated, but relevant article on Byzantine architecture and liturgy published in *Diakonia* in 1983.[64] Chirovsky analyzed a series of interviews with Ukrainian architects published by the *Ukrainian Weekly* in 1981 on the future trajectory of Ukrainian Greco-Catholic church architecture. He lamented the ignorance of parish planning committees and architects in consulting the requirements of the Byzantine liturgy when establishing architectural designs and constructing the buildings. In inaugurating a discussion on establishing liturgical principles for architecture, Chirovsky invokes the traditional trinal nature of Byzantine buildings: buildings must contain a narthex (representing the world), a domed nave (representing the redeemed world, or partially realized kingdom of God), a sanctuary (heaven's fulfillment), and an iconostasis, the basic structure traceable to the Middle Byzantine synthesis.[65] Chirovsky promotes the need for the Church to issue guidelines for architects on how the architecture should serve the liturgical requirements of the Byzantine rite. His review of the architect interviews yields several examples of fissure between architectural form and liturgical function.

A good example is Chirovsky's analysis of Radoslav Zuk's suggestions for church architecture. While he praises Zuk for recognizing the octagon as a significant theological shape that could be incorporated into architectural design, he critiques Zuk's vision of a sanctuary that is integrated into the main space (nave) of the church and Zuk's designs that grant the sanctuary the greatest height of all the church's components.[66] For Chirovsky, promoting the sanctuary over the nave violates the prominence of the dome above the nave as symbolizing the assembly's progressive citizenship in the kingdom of God:

> Theologically, the position of the main dome above the assembly of the faithful points to the anthropological optimism of Eastern spirituality which sees the human situation here and now as capable of openness to the inbreaking of the divine and divinizing. The highly-developed Byzantine liturgical symbol system sees redeemed humanity "on the way" and therefore insists on an Eastern axis, and the celebrant's position facing East as well. But the central position of the bishop at the beginning of pontifical liturgies (in the very middle of the congregation), the administration of many sacraments at that location and the positioning of the main dome over this space demands attention to the here and now, to this world and its possibilities when open to the power of God.[67]

A synonym for this idea of the Church's here and now is Vatican II's model of the Church as a pilgrim on a journey to God's kingdom.[68] Chirovsky views Church architecture as delineating the realization of the kingdom in the sanctuary, and the journeying Church in the nave, which requires a barrier drawing a visible line between the "not-yet" and the kingdom: the iconostasis.[69] So the iconostasis adds a fourth required component to the established trinal nature of Church architecture that would fulfill the requirements of liturgical celebration. The order of the liturgy establishes the guidelines for the architectural space in this paradigm, which suggests that the liturgy should guide the design of the space, its structural components, and the coordination between components (such as sanctuary, nave, and iconostasis).

Chirovsky's attempt to begin a discussion on guidelines for Byzantine Church architecture echoes Roman Catholic teachings on how liturgy shapes architecture. He refers to the Catholic "landmark" on architecture, *Environment and Art in Catholic Worship*, issued by the National Conference of Catholic Bishops in 1978, and also to the emerging work of Richard Vosko.[70] The United States Conference of Catholic Bishops' (USCCB) *Built of Living Stones* updated the guidelines for Catholic ecclesial architecture, and they represent the priority of liturgy in designing an architectural program for a church.[71] In 2005, the late Benedictine scholar R. Kevin Seasoltz surveyed the history of architecture in the West and offered several principles to sustain the tradition of Catholic theology rooted in the apostolic preaching of the gospel.[72] Seasoltz's principles emphasize the priority of liturgy in its symbiotic relationship with architecture. He stated that the architectural and artistic environment of the church must be beautiful, inviting, hospitable, and seemingly incomplete when the body of Christ is not occupying it for worship.[73] Liturgy's priority in guiding architectural design and coordination of elements is evident in Seasoltz's recommendation:

> In our own time and place, architects and artists should be given relatively free scope in the church, but they must have both a clear understanding of the requirements of the sacred liturgy and a profound understanding of the paschal mystery of Jesus Christ and the dignity and role of the community of the faithful who celebrate that sacred mystery. It is the responsibility of patrons who commission architects and artists to provide such a sound liturgical and theological brief to both architects and artists.[74]

Seasoltz's principles suggest that architecture and artistic programs are most effective for Church ministry when liturgy guides them.

SOCIAL DYNAMICS: ENVIRONMENT AND POWER

Two additional authors—Vincenzo Ruggieri and Jeanne Kilde—warrant brief mention here due to the significance of their methodological approaches. Vincenzo Ruggieri conducted an extensive study of Byzantine architecture from 582 to 867 CE noteworthy for its methodology and insights into analyzing religious architecture.[75] Ruggieri asserts that scholars have typically examined Byzantine religious architecture from two related perspectives. First, the relationship between religious architecture and typology is an approach frequently adopted, which Ruggieri disavows as a "poorly chosen and inappropriate" method for the historical period he covers in his study.[76] Ruggieri also comments on the presuppositions concerning the symbiosis between architecture and the liturgy, and their consequential application to analyzing architecture in any historical period.[77] At first glance, his comments seem to reject the notion of liturgical function following architectural form. However, an engaged reading of his thesis illuminates his desire to demonstrate that architectural principles and designs accounted for much more than the liturgy in Byzantium. In addition to his thorough examination of the geographical and historical context of the buildings belonging to the historical period he covers, he conducts an informed presentation on how Byzantine engineers attempted to construct buildings that could withstand frequent earthquakes.[78] Ruggieri's study convincingly demonstrates the complexity of the Byzantine architectural enterprise, including the social dynamics of key people involved in funding and finalizing designs.

Jeanne Kilde's recent introductory monograph analyzing the historical tendency for Christians to design sacred spaces by marking and inscribing them through powerful personalities also provides an informative contribution to developing a hermeneutic for analyzing contemporary architecture.[79] Her discussion of the architectural shifts following Vatican II effectively illustrates her thesis. She states that the spatial transformation of the building symbolized by the repositioning of the altar so the celebrant can face the people was actually grounded in "shifts in the social power of the laity," along with a new emphasis on particular theological ideas.[80] Kilde's study consistently shows how social dynamics of Christian communities in history shape paradigm shifts in the spatial arrangement of buildings. Despite the brevity of her comments on the spatial meanings of Orthodox buildings, Kilde's thesis is helpful because she insists on showing how the architecture and accompanying art programs represent the community's employment of power, and also its interpretation of the exercise of divine power.[81]

Ruggieri's and Kilde's studies are pertinent to these profiles because they expand the ecclesial architectural discussion beyond a narrow analysis of architectural form shaping liturgical functions, and vice versa. Their examinations show that communities with specific social, political, and economic dynamics build churches, and that these buildings become repositories inscribed with many of the historical and personal details of their native communities.

EXTRA-LITURGICAL SPACE AND ECCLESIAL IDENTITY

While the dialogical relationship between architecture and liturgy remains preeminent in Orthodoxy, this study emphasizes the need to expand this relational model to include the complex social, economic, political, and environmental factors that are ultimately imprinted on Orthodox architecture. In the contemporary context, a useful tool for analysis is broadening the interpretive lens to consider the multifunctionality of Orthodox architectural complexes. For example, we know that Christians participated in the liturgies celebrated in Hagia Sophia, the smaller churches of the Middle Byzantine period, and their successors in Orthodox history. Our discussion of the liturgy has occurred in the Eucharistic context, and the Hagia Sophia model, along with others, offers architectural components that illustrate a broad coordination of liturgical celebration.[82]

In the contemporary American context, one must also consider how a community's buildings are used for extra-liturgical purposes besides pre-liturgical arrival and gathering. Marinis's examination of Middle Byzantine churches unveils examples of the non-liturgical use of buildings, including private devotions, healings, and festivals, such as the female festival of Agathe celebrated in Constantinople on May 12, which entailed icon veneration, cloth making, and singing songs.[83] In many historical instances, a community's sacred space served as the burial place for its patrons as a way of honoring them and asking them for intercession. The Cathedral of Saint Sophia in Kyiv (Kyiv Sophia hereafter) is a good example because it is the architectural model for the first contemporary church in our study (St. Katherine Ukrainian Orthodox Church in Arden Hills, Minnesota). St. Katherine is modeled after the renovation of Kyiv Sophia that occurred in the sixteenth and seventeenth centuries under the patronage of Metropolitan Peter Mohyla and Ivan Mazeppa. Excavation of Kyiv Sophia's interior unearthed sarcophagi containing human remains that were believed to belong to the cathedral's Prince Yaroslav the Wise.[84] His burial in the church is not unusual for the later medieval context (eleventh century), but it also attests to the sensitive relationship between the leaders of the realm and the Church, in this case, the princes of the Grand Prince period in Rus'. The patron of the church is often laid to rest in the very building he financed.

Kyiv Sophia was also a repository for ecclesial relics, including precious episcopal panagias, vestments, chandeliers, iconostases, and coffins.[85] In addition to providing storage space for valuables, Kyiv Sophia had a unique architectural form leading to an unconventional function: its towers rising at the corners of the church emphasized the visibility of Kyiv Sophia to the city, provided a clear view of the city, and served as a location from which members of the princely entourage could observe the city and also take refuge from the threat of foreign attack.[86] Discussing such functions in an analysis of contemporary Orthodox architecture might appear irrelevant, but the copying of architectural forms invokes the memory of the historical contexts that contribute to the shaping of contemporary ecclesial identity.

Contemporary Orthodox Ukrainians in Arden Hills, Minnesota, might not need to literally seek refuge from invaders in the church buildings, but it is quite possible that their architectural forms represent, at least in part, their self-understanding as people who have been persecuted and besieged throughout their entire history. Here I am applying the notion of memory in Amy Papalexandrou's explanation of the significance of the Virgin and Child mosaic in Hagia Sophia (above).[87] Just as the mosaic is a multivalent symbol expressing theology and history and communicating values of the past, present, and future, the deliberate designing of St. Katherine in Arden Hills according to the archetype of Kyiv Sophia represents a contemporary instance of communicating a community's values through a multivalent symbol expressing ideas from the past with a view to the present and future. Papalexandrou's definition of cultural memory in Byzantium remains relevant to contemporary Orthodoxy in a new way. Since

Orthodoxy in America consists of a complex fusion of ethnic immigrants, the generations of their children and grandchildren, and converts, the contributions of community memory and current experience to identity result in strongly unique local ecclesiologies at the parish level.[88]

Architectural multifunctionality occurs in more common activities in the contemporary context. Socioeconomic shifts have defined a fairly established workweek for Orthodox, whose main day of gathering is Sunday. For immigrants, Sunday was the chief day to enjoy fellowship with people of the same region or country of origin, and the church building became their meeting place for post-liturgical fellowship. Orthodox parishes also adopted the practice of implementing organized church schools, and parishes were no longer solely liturgical but spaces for the people of the parish to share fellowship, educate, hold special events, and conduct business. Designating appropriate spaces for non-liturgical community activities became important, and this begins to define the multifunctionality of ecclesial space, which also represents ecclesial identity. Separate meeting spaces (called halls or centers) from the liturgical space, appropriate for class meetings (classrooms), playing music, and serving food and drink, served to sustain the identity of the people who gathered at the local parish. These areas are multifunctional and promote cultural retention and cultivation while providing space for immigrants and their families to gather for fellowship. The increased occupation and usage of secondary, non-liturgical space on a parish's property manifests a more complex development of becoming in the American Orthodox environment. Many communities continue to use these spaces for cultural retention, but as parishes evolve and internal demographics change with the Americanization of émigré children and grandchildren and the reception of converts into the Orthodox Church, catechetical and instructional activities are becoming more prevalent in these spaces.[89] The buildings of a given parish's property, then, communicate several layers of self-identification, some of which reveal internal demographic evolution while simultaneously representing the community's status in the American religious environment.[90]

Understanding the coordination of contemporary buildings on a property requires an illustrative example. An example furnished by Chirovsky examines the liturgical coordination within a building, between its space and its furnishings. The specific dimensions of the furnishings can have a significant impact on liturgical celebration. Chirovsky's survey of Ukrainian architects illumines the importance of specifying dimensions to facilitate worship. Referring to an interview conducted with Jaroslav Sichynsky, Chirovsky summarizes some of the obstacles in contemporary architectural models:

> inadequate altar space and [the] impossibility of placing an iconostas, overly steep steps which bar the handicapped and even healthy from easy access, narrowness of the main door, resulting in distress at funerals, inappropriate placement of loudspeakers, large windows that cause glare and distraction. The lack of private quarters for the Sacrament of Penance is also listed as a problem, as well as the banality of the interior ornamentation. While not all of Mr. Sichynsky's practical considerations are specifically liturgical in nature, they most certainly have bearing on the liturgical celebration.[91]

Chirovsky's summary of Sichynsky's comments demonstrates the impact apparently minor design details can have on liturgical celebration. His brief presentation elevates the importance of planning for strong coordination between the spaces within the church building that will be used for liturgical celebration. One can only imagine the distress that could result from difficulty in carrying a coffin through a narrow door and down steep steps, and how even isolated instances can distort one's experience of any given liturgical celebration.

As the previous example suggests, the need for tight liturgical coordination among sacred spaces also applies to the coordination of a community's buildings on a property site. The building in which liturgy is celebrated is not the only part of any given property that contributes to and reflects the community's ecclesial identity because the community does not assemble only in the church. Contemporary communities frequently gather in parish halls, or the assembly departs from the church at the dismissal, only to continue its activity elsewhere. The content of the community's Sunday activities poses serious pastoral challenges since many people attend only a portion of the Eucharistic liturgy, often just enough for them and their families to receive communion, before moving to the location of "coffee hour." The location of "coffee hour" depends on a community's use of its property. St. Katherine in Arden Hills meets in a cultural center adjacent to the church building and connected by a fairly lengthy corridor. St. Matthew Orthodox Church in Columbia assembles in its meeting space on the lower level of the church, accessible by stairs and elevators. Parishioners of Joy of All Who Sorrow Orthodox Church (JOY) mission in Culver City use the adjacent room for their post- and extra-liturgical meeting space. The use of these spaces for church school and other events will be analyzed with greater detail in the chapters devoted to each parish.

Post-liturgical community gatherings are significant in developing and expressing the community's self-identity. Certainly, many people depart for home or some other planned activity. Those who stay impart and receive instruction, celebrate special events, welcome visitors, extend hospitality and charity to those in need, conduct necessary parish business, and share fellowship. In summary, the dynamics of the community's experience after the liturgy in a different room or building on its property reflects the community's self-identity as it continues to evolve in the American religious context. If the community frequently uses a non-liturgical space for designated activities, which is now the norm in Orthodox America, discussion of how the space facilitates such activities must be integrated into an analysis of the architectural suitability for the liturgy. Also, some discussion of how the community understands its space and how visitors perceive their own experiences when entering every aspect of the space will contribute to a holistic examination of how all the property's buildings contribute to ecclesial identity.

PARADIGM SHIFT: ORTHODOX MISSIONS IN AMERICA

A similar situation presents itself for Orthodox mission parishes using meeting spaces that are either rented or purchased, without consideration of the Orthodox architectural synthesis. Numerous Orthodox missions were blessed and planted by multiple Orthodox jurisdictions in America beginning in 1970, and these communities often gather in rented space until they have saved sufficient funds to purchase their own land and build a church.[92] In these cases, ecclesial identity is in an earlier stage of development, depending largely on demographics and the particular stories of the people constituting the community. They assemble to celebrate the Divine Liturgy, and thus fulfill the main criterion for architecture and liturgy since they are the people of God who make the space they occupy sacred. They also contradict the prevailing Orthodox architectural synthesis because the preestablished buildings they occupy were not designed and constructed with the requirements of Orthodox liturgy in mind. Innovative interior furnishing of the space can make only a limited contribution to celebrating the liturgy in its fullness, even when the community attempts to fulfill the obligations of the order of services. This examination of contemporary Orthodox architecture includes an analysis of mission communities meeting in rented or purchased buildings since American Orthodoxy actively promotes the planting of new missions. Their experience of liturgical worship in humble spaces makes a significant contribution to the diversity of ecclesial identities comprising Orthodox America.

Alexander Schmemann provided an informative example by comparing stereotypical "cathedral" liturgy with worship celebrated in limited spaces and means:

> In the first years of Russian immigration, when worship had to be celebrated in cellars and garages converted into churches, we became aware of the complete impossibility of celebrating it "as it should be," according to all the canons of elegance and solemnity proper to the synodical style of Russian Orthodoxy. This became especially apparent on days of services conducted by the archbishop or on special solemn festivals. In a very short time a piety was created which was not only by necessity but also in essence opposed to any show of pomp or external solemnity in worship, which would endure such pomp with suffering, as something undesirable and inappropriate to the nature of the Christian cult. For many people these wretched garage churches will remain forever connected with the fullness of liturgical experience, something which becomes impossible in churches of magnificent and grandiose design.[93]

Schmemann's example of worshiping in a garage illustrates a paradigm shift in the symbiosis of spatial context and the community's liturgical piety. He uses this example as a polar opposite of what transpired in the fourth century and beyond with the construction of large and ornate basilicas, and their impact on the community's piety.[94] His example provides a foundation for understanding the ritual context of mission communities worshiping in buildings that were not designed for worship. This study consults the realities presented by mission parishes in considering how they experience sacred space in properties they usually do not even own.

CONCLUSION

This chapter investigated select architectural models in Orthodox history to establish a working synthesis of principles serving as a hermeneutic for analyzing the contemporary parish profiles presented in this book. I examined Constantinople's Hagia Sophia because of the cathedral's influence on urban architecture and liturgy. The analysis included several references to the symbiosis of liturgy and architecture, the theological interpretation of sacred space, and the lasting imperial patronage of the Church. In developing the argument, the analysis demonstrates how a convergence of historical events such as theological controversies and foreign invasions simultaneously impacted architecture and liturgical celebration, resulting in a Middle Byzantine structure. Chirovsky's survey on the state of architecture in the Ukrainian Greco-Catholic Church identifies a trinal-structured church as the model for Byzantine worship in the contemporary American milieu, which confirms the Middle Byzantine church as an appropriate model for Orthodox structures, with the knowledge that the creative process of artistic freedom and retaining ethnic architectural traditions allows for flexibility in the application of this model.

The section introducing the dynamics of ecclesial identity demonstrates the necessity of considering the complete context of the liturgical community in an analysis of its architecture. The multifunctionality of the church building and its reciprocal relationships with the other buildings on the same property all contribute to and reflect ecclesial identity. The way any given community uses its sacred space helps define its particular ecclesiology, rooted in its praxis. This consideration is particularly germane to a study of contemporary Orthodox architecture in America since many communities meet in rented or pre-owned structures, or have no particular historic-ethnic identity shaping their ecclesial identities.

Finally, the community's memory makes a major contribution to analyzing its architectural plan. Imitative copying of Hagia Sophia, Kyiv Sophia, or churches constructed in the Middle Byzantine style includes, as part of the copying process, the memory of the events that shaped and influenced new architectural styles. For Orthodox, the prominence of Hagia Sophia always includes the Church's thorny and steadfast relationship with imperial officials and their patronage of the Church. For obvious reasons, today's churches are unable to precisely duplicate the same architectural methods and scale of building to honor the past. The current sociopolitical context of Orthodoxy in America provides new territory that the Church is still learning to navigate.

For many of these churches, however, the memory of patronage and history is so strong that much more is woven into the fabric of the community that uses the building space than the inherited liturgy. Orthodox in America are still learning how to reconcile their memories of imperial Byzantium, medieval Rus', imperial Russia, and other related personalities and institutions (like lay brotherhoods) with their new contexts, and this is often expressed by their architectural styles and also forms a layer in their ecclesial identities. The lesson from the past is that the work of art and liturgical historians on the contributions of architecture to the shape of the liturgy are accurate and informative, and when they are able, Orthodox in America attempt to copy most elements of the model. I am arguing that in the process of copying the model, Orthodox in America retain and sustain more than architectural paradigms and liturgical orders. The memory of their ecclesial past, shaped by history and prominent patrons of the Church, contributes to their contemporary ecclesial identities and thus shapes their ecclesiological praxis. The architecture expresses the entirety of the content woven into both the edifices the communities occupy and the people themselves.

The tendency for Orthodox to copy models from the past poses an intriguing challenge to architectural priorities in the context of ecumenical dialogue. In his response to receiving the Berakah Award from the North American Academy of Liturgy in 2011, Richard Vosko, a leading voice in Catholic architecture, bemoaned the re-emergence of an architectural movement in global Catholicism toward architectural clichés.[95] Vosko implies that the absence of creative architectural edifices that communicate the presence of the sacred to today's generation contributes to decreasing interest in and engagement of historically established Christian denominations in America.[96] Vosko calls for the design and building of architectural archetypes instead of reproducing banal copies of buildings unable to engage today's Christian.[97] Central to Vosko's thesis is that architectural forms must resonate with the self-identity and self-esteem of the people who engage them and make their buildings second homes.[98] Consequently, such buildings must bear the people's identities of past, present, and future.[99]

An application of Vosko's analysis to the situation of Orthodoxy in America appears to point to the preponderance of clichés in Orthodox American architecture. However, one must pause before affirming this conclusion too hastily, as Vosko's call for building programs to bear the people's past, present, and future identities is acutely germane to the architectural mosaic representing American Orthodoxy. For this study, Vosko's insights provide a useful contribution to analyzing the situation of American Orthodox architecture.[100] Vosko's discussion also opens opportunities for ecumenical reflection on how the future trajectory of Orthodox American architecture compares to the situations of other Christian denominations.

This overview of the Orthodox architectural heritage and discussion of contemporary methods for analyzing Christian architecture results in a list of hermeneutics for studying the architecture of the parish profiles in the following chapters.

1. Archetype or cliché: identification of specific historical architectural models used to design the contemporary building, with an analysis of how the current structure differs from its parent, and consideration of Vosko's archetype versus cliché question.

2. Architectural form and liturgical function: analysis of the community's liturgical celebration, how the architecture facilitates liturgy, and examination of obstacles, limitations, and opportunities.

3. Multifunctionality: study of community life in other buildings or designated areas of the property, and how the community's activities in these areas compare to its use of the building for worship, followed by a theological discussion of the relationship between the community's liturgy and its extra-liturgical activities.

4. Community memory: examination of local particularities expressed by the architectural design, decoration, or program, and how these contribute to community memory.

5. Conclusions on how architecture, liturgy, history, and memory reciprocally shape and are shaped by parish ecclesiology.

CHAPTER TWO

ST. KATHERINE UKRAINIAN ORTHODOX CHURCH

The Ukrainian Orthodox Church has a complicated history, and its story is not adequately told by scholars of Orthodox history and theology.[1] Usually, discussion of Ukrainian Orthodoxy consists of a few paragraphs in monographs on the Russian Orthodox Church.[2] Currently, there are three large Ukrainian Orthodox Churches centered in Ukraine: the Ukrainian Orthodox Church under the jurisdiction of the Moscow Patriarchate,[3] the Ukrainian Orthodox Church under the Kyiv Patriarchate[4] (a self-identified autocephalous church), and the Ukrainian Autocephalous Orthodox Church.[5] The fairly recent history of the emergence of the three competing Orthodox Churches in Ukraine is quite complex, and is not the subject of this study.[6]

St. Katherine Ukrainian Orthodox Church (Arden Hills, Minnesota) belongs to the Ukrainian Orthodox Church of the USA (UOC/USA), which is currently a part of the Ecumenical Patriarchate of Constantinople.[7] The UOC/USA was established by groups of Ukrainians living in the United States in 1924.[8] A large, second wave of Ukrainian immigrants enlarged the UOC/USA in the late 1940s and early 1950s, settling in America in the aftermath of World War II. Ukrainian immigrants who settled in Minneapolis and St. Paul blended into an existing parish, St. Michael Church in northeast Minneapolis, which had been established in the 1920s. Post–World War II Ukrainian immigrants established two new parishes: St. George parish in Minneapolis, near the University of Minnesota campus, and Saints Volodymyr and Ol'ha parish in St. Paul, established in 1951. The three parishes worshiped primarily in Ukrainian, although St. Michael celebrated occasional English services for first- and second-generation descendants of the original immigrants.

Saints Volodymyr and Ol'ha parish occupied a historic building that had served as a church and theater into the early 1990s, but it no longer desired to finance repairs of its structure on Portland Avenue in St. Paul, so the parish established its own building committee in 1987. The parish procured funding from private benefactors, including a substantial donation from parishioner Vera Tanasichuk, and proceeded with its plan for a new church. It purchased vacant property in Arden Hills in 1988, broke ground, and blessed the foundation in 1990. During the process of constructing the new building, Saints Volodymyr and Ol'ha convened representatives of the three local parishes in an effort to create one, unified Ukrainian Orthodox community for the Twin Cities metropolitan area. From the beginning of both the unification process and the preparation for the new building, the primary motivation for the new church was clear. A new church, located in the suburbs, would halt the membership attrition afflicting the three communities and provide a space that bridged the immigrants' memory of the past with the hope for future parish vitality. Sustaining a vibrant cultural identity was a top priority for the founders of the new parish. Tanasichuk stated, "we not only wanted a place for youth to have Bible studies, pray and worship, but to learn about Ukrainian culture, history and language."[9] The community's cultural identity emerges as a leading motif inscribed on the complex's architecture and artistic decoration, and significantly contributes to its ecclesial identity.

UNIFICATION NEGOTIATIONS AND CONSTRUCTION

In a meeting on December 15, 1996, the representatives of St. Michael and St. George parishes offered effusive praise for Tanasichuk's donation.[10] This meeting yielded a preview of the priorities and self-identity of St. Katherine as the parish prepared to occupy its new property. St. Katherine would provide a space where members could preserve Ukrainian culture and provide a source of pride for the members' children.[11] As unification discussions led by representatives of the three parishes continued into 1997, the prospects of unification darkened for several reasons. Concerns about paying the mortgage and the lack of public transportation for elderly parishioners to attend worship services were frequently mentioned, but an underlying tension on the social dynamics of the proposed unified parish became heated.[12] Tanasichuk and her sister, Neonila Maeser, were the primary donors of the building campaign, and representatives from other parishes felt that their prominent social stature might prohibit a sense of equal belonging among all members of a united parish.[13]

Despite repeated attempts to negotiate unification, the three parishes failed to achieve a union into one parish. Leaders at Saints Volodymyr and Ol'ha had hoped for a stream of income from the other two parishes, and the absence of additional significant donations, along with unanticipated construction costs, delayed the opening of St. Katherine until the parish was able to raise the cash to pay the contractor.[14] In January 1997, the parish was indebted to the contractor in the amount of $550,000, and hoped to raise money by hosting an ethnic festival featuring food and Ukrainian Easter eggs.[15] According to the minutes from a meeting of the Saints Volodymyr and Ol'ha board on October 27, 1996, the parish's struggle to find reliable financial sources to pay the contractor ignited serious tensions among the community's leaders, with several parish council members and parishioners requesting a general meeting to establish new parish leadership.[16] These financial struggles persisted until April 7, 1997, when the parish obtained a loan from Premier Bank in Maplewood, Minnesota, and settled the debt with the contractor.[17]

In August 1997, the parish completed construction of the church and parish hall, and celebrated the dedication of the church and the complex in a hierarchical liturgy presided over by Metropolitan Constantine, then head of the UOC/USA Synod of Bishops. Upon occupying the church, the parish changed the name from Saints Volodymyr and Ol'ha to St. Katherine, in commemoration of the Alexandrian martyr of the fourth century.[18] The parish paid the mortgage in full in 2005. As of February 2012, the parish has one full-time priest, with 70 official member families who pay monthly dues of approximately $120 to $150, depending on their status.[19] Its current liturgical cycle follows the basic order of the Byzantine liturgical year governed by the Typikon, Menaion, Triodion, and Pentecostarion, according to the Julian calendar. On April 17, 2011 (Palm Sunday), Bishop Daniel Zelinsky made an archpastoral visit to the parish and consecrated a new iconostasis.

St. Katherine Ukrainian Orthodox Church is the result of a complex convergence of ecclesial environmental factors motivated by an attempt to restore community vitality. The authors of the plan to establish a unified Ukrainian Orthodox community in the Twin Cities metropolitan area envisioned a space that would accommodate both Orthodox liturgical requirements and the continued cultivation of cultural identity in the community's younger generation. When the unification of the three parishes failed, St. Katherine's leaders moved forward with the building of the new church and its large hall, even though they had the option of reducing costs by forgoing the hall and kitchen. While the hall was a potential source of rental income, its potential for hosting public cultural events underpinned the community's adherence to retaining cultural identity.[20] St. Katherine described the achievement of the new church as the establishment of "the greater visibility of the Ukrainian presence in the Twin Cities," a statement that punctuates its cultural priority.[21] The following analysis of St. Katherine's architectural complex will reveal the parish's ecclesial identity as a demarcation of its cultural memory with minimal adherence to Orthodox liturgical requirements.

ST. KATHERINE AND KYIV SOPHIA

St. Katherine employs the style of Ukrainian baroque architecture, the renovated Kyiv Sophia in particular. Ukrainian baroque was a renaissance movement permeating Ukraine's artistic and intellectual life in the seventeenth and eighteenth centuries.[22] The emergence of baroque in Ukraine occurred because of the country's position as a borderland. Polish influence on Ukraine in the sixteenth century, up until Ukraine's annexation to Moscow in 1686 CE, created an influx of Western European talent into the country influencing its art, music, and architecture. Baroque architecture flourished in Ukraine under the patronage of Ivan Mazeppa, the hetman of the Zaporizhian Cossacks in the late seventeenth and early eighteenth centuries.[23] Mazeppa's patronage of constructing new churches and renovating old ones in the baroque style is renowned among Ukrainians.[24] Mazeppa studied in the Kyiv Academy, attended college in Warsaw, and served the Polish king, so he had a broad education. He was wealthy and accumulated nearly 20,000 estates, demonstrating his ability to support the construction of new churches. James Cracraft, in his study of Russian architecture under Tsar Peter I, divides Ukrainian baroque architecture into three distinct groups: vertical, mostly wooden churches of the three- to five-cupola type, "dressed in baroque finery"; basilican in form complete with transept, polygonal apse, and twin towers rising on the west front; and hybrid, traditional in structure with extensive baroque additions.[25] Thus, Ukrainian baroque produced a multivalence of architectural styles, of which Kyiv Sophia represents just one.

The baroque period in Ukraine was marked by intense decoration of the interior, especially of the iconostasis. Orest Subtelny identifies the attractive features of this style: grandeur; sumptuousness; decorativeness; and stress on form over content, complexity over simplicity, and synthesis over originality.[26] He concludes that Ukrainians prefer synthesis because of their historically precarious position between the Orthodox East and the Latin West, particularly appealing to the Ukrainian elite.[27]

The adoption of Kyiv Sophia, which celebrated its millennial anniversary in 2011,[28] as the model for St. Katherine's architecture is interesting because while for much of its history Kyiv Sophia was the cathedral church of the Kyivan Metropolia, the Dormition Cathedral of the Monastery of the Caves and the main church of the Brotherhood Monastery of the Epiphany in Kyiv exemplify Mazeppa's baroque restorations.[29]

Kyiv Sophia was originally constructed under the patronage of Grand Prince Yaroslav the Wise in 1037 CE.[30] Its position on a high hill overlooking the Dnipro River emphasizes its visibility, and it was the location of important events in Ukraine's history, including the reception of Hetman Bohdan Khmelnitsky following his victorious campaign over the Poles in 1648 CE and Ukraine's first declaration of independence in 1919.[31] The cathedral also housed the first independent movement of Ukrainian Orthodoxy: the autocephalous church headed by Metropolitan Vasyl Lypkivsky in 1921. Its twentieth-century history is probably the stronger motif shaping the memory of Ukrainian immigrants to the United States and Canada. Considering its function as the resting place for its patron, Yaroslav the Wise, and also other princes and metropolitans of Kyiv, Kyiv Sophia was an integral part of the Ukrainian people's collective memory.[32]

Like many of its sister churches, Kyiv Sophia was damaged by foreign invasion and fire, first in 1169 CE during the invasion of Suzdal Prince Andriy Bogoliubsky, then by fire in 1180 CE, and finally by the Mongol invasion of 1240 CE.[33] Kyiv Sophia was frequently renovated and repaired until the nineteenth century. The first significant renovation was implemented by Metropolitan Peter Mohyla around 1642 CE, with baroque renovations continued under Mazeppa between 1690 and 1707 CE.[34] Olexa Powstenko states that the current version of Kyiv Sophia is the result of Mazeppa's baroque restorations.[35] The original Kyiv Sophia was based on a domed Greek-cross plan, with thirteen cupolas. Powstenko opines that the cupolas represent Christ and the Twelve Apostles, with the four larger cupolas surrounding the dome representing the evangelists, and with a spherical shape representing Sophia's Byzantine heritage.[36] Cyril Mango, however, provides a more intuitive explanation based on the motivations of the church's patron and Kyiv's relationship with Constantinople, stating that the thirteen domes are the result of the Byzantine architect's adaptation of the smaller, five-domed church he knew in Constantinople to a much larger model in Kyiv, resulting in a thirteen-domed church, which provides proportionality to the structure.[37]

The restoration funded by Mazeppa included the building of pear-shaped cupolas and the construction of the bell tower.[38] An extensive restoration and decoration of the iconostasis occurred in the eighteenth century, as Metropolitan Raphael Zaborovksy replaced the wooden iconostasis of the Mohyla era with a new iconostasis featuring a rose motif.[39]

Kyiv Sophia functions as a symbol of the finest efforts to restore the central cathedral of the Kyiv Metropolia. The cathedral functions as a repository of the Ukrainian people's history, beginning with the period of the Grand Princes, through the reforms implemented by Peter Mohyla, the victories and defeats of the hetmanate, and a resurgence of Ukrainian identity in the twentieth and twenty-first centuries. It is thus fitting that a Ukrainian immigrant community would look to Kyiv Sophia as the model for its new church building. The key impetus here is not architectural functionality, but the people's memory. Kyiv Sophia is the symbol of the memory of Ukraine's finest moments, especially Ukrainians' accomplishments in the Ukrainian baroque intellectual and artistic movement. The desire of the people of St. Katherine parish to use Kyiv Sophia as the model for their church testifies to their mission of retaining and sustaining their identity as immigrants in America.

ST. KATHERINE'S CHURCH ARCHITECTURE

St. Katherine's church is a recent structure modeled after the Ukrainian baroque style, but certainly not the only one. Ukrainian immigrants have a history of incorporating elements of the Ukrainian baroque style into newly constructed or renovated churches in America.[40] By 1907, there were already more than one hundred Ukrainian churches in America that "possessed architectural features recalling, in one way or another, the appearance of the churches in the old country."[41] The architectural design of Ukrainian parish churches in America adapted to the needs of the times as new immigrants arrived immediately before and after World War II. Church structures needed to serve as multifunctional locations accommodating all of the immigrant community's needs, including education and other activities promoting cultural sustenance and awareness.[42] Liturgical celebration is one among many activities in which the local Ukrainian parish community engages.

St. Katherine Church was designed by Oleh Gregoret, American Institute of Architects (AIA), and in many ways follows the pattern described by Julian Jastremsky.[43] Table 2.1 lists all the components of the church's architectural plan. Gregoret described the overall setting

Table 2.1   Architectural Plan of St. Katherine Ukrainian Orthodox Church

Component	Description (includes capacity and square footage)
Church	4,400 square feet, capacity = 180–200
Connector	3,120 square feet
Parish hall	6,200 square feet, capacity = 300
Landscaped plaza	1,400 square feet
Lot area	209,914 square feet
Classrooms	capacity = 40
Parking	capacity = 124 cars

of the complex at the end of his statement for the parish's sixtieth anniversary book: "The approach to the Church is from Snelling Avenue by means of a curved road. The white stucco Church with copper cupolas is visible to the left across a beautiful wetland area and is framed by trees on all sides [fig. 2.1]. The western and northern portion(s) of the site have a large parking area. The south side of the Church has an extensive lawn area suitable for picnics and other outdoor events."[44] St. Katherine's property also includes a preexisting residence for the pastor (2,000 square feet) with a garage that is currently rented to tenants. The property is parallel to State Highway 96 to the immediate north, and accessed via Snelling Avenue to the east in Arden Hills, near the main arteries of Interstate 35W and 694 connecting the suburbs of Minneapolis and St. Paul. Thus, the church is accessible to parishioners and visitors who live throughout the Minneapolis–St. Paul area since Arden Hills is near both cities. The large parking lot borders the parish hall to the west and the hall, plaza, and church to the north. The rectory is on the northwest corner of the property (currently occupied by tenants). See fig. 2.2 for a site plan of the property.

The church maintains the traditional Orthodox orientation facing eastward. Five domes crown the church: four smaller pear-shaped cupolas with three-barred crosses are at each corner, and there is a larger dome over the nave. The top of the cross on the central cupola of the church is ninety feet high. The overall shape represents the traditional Orthodox trinal architectural plan, with a sanctuary and apse, an ico-

Figure 2.1   St. Katherine Ukrainian Orthodox Church, exterior (courtesy of Maya Gregoret)

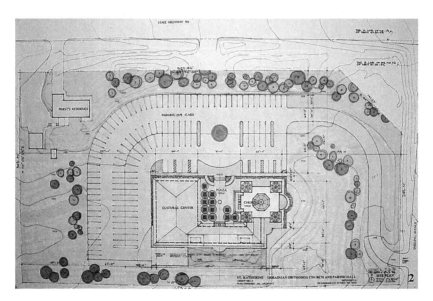

Figure 2.2   St. Katherine Ukrainian Orthodox Church, site plan (courtesy of Oleh Gregoret)

Figure 2.3   St. Katherine Ukrainian Orthodox Church, interior (courtesy of Maya Gregoret)

nostasis, a nave, and a narthex (fig. 2.3). The sanctuary is quite spacious, with the vestry to the immediate north and a restroom to the south, easily accessed from the sanctuary. The architectural plan does not indicate the sanctuary's occupancy, but the space is conducive for concelebrated liturgies, with ample room for approximately twenty clergy and altar servers.

The nave is the largest space within the church complex, but not proportionately larger than the sanctuary and narthex as one might expect. Pews brought from the previous structure owned by the church in St. Paul constitute the seating. The building has one large loft, used by the parish's choir, with a capacity of approximately forty to sixty people, over the west end of the nave. Singers and parishioners can use either one of two staircases or an elevator to access the choir area. Doors separate the nave from the narthex, which is quite large. A small "quiet room" is available for families with small children in the southwest corner of the nave. St. Katherine repurposed the interior furnish-

ings used in the St. Paul property. The frame for the iconostasis originally painted by parishioner Michael Mychalevych and carved by Igor
Kubik was dismantled and reset, with the same icons decorating the
interior. A new iconostasis painted by Volodymyr Hordiiv was consecrated on April 17, 2011.[45]

The "connector" literally connects the church and the parish hall,
so parishioners can easily move from church to hall without difficulty in
inclement weather, a reality in harsh Minnesota winters. The connector
also contains space for three classrooms, a library, a large coat area, two
restrooms, and a museum in the lobby. Currently the museum contains
many memorabilia from the parish's history, along with photos of the
ruling bishops. People can access the lobby via the outdoor plaza, the
church, or the parish hall.

The parish hall is quite large (6,200 square feet), containing a fellowship area, a large kitchen, a stage for performances, and storage areas
(fig. 2.4). St. Katherine's community uses the hall space frequently. A
luncheon is served on most Sundays after the Divine Liturgy. Special
meals are served to the community annually on Christmas Eve (January
6 in the Julian calendar) and following the Paschal Orthros and Divine
Liturgy. The parish also uses the hall for special feasts, such as the annual patronal feast day of St. Katherine on December 7; the annual pre-
Lenten "maslyana" associated with Cheesefare week, which constitutes
the last chance to eat dairy products before Lent and is very popular
among Eastern Slavs; a Palm Sunday bazaar and bake sale open to the
public; and other special occasions. St. Katherine features its parish hall
and promotes it to the broader community as a space to be rented for
special occasions, so the hall serves as a source of income when the parish rents it for wedding receptions, meetings, or banquets.

St. Katherine was built with the explicit intention of retaining the
Ukrainian baroque-style Ukrainians cherish. The church's high, pear-
shaped cupolas are visible from a close distance through the trees on the
border of the property, with the central cupola reaching a height of
ninety feet. The finished, white-painted stucco exterior with precast art-
stone trim offers a sense of elegance that coheres well with the Ukrainian
baroque style. The church's backdrop against the sky during a good
weather day creates a lovely setting and photo op.[46] The renovated

Figure 2.4   St. Katherine Ukrainian Orthodox Church, parish hall (courtesy of Maya Gregoret)

iconostasis also evokes the Ukrainian baroque style, with its consistently flowing motif of vines and roses in gold, set against a white background. Thus, the most visible elements of the church exterior and interior integrate elements from the Ukrainian baroque style: the high, copper cupolas; the white building; the windows in the cupolas promoting a solid balance of shade and light; and the renovated iconostasis.[47]

ANALYSIS OF ST. KATHERINE'S CHURCH

Obviously, St. Katherine is not an exact replica of Kyiv Sophia. The absence of wall-to-wall frescoes or sarcophagi containing the remains of its patrons and the numerous buildings of the Kyiv Sophia (bell tower, Metropolitan's residence) do not re-emerge in Arden Hills. But St. Katherine has created a space that retains the core of the spirit of Kyiv Sophia with its spacious property, cupolas, artistic renderings on the exterior and interior, and inclusion of a plaza. Kyiv Sophia was the center of the Kyiv Metropolia for centuries, and St. Katherine does not have the resources to replicate every aspect of Kyiv Sophia. However, its location bridging Minneapolis and St. Paul and its architectural program capacitate it to serve as the central location for the Orthodox Ukrainians who live in the Twin Cities. From the perspective of the community's context, St. Katherine has accomplished its goal of integrating Ukrainian baroque exemplified by Kyiv Sophia most effectively in its core exterior and interior features.

St. Katherine's Liturgy

St. Katherine follows the Byzantine rite used by the Orthodox Church. Its liturgical celebration follows the general direction of the Typikon.[48] For the movable cycle of feasts, including pre-Lent, Lent, and Holy Week, St. Katherine follows the Lenten Triodion.[49] The Pentecostarion is used for the post-Paschal period (through Pentecost), and for the fixed cycle of the twelve months it follows the Menaion.[50] With one pastor serving the parish, St. Katherine does not slavishly follow the Typikon's order of services.[51] The assembly meets on Sundays for the Divine Liturgy. For particularly solemn feasts, such as Christmas and Theophany, a broader cycle of services is celebrated when these feasts fall on weekdays. The parish begins to celebrate Holy Week on Thursday (the Gospels and Orthros of Great and Holy Friday), with one Vespers celebrated on Good Friday evening; the vesperal liturgy celebrated on the morning of Holy Saturday; and Nocturnes, Orthros, and the Divine Liturgy celebrated on Pascha Sunday.

   The description of St. Katherine's liturgy illustrates the community's use of its facilities and shows the harmony between its architecture and liturgy. Its liturgy represents the basic notion of architectural form shaping liturgical function. The liturgical celebration of the Divine Liturgy on Sundays is a faithful representation of the customary Divine Liturgy celebrated by Orthodox in the twentieth and twenty-first centuries described in chapter 1. St. Katherine features a few notable practices in its variant of the Divine Liturgy. The celebrant reads the Gospel facing the people at St. Katherine, even if a deacon is present. At the conclusion of the distribution of Holy Communion at St. Katherine, the celebrant follows a Ukrainian tradition of touching communicants on the head with the chalice containing the remnants of the consecrated gifts before returning them to the table of oblation.

After the Divine Liturgy, brief memorial services commemorating the loved ones of St. Katherine's parishioners are often celebrated. Thus, the celebrating clergy perform the vast majority of the liturgical movements at St. Katherine. The people are largely static, observing the liturgy from the pews, with the choir singing the responses from the loft overlooking the nave. With the exception of personal business, the people move on two occasions. The first movement is to receive Holy Communion. At St. Katherine, a small but growing number of people regularly receives communion. The second movement occurs at the dismissal, when the people leave the church building.

This description of the regular Sunday liturgy at St. Katherine might seem banal, though this is not the intention. The description of this liturgical celebration represents the core of the normal Sunday liturgical celebration in the Orthodox Church. Certainly, prevalent traditions in local communities and special occasions such as a hierarchical liturgy break the rhythm of the norm, and liturgical scholars are calling for restorations of particular historical models, adapted to meet the needs of the contemporary Church, to renew the broader tradition of Orthodox liturgy.[52] From the perspective of the Byzantine rite historian, St. Katherine's liturgy represents a minimalist approach to the liturgical cycle. Each liturgical movement is limited in space; the choir is separate from the people; and the vast majority of liturgical orations are recited quietly, with only the doxologies and the Liturgy of the Word proclaimed aloud. However, St. Katherine celebrates all the aspects of the Orthodox liturgy attractive to scholar and visitor alike. Multiple incensations; chanting of litanic biddings and orations; veneration of icons; lighting of candles; and the singing of a choir familiar with "stock" musical compositions spanning the sixteenth through the twentieth centuries, including numerous gems from the Ukrainian Orthodox resurgence in the early twentieth century, enhance the liturgy's aesthetical dimension. The variety of music employed by the choir when it sings in Ukrainian adds to the liturgical aesthetic. St. Katherine's choir is progressively expanding its English repertoire and nuances in establishing the proper mutual influence between English liturgical texts and music adapted from the original Ukrainian or Slavonic, so on the Sundays when English is the liturgy's language, the choir usually uses more simple works. Thus, the parishioners of St. Katherine are most familiar with the standard Sunday liturgy, and the inclusion of English in the liturgy sets them apart from their sister Ukrainian Orthodox parish.

Iconographic Blends

St. Katherine's iconography is somewhat limited, given the vast wall space of the church's interior. The worshiper's visual experience is dominated by the large iconostasis and impacted by a polyphonic blend of procured and donated icons. When the church was constructed in 1997, the parish reconstituted the original iconostasis from its previous building on Portland and Victoria in St. Paul. Parishioners designed the iconostasis frame and painted the icons, dating from 1963. A team consisting of Michael Mychalevych, Eugene Pysarsky, Ivan Ilievsky, and Igor Kubik performed the painting, gilding, sculpting, and carving of the icons and iconostasis frame, which was built in a Romanesque style to accord with the older and historic building occupied in 1963.[53] In 1997, St. Katherine hired Volodymyr Hordiiv, an iconographer and restorer of church art, who rebuilt the iconostasis to fit the new space, added rich wood carvings to enhance the baroque quality of the iconostasis, and repainted damaged icons.[54] St. Katherine hired Hordiiv again, in 2010, to renovate the iconostasis one final time.[55]

The restored iconostasis significantly updates St. Katherine's iconographic program because several new icons were added, including an icon of St. Katherine of Alexandria on the southern end of the iconostasis and new icons of the archangels Gabriel and Michael for the deacons' doors. The iconostasis is much more decorative with the weaving of extensive gilded woodcarving, especially in the two deacons' doors and the royal doors. Greek crosses adorned with a vine theme are at the bottom of each icon frame. Hordiiv's new icons promote more visibility as he employed traditional materials such as gold leaf, which enhance the lighting and visibility of the icons. Hordiiv's restoration both updates the iconographic program and significantly enhances its baroque quality. Since the seating arrangement and longitudinal axis of the church orient the worshipers toward the sanctuary and, consequently, the iconostasis, one can only conclude that the primary visual liturgical experience promotes encountering Christ and the saints in a holy setting enhanced by creation's beauty, a hallmark of baroque iconography.

Several other icons adorn the walls of St. Katherine, resulting in a polyphonic visual blend because they utilize completely different materials and were created by different artists. Several large icons were donated by the Olishkevich family, unique because the icons are embroidered, not painted.[56] The icons are also significant because they are the only ones adorning the spacious walls of the nave, and consequently draw the attention of the participant. The embroidered icons in the nave were created by an immigrant priest of the Ukrainian Greco-Catholic Church (UGCC), Father Dmytro Blazhejowsky, a native of the Lemko region of Ukraine who studied theology and history in the Urbanian and Gregorian universities in Rome in the 1940s.[57] Blazhejowsky's iconographic work was devoted to sustaining particular elements of Ukrainian Christian culture and the legitimacy of embroidered icons in the diaspora.[58] After the legalization of the UGCC and the independence of Ukraine in 1991, Blazhejowsky traveled to Ukraine and displayed samples of his work in Kyiv museums, with a museum devoted to his work opening in L'viv.[59] The diffusion of Blazhejowsky's work and the tradition of embroidered icons in Ukraine and among Ukrainian parishes abroad are unknown.

At St. Katherine, seven of Blazhejowsky's icons adorn the walls of the nave. The most prominent icon hangs on the northern wall, an embroidered protection of Kyiv Sophia and Theotokos Oranta (fig. 2.5). The southern wall has three large embroidered icons: Saints Volodymyr and Ol'ha positioned side by side, and St. Katherine a few feet away. An embroidered icon of the Theotokos Oranta hangs on the western wall at the entrance of the nave, facing the narthex, and flanked on both sides of the narthex door at the interior wall of the nave by smaller icons of Christ and the Theotokos with Child (which mirror

Figure 2.5   Icon of Kyiv Sophia (photo by author)

Figure 2.6 St. Katherine Ukrainian Orthodox Church, sanctuary, icons (photo by author)

the same icons of the iconostasis). The sisterhood of St. Katherine also purchased two embroidered icons following this tradition for the sanctuary, with a painted icon of the Risen Christ in between the embroidered Theotokos (north, to the left) and the Risen Christ (south, to the right) (fig. 2.6). The embroidered icons in the sanctuary were not created by Blazhejowsky.

The embroidered icons make four significant contributions to St. Katherine. First, they deliberately include a regional iconographic tradition (Lemko) varying from the customary painted icons or mosaics traditionally adorning Byzantine rite churches. The presence of the embroidered icons in St. Katherine embellishes the community's mission of sustaining and cultivating Ukrainian cultural traditions representing multiple Ukrainian regions. Second, the prominence of the Kyiv Sophia Oranta again emphasizes the community's veneration of Kyiv Sophia as its mother temple and model for its architecture since St. Katherine is modeled after Kyiv Sophia. Third, the icons on the southern wall represent the entirety of the parish's history in a type of progression, in homage to its past as Saints Volodymyr and Ol'ha parish and another representation of its present and future as St. Katherine. Fourth, the fact that a Greek Catholic priest authored the icons of the nave was not prohibitive, and aptly represents St. Katherine's American context, where relations between Ukrainian Greek Catholics and Orthodox are generally warm due to their shared circumstances and common cultural mission. The presence of embroidered icons in the apse of the sanctuary illustrates the permeation of the community's mission of cultural cultivation into every architectural segment. This detail is important because it illustrates the legitimacy of this style of sacred art to occupy the walls nearest the Eucharistic table in the sanctuary. The embroidered icons of the sanctuary could be construed as representing the community's offering the entirety of its cultural heritage to God at the liturgy, an authentic manifestation of theologizing the community's self-identity in its architecture and its art.

In summary, St. Katherine's current iconographic program is polyphonic due to the varying styles of icons adorning the church. The parish's recent investment in renovating and updating the iconostasis punctuates its grounding in the Ukrainian baroque artistic heritage of the past. The orientation of the church focuses the primary visual experience toward the iconostasis, but the prominence of the embroidered icons introduces a worship experience of variety and contrast, and emphasizes the parish's mission to retain and cultivate the entirety of its Ukrainian heritage. An attentive liturgical participant will encounter the breadth of the parish's self-identity in the iconographic program. The iconostasis offers a legitimately mainstream Orthodox worship experience decorated by Ukrainian baroque, whereas the embroidered icons illustrate the community's goal to establish icons representing the Lemko embroidered iconographic tradition generously donated by benefactors, unusual for its prominent display in an Orthodox church.

The worshiper consequently recognizes the newness of the parish, as there is plenty of space on the walls for iconographic expansion, and will also experience worship as permeated by the parish's ecclesial identity seeking to retain its past heritage, which includes the community's history as Saints Volodymyr and Ol'ha parish. The parishioner experiences an environment where the community includes its hopes and aspirations for the cultivation and proliferation of its self-identity in its liturgical offering to God, as these elements are permanently inscribed in the interior architectural adornment of the church. The saintly patrons of the past and present (Volodymyr, Ol'ha, and Katherine) all bear witness to the community's self-offering to God in the present. The architectural design and icons of St. Katherine evoke Amy Papalexandrou's notion of memory in architecture.[60] Papalexandrou mentioned that the icons in Hagia Sophia referred to the memory of violence in the recent past. These design motifs implicitly refer to past struggles at St. Katherine as the decoration of the temple's exterior and interior speaks to the community's resilient cultural cultivation made possible by freedom in the West and protection from the Soviet past.

In conclusion, St. Katherine's liturgical celebration offers the participants a comprehensive view of the community's status and self-understanding. Architecturally, the liturgy utilizes only a limited portion of the church's space. The spaciousness of the sanctuary is largely irrelevant because there is normally only one celebrant assisted by a handful of acolytes and the pews do not encourage free movement by the people during the liturgy (with the exception of major feasts of the liturgical year). The community follows the minimal requirements of the established liturgical ordo of the Byzantine rite by regularly celebrating the Sunday Eucharist and offices of the major feasts, placing it in the mainstream of American Orthodoxy. The parish's iconography and liturgical music represent its status in the tension of the present, beholden to its past and wishing to retain and cultivate it for the future. The interior height and large choir gallery promote the quality liturgical singing and musical repertoire precious to Ukrainian émigré communities. While the parish choir employs many compositions from Ukrainian composers of the late nineteenth and early twentieth centuries, it also gradually introduced English into its liturgical celebration. One may view the increasing use of English as an instance of pastoral transition or a concession to an internal constituent, but the result is still a tension between retaining the Ukrainian past and embracing the future parish trajectory, which, barring an influx of new Ukrainian immigrants, will be English-speaking.[61]

Likewise, while many of the interior walls offer space for an expansion of the iconographic program, the dominance of the renovated iconostasis and embroidered icons offer a polyphony that is interesting but not necessarily harmonic. With the renovated iconostasis offering a prominent display of the finest Ukrainian baroque woodcarving, and the embroidered icons highlighting the parish's breadth of immigrant ethnic identity, the liturgical arts adorn the space by offering the participant a selection from the best works of the Ukrainian past. From the perspective of St. Katherine's self-identity and goals in building the church, which equated the cultivation and retention of cultural heritage with the practice of the Orthodox faith, the harmony of architecture and liturgical arts aptly represents the parish's self-identity as a community retaining its past and desiring to project it safely into its future.

PARISH HALL

Chapter 1 introduced possible components of parish ecclesial identity. For many Orthodox in America, the experience of immigration created a need for them to find fellowship with people of their native countries. The parish community was not only a place for liturgical worship, but also for special schools where children of the immigrants would learn the intricacies of their native country's history, culture, and language.[62] Suitable space for holding such meetings and events, essentially incarnating the life experience of immigrants, was necessary and outside the liturgically defined trinal space of the church building.

At 6,200 square feet, St. Katherine's parish hall (also called a cultural center) is considerably larger than the 4,400 square-foot church building. One can rent the parish hall, and St. Katherine is a popular venue for various events. The connector serves as a literal and definitive bridge for understanding St. Katherine's self-identity. At 3,120 square feet, the connector, containing the classrooms and museum, combines with the parish hall to more than double the size of the church. Thus, the architectural plan of the complex assumes that the hall will be occupied with greater frequency and by larger numbers of people than the church itself. On Sundays and solemn feasts, the connector provides a convenient way for parishioners and visitors to continue their fellowship in the parish hall without encountering Minnesota's frequently inclement weather. The Twin Cities has a local tradition where the clergy and people from the sister Ukrainian Orthodox and Catholic parishes gather together to honor the host parish's temple feast. Usually, visitors from the sister parishes will celebrate liturgy in their home parishes and then attend the post-liturgical banquet of the host parish. The size of the parish hall accommodates a larger number of visitors without expecting them to participate in the liturgical celebration. The connector and the parish hall also facilitate the multifunctional architectural quality of the complex. People participating in a wedding reception or banquet who have no interest in Orthodoxy can access their gathering without entering the sacred space of the church. At a surface level, there is absolutely nothing unusual or remarkable about these circumstances. They represent a common practice among church communities of varying sizes and backgrounds.

The architecture's multifunctionality exposes the community's mindset. St. Katherine depends on income generated by its superior parish hall to help pay property costs. The community extends hospitality to outsiders to celebrate their own joy with minimal contact with the host community (St. Katherine). Visitors attending an event at St. Katherine have no obligation to consider the parish's ecclesial identity. They can participate in their event and depart without experiencing the gathering of Christ's body in the temple devoted to glorifying him. In this regard, St. Katherine's outreach is attached to its expectation of an economic return on investment. For those not belonging to the community, the parish hall and its possibilities are the chief draw. Certainly, the church's exterior design and the community's story depicted by its interior art ignite interest in some visitors, who want to learn more about the unique structure. The overall trajectory of the complex's plan speaks to separating liturgical and extra-liturgical gatherings, a real, if unintentional, demarcation of sacred space.

The museum of the connector demonstrates St. Katherine's mission of retaining and sustaining Ukrainian identity.[63] For example, the central exhibit case contains a bandura (the Ukrainian national instrument) made by deceased parishioner Volodymyr Wowk, who taught

Figure 2.7   St. Katherine Ukrainian Orthodox Church, museum, bandura (photo by author)

bandura to parish children for many years (fig. 2.7).[64] Prominently displayed for all to behold, the bandura is a symbol of the parish's historical cultivation of its Ukrainian heritage, a bridge from past to present. Another example of the parish's inner dynamic is an oil painting titled *Democracy* by Orysia Sinitowich-Gorsky from Winnipeg, Canada, donated to the parish following an exhibit of her works in 2006 (fig. 2.8). The picture depicts a scene in Ukraine during the country's so-called Orange Revolution of 2004. These examples are but a small sampling of the museum's holdings, and demonstrate the parish's inscription of its cultural self-identity and cultivation on its architectural program, as the connector serves as a natural highway for visitors.

In summary, the dynamic program of church, connector, and hall illuminates St. Katherine's intra-ecclesial identity. One can attend the post-liturgical gathering without entering the sacred space of the church. The space's multifunctionality seems to anticipate this occurrence. Clearly, on occasions where visitors will join the community

Figure 2.8 St. Katherine Ukrainian Orthodox Church, museum, *Democracy*, oil painting by Orysia Sinitowich-Gorsky (photo by author)

after the liturgy, the larger size of the parish hall is advantageous, as it can readily accommodate extra people. In St. Katherine's case, the larger size of the parish hall represents the immigrant hybrid priorities of having space serving several community priorities. The community will do much more than worship. At St. Katherine, the community uses the parish hall for cultural festivals, meetings, and education. The hall's large size shows that the parish expects more people to use the space for extra-liturgical activity, and outside the connector, there is no organic connection to the liturgical assembly. In contrast, the limited size of the church indicates a plateau in community growth. With a maximum occupancy of 180 to 200 people, the size of the liturgical assembly is not expected to significantly increase. The contrast between the church building and the hall represents the Orthodox immigrant mission of sustaining and promoting identity. The community is not expected to grow because an influx of new immigrants is not anticipated, though many new Ukrainian-language immigrants have settled in the Twin Cities since 1997. Evangelistic mission to the unchurched is not a priority. Visitors will be welcomed but are under no pressure to participate in the liturgical assembly. Thus, the building program itself reveals the parish's comfort with the status quo and its interest in promoting and cultivating its ethnic heritage.

CONCLUSION

St. Katherine's architectural program stands out among those of many of its Ukrainian predecessors in America by finding a space that most suitably reflects and allows parishioners to nurture their complex ecclesial identity. St. Katherine's multifunctionality reveals this ecclesial identity: a community of immigrants devoted to sustaining their heritage in diverse community gatherings, of which liturgy is a part, but not necessarily the center.[65] For St. Katherine, the beauty of the church structure ignites interest in the visitor, but provides him with the option of forgoing the church and entering the hall instead. Encountering God through the liturgy celebrated by Christ's body is one option among many. The parish's liturgy retains the Byzantine synthesis it inherited.

While the liturgy itself has progressed with increased frequency in the liturgical use of English and people partaking of Holy Communion, St. Katherine represents, in some ways, the parish models discussed by Chirovsky. The parish adheres to the favored Ukrainian baroque style represented by Ivan Mazeppa's renovated Kyiv Sophia, a gesture of honor to its past, sustained by the community's life in the parish hall. Some might critique St. Katherine's architectural plan as a cliché, too nostalgic, slavishly "xeroxing the past,"[66] given its fidelity to the height of Ukrainian culture and emphasis on extra-liturgical community gatherings. The architecture, however, reveals parishioners' own expression of ecclesial identity. Their strong memory of resilient Ukrainian identity, preserved under severe duress during the Soviet period and liberated in the West, is fiercely and proudly displayed for visitors to see as they drive by the property, in formal liturgical worship, and on other occasions.

For St. Katherine, the body of Christ is mobile, and is equally vibrant in its extra-liturgical gatherings in the parish hall as it is in the church. Its particular manifestation of Christ's body must gather frequently in both locations. The absence of its local body is noted not only in the church, but also in the parish hall and throughout its property. St. Katherine's architectural plan and style represents the complex mosaic of its community's memory. The symbiosis of architecture and liturgy at St. Katherine is quite elementary, as the liturgical ethos is somewhat minimalist. The architecture, however, helps to tell the entirety of the community's story. This story is inscribed throughout the exteriors and interiors of the property's buildings, beginning with the church as a copy of Kyiv Sophia and including the prominence of Ukrainian baroque in the iconostasis, the retention of cultural heritage in the embroidered icons, and the tension between past and future in the hybrid liturgical use of Ukrainian and English. Thus, while the people of St. Katherine gather for the liturgy and honor it as the center of the Orthodox life, their architecture reveals a much broader ecclesial identity sharply influenced by their unique memory. Liturgical participants experience the community's architecture as an offering of their self-identity to God, rooted in the past, with the hope that God will preserve it in the community's future.

St. Katherine's contribution to the future trajectory of Orthodox architecture in America might fall on the side of exception, but is still important. The parish exemplifies the attempt to sustain and promote local ethnic identity still current among many Orthodox groups in America. What is unknown is its community trajectory. Assuming a plateau of new immigration at minimum, its community development depends on its success in retaining all of its community constituents and also initiating new people into its community, which could increase the inner tension between past and future in the present. With the introduction of new people, St. Katherine's own ecclesial identity will be shaped by the experiences and memories of new people, which could result in a future architectural adjustment.

CHAPTER THREE

ST. MATTHEW
ORTHODOX CHURCH

St. Matthew Orthodox Church, founded in 1988 as a mission and located in Columbia, Maryland (Howard County), is part of the Diocese of Washington in the Orthodox Church in America (OCA). The community assembled in various locations of Howard County near Fort Meade and Columbia, and gathered for approximately twelve years in the Slayton House, a temporary rented space that accommodated growth. The parish community built a home for physically disabled adults at King's Contrivance Interfaith Campus (KCIC) in Columbia in 2001 called St. Matthew House. St. Matthew House has 15 units for residents, along with 2 apartments for managers in a building with 3 floors, consisting of 18,500 square feet. In 2000, the community began the process of purchasing available property at KCIC, which had been set aside for church building use by a Columbia development group. Charles Alexander, American Institute of Architects (AIA), who owns and operates the design studio of Broken Boxes in Ellicott City, Maryland, designed the architectural plan for the church of St. Matthew. Construction began in December 2005 and the property was ready for worship in 2007, with the first Eucharistic liturgy served on the first Sunday of Lent. St. Matthew parish received a $1.6 million loan from

Howard Bank to finance the church's construction. Metropolitan Herman (then-primate of the OCA) consecrated the building in May 2008.

St. Matthew Orthodox Church has a unique sense of self-identity. The community embraces people of diverse ethnic backgrounds, but the core of the community's mission and worship is exclusive ministry in the English language. As a parish of the OCA, using English as the official language of community life and liturgy is not unusual since the OCA has largely emphasized English as a core component of its strategy for mission and outreach. From its inception, St. Matthew deliberately avoided associating with any particular Orthodox ethnic group.[1] The mission's chief objective was evangelization of new people, and it purposefully eschewed propositioning parishioners from other Orthodox parishes in the general area, though the parish welcomed people who came from area Orthodox parishes. The OCA's Diocese of Washington is quite small, with only eleven parishes and one mission serving OCA communicants in Delaware, Virginia, Maryland, and DC. Parish options for residents on the western shore of Maryland near the two beltways of Baltimore and DC are limited, with St. Nicholas Cathedral, a trilingual parish (English, Russian, and Georgian) near Georgetown in DC; St. Andrew parish in Baltimore; and St. Mark Church in Bethesda (near DC).[2] Until a mission parish was established in Annapolis in 2010, the OCA faithful of Howard and Anne Arundel Counties had to commute to St. Nicholas in DC (which has only on-street parking), St. Andrew in Baltimore, or Saints Constantine and Helen Greek Orthodox Church in Annapolis. St. Matthew parish provided an English-speaking Orthodox presence for the OCA faithful in between the other Orthodox communities. One can easily access St. Matthew parish without using the Baltimore or DC beltways since St. Matthew is located right off Route 32, easily accessible via a network of state highways and county roads. Parishioners stated that St. Nicholas, St. Andrew, and St. Mark, the neighboring OCA parishes, all voiced strong support for the creation of St. Matthew without any overt concern that the new parish might attract their own parishioners.[3] Father Raymond Velencia was the rector of the parish from 1989 to 2010, and he oversaw the process of parish mission and church construction. St. Matthew parish supported two priests from 1997 to 2010, and currently supports one priest and two deacons.[4]

St. Matthew parish is a relatively young Orthodox community. The community's mission emphasizes outreach to native people in the Columbia-Laurel area, and provides a home for Orthodox of diverse backgrounds, united by the liturgical use of English. The parish has a relationship with St. Matthew House, a home for physically disabled adults, and shares a campus with St. Matthew House and Cornerstone Church.

DESCRIPTION OF CHURCH ARCHITECTURE

St. Matthew's architecture is designed to maximize community activity driven by its mission and logistical realities. St. Matthew is part of a larger complex of buildings (KCIC), with St. Matthew House to the immediate north and Cornerstone Church to the south. The three communities share one parking lot. The campus is adjacent to the Columbia Village Center, a strip mall with several businesses, including Amherst House (its place of meeting for six years, 1990–96), several small eateries and convenience stores, a bank, an auto service station, and a large grocery store (Harris Teeter) on the farthest western end of the whole complex. Thus, St. Matthew is at the center of a visible and public neighborhood in Columbia, which draws much automobile and walking traffic from local residents.

St. Matthew's architectural plan was impacted by the rules of the Columbia Village Center, which prohibit the public display of overtly religious symbols and require multiple religious expressions, hence the presence of two Christian churches belonging to different parent organizations.[5] The religious structures on the property must also be built from the same materials. The exterior of St. Matthew's church is brick and does not have an explicitly Orthodox visual characteristic except for a simple cross crowning the tower (fig. 3.1). The entrance to the building is accessible via the shared parking lot on the east side. The building sits on a downward sloping hill on a neighborhood street and has two levels, with the church on the second level and the parish hall on the lower level. As one enters the complex from the parking lot, the narthex functions as an area of assembly leading to a staircase and an elevator that provide access to the hall on the lower level, with the main entrance to the church through double glass doors to the left, and a hallway with

Figure 3.1   St. Matthew Orthodox Church, exterior (photo by author)

coatrooms, a reception area, and offices for the rector continuing past the church (fig. 3.2). The entrance point has three Greek arches, a design motif honoring the multivalence of the parish's ethnic heritage. The tower at the entrance contains a small bell that calls the assembly to worship. The size of the entire upper level is 6,300 square feet.

The parish hall is on the lower level, and has a large area for assembly and fellowship, a kitchen, six classrooms of varying sizes for the parish's large church school, a music room, and storage areas. Doors from the lower level lead out to a cement patio on the west end, with a walking path ascending around the church to the parking lot. The periphery of the church descends sharply from east to west. The size of the entire lower level is 6,300 square feet. The lower level of the church building provides the space for post- and extra-liturgical assembly. The architectural design illustrates the main assembly area of the lower level as octagonal, functionally following the church design on the upper level. Sunday coffee hours, church dinners and special affairs, church

Figure 3.2   St. Matthew Orthodox Church, narthex (photo by author)

school instruction, and meetings all occur in this common area. St. Matthew parish built the hall on the lower level for purely functional purposes; there are no hallways to classrooms, and there is ample access to the exterior.[6] The lower level also provides immediate access to the lower loggia, which was designed to accommodate liturgical processions. The parish shares the parking lot with Cornerstone Church, with approximately one hundred spaces available to both communities.

The overarching goal of St. Matthew's architectural plan is to create a space facilitating the most salient points of Orthodox liturgy within the context of the church's position in the interfaith campus. Alexander describes the goal as follows:

Because this church is to be connected to two other structures, the accommodation of the traditional circumnavigation of the "church" used in so many Orthodox rituals became a key design feature. To shorten the path that would have required circling three buildings, this scheme creates loggias on the upper and lower level[s] that allow passage around the sanctuary yet within the confines of the church's footprint. The sequence starts in the narthex, descends to a lower loggia along the rear of the building, up a garden path to the entry loggia, and back to the narthex. The various structures and streets that make up this interfaith center create a context with a clear organizing geometry. Because of the desire to maintain a traditional east-facing apse, the design rotates the sanctuary within the overall geometry of the building. The result is a building that establishes a street façade that is animated by the curve of the apse and the angled direction of the main roof. It is at once a part of a larger built order, yet also oriented to its symbolic compass.[7]

Alexander also offers the following elements as points of emphasis in the parish's architectural plan: an octagonal orientation, a centralized dome, an apse, aisles, and arches. Many of these elements are visible from the exterior, particularly the apse, as it protrudes from the eastern end immediately facing the parking lot, and also the four prominent arches forming the upper loggia at the main entrance to the building. The loggia with its arches on the lower level is also quite attractive, though not visible to people entering the church from the main parking lot entrance. The angled direction of the main roof is unique to St. Matthew's architecture, and while it does not follow the Middle Byzantine model, it accommodates the interior dome and emphasizes a central point in the entire interfaith complex. The bell tower crowns the northeast corner of the building and punctuates the upper loggia.

Nave: Octagon and Dome

The interior architectural plan emphasizes space, especially providing room on the walls for an iconographic program still in progress. The nave is spacious and resides underneath an octagonally shaped dome (fig. 3.3). The selection of the octagon as the main shape for the interior design is telling, an homage to the significance of the octagon in the history of Christian architecture, but also because the octagon works particularly well with an eastern-oriented apse in St. Matthew's

Figure 3.3   St. Matthew Orthodox Church, dome (photo by author)

interfaith campus context.[8] The domed octagon and the Greek cross domed octagon were church plans that began to emerge in Byzantine architecture in the tenth and eleventh centuries, alongside the more prevalent basilica, cross-domed, and cross-in-square church plans.[9] The domed octagon plans were used in the Nea Mone monastic communities in Chios and Thessalonike, and in the katholikon of Daphne.[10] The octagon stood alongside the cruciform as a favored shape for the baptismal font of antiquity.[11]

St. Matthew's octagon holds the nave together, and the octagonal motif repeats itself in the church's dome above the nave. The dome consists of rotating octagons that ascend in a parabola, leading up to a painted icon of Christ the Pantocrator.[12] The parabola enhances the visual experience of verticality in the dome, as the parish was not able to finance a more elaborate and traditional domed-ceiling. Several skylights are attached to the rotating octagons to illuminate a halo around the Pantocrator, and provide light in addition to the natural light flowing into the church. The vast space of the nave represents St. Matthew's understanding of its current status and hope for growth, as it has a maximum occupancy of five hundred, with connecting chairs (including folding kneelers) serving as seating. The octagon facilitates maximum interior visibility within the nave, creating an atmosphere conducive to vibrant visual liturgical participation. The outer rim of the dome's wooden, rotating octagons parallels the nave's octagonal borders, and each wall of the octagon has a large arch, which provides some sense of separation of the nave from the north and south aisles, and also visibility to those walls. The framework facilitates subtle entrances to and exits from the church along the north and south aisles. The architectural plan provides much space for occupancy but does not designate a specific space for the singers. When the parish initially began using the church for liturgical celebration, the choir used the aisle on the south end of the church, as there is no gallery or other area set apart for the singers. The altar table was a gift from a parishioner, handmade of wood, and was consecrated with the dedication of the church in May 2008. The sanctuary area is spacious, and the vestry is in a room just outside the sanctuary.

Interior Iconography

The iconostasis emphasizes height in a simple structure (fig. 3.4). St. Demetrius Greek Orthodox Church of Baltimore donated the iconostasis frame to St. Matthew, and the parish is considering updating the frame with a custom-built one.[13] The iconostasis consists of two wooden platforms holding three life-size icons each. The northern portion of the iconostasis has icons of Archangel Gabriel, St. Matthew (the parish's patron saint), and Mary Theotokos. The southern portion of the iconostasis has icons of the Risen Jesus, the Forerunner and Baptizer John, and the Archangel Michael. The iconostasis has only the one level, and there are no plans to add layers. Initially, St. Matthew did not have royal doors between the icons of the Theotokos and Christ on the iconostasis, leaving a large opening between the two portions of the iconostasis that maximized visibility of the sanctuary from the nave.[14] Deacons' doors are absent, so deacons must enter and exit the

Figure 3.4   St. Matthew Orthodox Church, iconostasis (photo by author)

sanctuary via the open spaces on the outer edges of the iconostasis. Parishioners have collaboratively painted all of the parish's icons, and continue to paint the icons, fulfilling the iconographic program plan.

An extensive iconographic program is currently in progress and will adorn the church's walls. A prominent icon of Jesus's Descent into Hades (the Resurrection) occupies the space on the northeast corner, bordering the sanctuary. An icon of the Theophany, the feast celebrated on January 6 in the Orthodox liturgical calendar, adorns the southeast corner nearest the sanctuary (fig. 3.5). An icon of the Transfiguration of the Lord adorns the south arch, immediately behind the place designated for the choir. The Triumphal Entry of Jesus into Jerusalem is currently in progress (as of this writing), and an icon of the Dormition of Mary Theotokos adorns the arch over the main entrance into the nave.[15] An icon of the Platytera and the Mystical Supper of Christ occupies the apse at the high place of the sanctuary (fig. 3.6). Another icon of the Mystical Supper is on the front of the wooden

Figure 3.5 St. Matthew Orthodox Church, Theophany icon, painted by
Wayne Hajos (photo courtesy of John Hudak)

Figure 3.6   Icon of Platytera and Mystical Supper (photo by author)

altar. As of this writing, more icons are planned for the inside walls above the arches, including the Nativity of Mary Theotokos above the Crucifixion and the Presentation of Mary in the Temple over the Theophany icon. So the large spaces created by the arches on the outer walls are reserved for feasts of the Lord, whereas the smaller spaces on the inside walls above the arches are designated for feasts of Mary, representing a hierarchical program featuring dominical feasts primarily, with Marian feasts secondary.

In summary, St. Matthew's church architecture honors the past while confidently preparing for the future.[16] The parish's veneration of its Orthodox heritage is represented by the repetitive octagons, the dome, the arches, and space allotted for an extensive iconographic program. The structure maximizes efficiency given the space constraints in the shared interfaith campus with Cornerstone Church and St. Matthew House.[17] Its public location is an important feature in the architectural plan, with the assumption of community growth dependent on the parish's mission to the native population of the Columbia-Laurel area.

ST. MATTHEW'S ARCHITECTURE: ANALYSIS

Prior to moving into the new complex, St. Matthew Orthodox Church was a mission parish for most of its history, and had already developed a local liturgical style and tradition. St. Matthew's leaders were proponents of active lay liturgical participation, which they hoped would directly influence lay participation in every aspect of parish life. The parish's long history as a mission parish, its operation within the limitations of rented space, and its emphasis on strong lay participation established its liturgical style and cycle.

When St. Matthew was occupying the space at Slayton House, the liturgical cycle was somewhat limited. The Divine Liturgy was celebrated every Sunday at 9:30 a.m., preceded by the reading of the Third Hour. Vespers was not customarily celebrated on Saturday evening, unless the liturgical calendar designated a major feast. St. Matthew attempted to observe the major dominical feasts of the liturgical year by celebrating evening Divine Liturgies with Vespers, an alternative to the standard Orthodox cycle of evening Vigil followed by Eucharistic Liturgy on the day of the feast.[18] Christmas consisted of Great Compline followed by the Eucharistic liturgy on the evening of December 24, and Theophany included the blessing of waters with the Eucharistic liturgy on the evening of January 5.[19] Lenten services consisted of the Liturgy of Presanctified Gifts on Wednesday evenings, in addition to the usual Sunday morning Divine Liturgy.

Holy Week and Pascha, the center of Orthodox liturgical life, was the most complicated order to follow given the parish's mission situation.[20] On the evening of Holy Wednesday, St. Matthew gathered for the mystery of Holy Unction. The twelve Passion Gospels with Orthros were celebrated on Thursday evening, with Holy Saturday Orthros and the veneration of the Epitaphios celebrated on Friday evening.[21] The Divine Liturgy of St. Basil with Vespers (originally the Paschal Vigil in the Byzantine tradition), customarily celebrated on Holy Saturday, was omitted from St. Matthew's Holy Week cycle.[22] Pascha began with Nocturne at 11:00 p.m., followed by Orthros, the Eucharistic liturgy, and a festive community agape meal. This description of the parish's calendar is relevant due to its adaptation of the Orthodox liturgical order during its history as a mission parish using rented space. St. Matthew's leaders created an order of services they could realistically manage given their accessibility to the rental property during their time as a mission and in accordance with parishioners' schedules. The current pastoral leaders are gradually expanding the schedule of festal services.

The liturgical style at St. Matthew also developed during the mission period. For the Sunday liturgy, the choir had two sets of preestablished musical repertoire, with only the weekly and festal propers of the liturgical year changing the music. The music remained the same from one week to the next because books containing the musical settings for the liturgy were distributed to all the lay faithful to sing along with the choir. The people also received music booklets for all of the seasonal liturgical celebrations of Christmas, Holy Week, and Pascha. Currently, the parish choir is expanding its musical repertoire.

When the parish moved from its rental space into the current church building in Columbia, it transferred its established liturgical cycle to its new environment. The choir occupied the exact same position it had in the rental space. For the first year, the liturgical cycle remained largely unchanged with a few exceptions. Three liturgical celebrations were added to the Holy Week cycle: Eucharistic liturgy with Vespers on Holy Thursday, Friday Vespers with the burial of Christ, and the Holy Saturday Eucharistic liturgy with Vespers. For its first Christmas in the new building, the parish moved the Eucharistic liturgy of Christmas to the morning of December 25.

The parish's most significant liturgical change occurred with the addition of regular Saturday evening worship, the Vigil. In adding the Vigil, the parish remained consistent with its liturgical style of promoting active lay participation in distributing preestablished music to attendees. From 2007 to 2010, the parish adopted the order of the Vigil celebrated by New Skete Monastery in Cambridge, New York, an Orthodox monastic community well known for implementing liturgical reform.[23] New Skete's variant of the resurrection Vigil restores many of the ancient prayers of light that came to be suppressed in Byzantine liturgical celebration when the cathedral and monastic liturgies began to be fused in the eighth through the thirteenth centuries. The New Skete Vigil emphasizes responsorial psalmody and the recitation of all the prayers aloud for participants to hear, along with the more participatory components of Saturday evening worship such as hymns of resurrection and the Polyeleos (responsorial singing of Psalm 136).[24] The above examples of liturgical change represent St. Matthew's initial attempts to adapt to its new liturgical environment by adjusting the schedule of the liturgical year while remaining faithful to its pattern of emphasizing lay liturgical participation.[25]

One of the priorities in the erection of the new building was facilitating liturgical processions. The connections between the upper and lower loggias of the building were constructed so the assembly could circumambulate their own building and also bear witness to the interfaith campus to which they belonged in the frequent processions that Orthodox liturgy engages. At this point in its history, St. Matthew continues to attempt to navigate its future liturgical trajectory given its architecture and place. Some examples from recent parish history help to illustrate the current dialectic between architecture and liturgy. The liturgies of Holy Week allow for liturgical processions on the evening of Good Friday, the Orthros of Holy Saturday, and prior to Paschal Orthros. From 2007 to 2010, St. Matthew engaged in outdoor processions, but it did not follow the architectural plan of circumambulating the building using the upper and lower loggias. Instead, the procession began at the narthex, exited the main entrance at the northeast corner of the complex, and walked in a rectangle alongside the portions of the shared parking lot. Thus, the processions did not follow the plan facilitated by the architecture and only engaged a limited portion of the shared interfaith campus. However, the direction of the liturgical processions made the community much more visible to people frequenting businesses in the adjacent retail Columbia Village Center.

The result of this liturgical innovation was a missiological opportunity, where the body of Christ left the building and deviated from its preplanned processional path to instead use the more public area of the parking lot and introduce the liturgical celebrations of Holy Week, with icons, incense, epitaphios, Gospel book, and the whole assembly to everyone nearby who could clearly see the liturgical celebration. The parish's deviation from the architectural plan that facilitated a procession appears to be an innovative way of mitigating the restrictions on religious expression stipulated by the Columbia Village Center. If the procession followed the planned route, exposure to the public would be limited. Processing through the parking lot maximizes the community's exposure to and engagement with the local neighborhood. This liturgical innovation demonstrates the parish's retention of its liturgical outreach to visitors from the mission period in its history despite the parameters of the architectural plan.

Iconography: A Lay Ministry

The performance of the liturgical arts at St. Matthew parish is also faithfully representative of its lay-centered ecclesiology formed during the mission years. In creating the iconographic program, the parish leaders turned to several talented parishioners to paint the icons. Select lay parishioners collectively painted the icon of Christ the Pantocrator in St. Matthew's unique octagonal dome. Parishioner Eugenia Ordynsky stored the icon in her home until it could be installed in the dome. Wayne Hajos painted the six icons on the iconostasis, as well as seven additional icons, including the Mystical Supper in the apse, and on the walls of the church, the Descent into Hades, the Nativity, the Baptism of Jesus in the Jordan, and the Crucifixion.

Hajos learned Orthodox iconography from Valentin Streltsov of Toronto and Peter Pearson of Pennsylvania, and frequently offers workshops on iconography to parishioners and others interested in learning the liturgical art.[26] Hajos himself learned iconography by attending several series of workshops from these two teachers, as access to learning iconography through formal programs in America is difficult for Orthodox who wish to learn.[27] Streltsov, who has been an iconographer for more than twenty-six years, confirmed that it is both convenient and best to learn iconography through apprenticeship.[28] After studying monumental painting at the State Institute of Applied Arts in Ukraine, Streltsov studied a variety of iconographic styles under the tutorship of Father Theodore Koufos, who mentored other prominent iconographers of the Russian Orthodox Church Outside of Russia (ROCOR), and thus considers himself an adherent of the Jordanville school. Pearson's preference is to employ the fourteenth-century style from Novgorod due to the "simplicity of the lines, the boldness of the brush strokes, and the strong graphics," though he admits that his own style is eclectic due to the number of teachers with whom he has studied.[29] Hajos also prefers and employs the Novgorodian style, as he favors its directness, simplicity, and revelation of the truth without unnecessary ornamentation.[30] He described the benefits of the Russian iconographic school as depicting a more human and compassionate face, as opposed to the Byzantine style, which accentuates sternness.[31]

A more comprehensive analysis of the parish's iconographic program can occur once it is complete, as the eight arches in the nave reveal broad wall space for the program to expand, and the parish has plans to gradually add more icons to the interior walls.[32] The inflow of exterior light into the building, along with the skylights, effectively harmonizes with the interior iconography due to a solid balance between the vast interior space, the natural and electric lighting, and the icons. Visual access to the icons is promoted by the octagonal interior, which draws attention to the vast walls. The church's emphasis on heightening horizontal interior decoration promotes an enriched visual experience since the modest verticality does not overemphasize the Pantocrator in the modified dome. Participants view salvation history as celebrated by Orthodoxy's liturgical year, with the highest-ranking feasts holding the prominent places, as worshipers stand together *ad orientem* and thus have the icons of the Descent into Hades, the Nativity, and the Theophany of Jesus in view. Combined with the parish's emphasis on lay participation, the iconographic program promotes a visual catechesis on salvation history through the icons, on account of their accessibility, size, and simplicity.

The interior decoration represents a minor deviation from the traditional architectural synthesis. While St. Matthew honors the tradition of having a dome, the increased emphasis on maximizing interior horizontal visual access to all components of the nave and sanctuary creates a balance that softens the perception of Christ as remote, which is suggested by a Pantocrator elevated to a great height. Essentially, Christ is among his people, who encounter no obvious barriers to approaching him. Contemporary economic and municipal limitations certainly contribute to this revision, but the revised interior also speaks to a certain sense of conforming to ecclesial phenomena prevalent in American culture. Jeanne Kilde suggests that architectural modifications in Roman Catholic structures represent shifts in the social power of the laity.[33] The overtly lay-oriented approach present at St. Matthew parish coheres with the trans-denominational notion of an empowered laity. For Orthodox Christians, the shift toward restoring the priesthood of the laity and making adjustments so the lay priesthood would be manifest in the liturgical structures began in the late nineteenth century and continued throughout the twentieth century with the teachings of theologians such as Nicholas Afanasiev, Alexander Schmemann, and Paul Evdokimov, among others.[34] It is likely that St. Matthew's preference for a lay ecclesiology was established by Orthodox theologians and the restoration of the laity that prevailed in ecumenical circles.

The parish's current iconographic trajectory indicates that Hajos will paint most, if not all of the icons, at least in this early phase of the parish's history in the new building. Hajos's creation of St. Matthew's iconography offers a keen insight into a possible trend in American

Orthodoxy: the employment of lay amateurs who have learned from select mentors as apprentices to provide the liturgical art adorning the architecture. While Hajos prefers and employs a medieval Russian iconographic style, a brief overview of his teachers' backgrounds suggests that his style might be an amalgamation of multiple compatible styles. In the case of St. Matthew, an eclectic iconographic style accentuating the Novgorodian school introduces a mosaic of Orthodox tradition in the parish's program of liturgical art. The use of a Native American parabola to create a halo around the dome only embellishes the eclecticism of the overall art program. Eclecticism reflects the parish's liturgical styles and also the present and future people of St. Matthew's parish, who hail from a variety of Orthodox ethnic and convert backgrounds. What is unknown is whether or not the convergence of these backgrounds might someday crystallize into an organic, native family of American Orthodox liturgical schools.

The intentional omission of deacons' doors at St. Matthew poses a unique dilemma. Originally, the large, open space leading from the solea to the area on the front of the altar table maximized visibility of the liturgy celebrated in the sanctuary, which in turn removed the customary visible barrier between sanctuary and nave caused by a high iconostasis. The current absence of deacons' doors causes some minor liturgical irregularities, especially for clergy who are familiar with liturgical celebration in parishes that retain these components. In the absence of deacons' doors, the deacons are obliged to enter and exit the sanctuary at the north and south edges of the iconostasis, which makes for a lengthy liturgical movement. In general, this is a minor issue that requires adjustments on the part of celebrants. The lack of a designated space for the choir can cause minor liturgical "traffic jams" when the church has interior processions (such as the incensation of the church performed by deacon or priest), and the parish has no easy way to communicate with the choir (which, admittedly, is an issue in many Orthodox parishes worldwide). The building's architecture does facilitate a quality acoustic for the Orthodox tradition of singing without accompanying musical instruments. The combination of acoustics and lighting encouraged the parish to rent the facility for amateur and professional music recitals, and also two public and well-attended concerts of Christmas music, with the proceeds going to the building fund.

In summary, the building's architecture effectively serves the parish's liturgical arts by providing plentiful natural lighting, ample interior wall space designated for the iconography, and maximum visibility of the church's interior with the octagonal orientation of the nave originating in the modified dome and its parabola. The parish's particularities in the placement of the choir and the absence of the customary deacons' doors cause some minor irregularities, but more important, they represent St. Matthew's commitment to promoting lay participation. A comprehensive examination of the parish's architecture manifests its ecclesiological underpinning. The parish's native laypeople paint the icons themselves, sing the responses to the liturgy, and are not physically separated from the officiating clergy. The laity exercises these liturgical ministries by receiving training, such as attending workshops provided by experts. For St. Matthew, the creative process exercised by lay leaders is not merely a representation of the community's mission, but mirrors the intonation exclaimed by churches of the Byzantine rite at the anaphoras of Saints Basil and John Chrysostom: "offering you your own of your own, we praise you."[35] At St. Matthew, the laity fully participates in this offering, and the worshiper beholds it in the interplay between architectural design and artistic performance. The prominence of the nave's octagon, with its elegant arches and the Pantocrator crowning the dome, actualizes Chirovsky's vision of the nave as representing the "anthropological optimism" of Eastern Christian spirituality, an optimism experienced by the faithful who stand beneath the dome.[36] At St. Matthew, the dome's relative proximity to the people and the general open visual nature of the nave promotes a strong sense of Christ's presence. More important, the parish's celebration of the liturgy and construction of its iconographic program strongly facilitates a mobile and active royal priesthood of the laity. The general shift of social power to the laity and the restoration of the priesthood of the laity in ecumenical theology contributed to St. Matthew's empowerment of the people. It is equally notable that St. Matthew's memory of life as a mission where everyone must contribute to parish activities is a key ingredient in the dynamics of its current architecture and liturgy.

ANALYSIS OF PROPERTY: HALL, PARKING LOT

St. Matthew's hall has a rather perfunctory function. As with most churches and community centers, the hall provides space for extra-liturgical fellowship and events. It is the common area for educating children, choir rehearsal, and meetings. The hall's design is efficient, making the best use of space given the structure's location, and it also contains the artistic motifs of the church, connected by the lower loggia, the arches, and the octagonal shape of the nave, repeated in the hall. St. Matthew parish offers the hall for rent to the local community, and a bingo group gathers each week in the space. In 2010, at the evening celebration of the blessing of Epiphany waters, the celebrant brought the blessed water through the hall while the bingo players were gathered. Besides this isolated incident of liturgical evangelization, the parish's use of the hall is functional.

A high point in the life of the community is their annual fall festival, usually occurring in early October; it was originally organized in 2008 as a way to raise funds to make payments on the building's mortgage.[37] Like their use of the hall, organizing a fall festival might seem normal for an Orthodox community in America, especially one promoting the parishioners' ethnic heritage. In the case of St. Matthew, the festival is unique because the parish does not adhere to a particular ethnic heritage, but rather represents several groups. In this case, while one certainly encounters the ethnic food, music, and dancing one would expect at an Orthodox festival (Middle Eastern, Greek, and Slavic), Mexican heritage is also represented. The festival is public, with parishioners making appearances on the local public news and the event occurring in the parking lot of the interfaith campus. Visitors to the festival are free to take church tours and use the hall, but the parking lot is the event's arena, utilizing the efficiency of space and temporary equipment, but also providing a soft introduction to the parish community outside the liturgical context. St. Matthew offers a public witness to the local community through the festival and the liturgical processions that occur in the same space outside of the church building.

St. Matthew's fall festival reveals an inner tension within the parish given its mission background and orientation toward evangelizing the people of Columbia and Laurel. St. Matthew draws on the visible elements of Orthodox ethnicity to help pay off the balance of the building's mortgage and also to introduce visitors to the community. The promotion of ethnicity visitors find at the festival is quite temporary; those who become better acquainted with the parish community find that retaining ethnic flavors is not a priority in the parish's mission and identity. Thus, the festival occurs in a safe space, with the parish community, as the body of Christ, coming out from their building to greet people in a non-liturgical context. St. Matthew parish emphasizes the aspects of Orthodoxy all ethnic groups hold in common, such as the Byzantine rite liturgy, the liturgical arts, the doctrinal tenets of faith, and Orthodox variants of prayer and fasting. The common cultivation of these practices supersedes any external expression of ethnic identity.

ST. MATTHEW HOUSE AND CORNERSTONE CHURCH

The original architectural design of St. Matthew parish emphasized its unique place on an interfaith campus. St. Matthew's current neighbors are St. Matthew House and Cornerstone Church, comprising the KCIC campus. Officially, St. Matthew House is a ministry of St. Matthew parish, and the rector of the parish has traditionally served as the chief of its board of directors (fig. 3.7). The parish does not directly govern St. Matthew House, as it has full-time staff that handles the daily responsibilities. While its board of directors implements its mission vision, it does not conduct business that comes from parish community imperatives. Parish involvement with St. Matthew House is thus largely limited to its representatives from the board of directors, and an ongoing parish ministry of making and delivering meals to its residents. Residents of St. Matthew House are welcome to participate in the parish's liturgical life, and often attend services. In general, though, there seems to be a fairly clear line of delineation between St. Matthew parish and St. Matthew House on a daily basis. The community's act of building St. Matthew House before beginning construction on its own church building speaks to its priority as a mission parish. The parish essentially provided a home for people who are unable to completely care for themselves

Figure 3.7   St. Matthew House (photo by author)

before the community occupied its own home. The ministry at St. Matthew House retains and expresses St. Matthew's history as a mission community devoted to outreach, especially since St. Matthew House does not discriminate against applicants for residency. In other words, one does not have to be a practicing Orthodox Christian, or even a Christian, to apply for residency at St. Matthew House, a testimony to St. Matthew's fidelity to ecumenism in its interfaith campus.

St. Matthew's relationship with Cornerstone Church is largely limited to their monthly KCIC meetings. Members of the respective church communities encounter each other as they assemble for worship on Sunday mornings, but there is no official contact beyond parking lot encounters and the monthly meetings. The lack of contact is most likely due to the absence of commonality in the traditions to which the communities adhere. Their peaceful and cheerful coexistence on the interfaith campus fulfills the mandate of the Columbia Village Center, which prohibits overtly public religious expression and requires more than one church in a religious center, to promote an interfaith presence.[38] That the two church communities share this space in Columbia demonstrates an ongoing opportunity to collaborate in ways they might serve the native people of Columbia and Laurel together, despite the differences of their traditions.

CONCLUSION

St. Matthew Orthodox Church occupies a unique building in Columbia. On the surface, one might dismiss the authenticity of the architectural design because the exterior is not an obvious cliché of the Orthodox synthesis. St. Matthew does not have cupolas, a dome visible on the exterior, or exterior designs adhering to a particular motif in Orthodox history. One could similarly assess the interior decoration since the iconostasis currently lacks deacons' doors, has no clearly designated space for the choir, and has a single level on the iconostasis. In many ways, St. Matthew's architecture violates the idea of a prevailing Orthodox synthesis because while the interior incorporates some of the more robust theological aspects of Orthodox architecture in the octagonal dome and nave, the developing iconographic program, the organic connection of upper and lower loggias, and the arches, the design is innovative and simply does not conform to one model. This diversion from the Orthodox synthesis is also evident in the parish's processional direction, which eschews the planned circumambulation of the church and instead brings the people of the parish into public view in the parking lot.

As a recent construction project, St. Matthew does not promote the highest degree of environmental protection, an emerging motif in Christian architectural design.[39] As the community grows into the future, updating the structure with sustainable features could become a higher priority if the building is used more with regular frequency on a daily basis.

This chapter's analysis demonstrates that St. Matthew constructed its building employing genius innovation, given its logistical limitations, and in strong fidelity to its mission background. Despite the absence of an obvious Orthodox identity on the exterior, the design offers attractive features like the protruding apse, elegant arches, and a bell tower that invite visitors to investigate. The prominence of the octagonal motif throughout the interior, and especially in the nave, evokes the theology of the eighth day of God's creation, the transcendence of time when the community encounters the living God at the Eucharistic liturgy. This encounter is always driven by the whole community since lay members of the community have taken on a leadership role in contributing to the dynamics of architecture and liturgical celebration. St. Matthew's overt emphasis on encouraging lay participation in the parish's life coalesces with the architectural intent of uniting the ordained and royal priesthoods in the church. The architecture is a visual representation of the parish's mission to acknowledge the multivalent ethnic heritage of its parishioners, and evangelize the native people of Columbia and Laurel.

While St. Matthew's architecture is not a stereotypical Orthodox cliché, it advances the parish's mission, promotes a mission-oriented ecclesiology, and adheres to the local secular ecumenical priority. The architecture of St. Matthew is thus an apt representation of the parish's mission-driven ecclesial identity, which includes an attitude of providing hospitality to people who have no past connections with Orthodoxy.

St. Matthew is a potential archetype for the future trajectory of Orthodox architecture in America because of its eclectic blend. The architecture attempts to address most of the areas of traditional importance to Orthodox. The design attempts to accommodate quality liturgical celebration with its spacious interior and procession-enabled exterior. St. Matthew's long tenure as a mission shaped its liturgical ethos, which was minimalist by necessity. The liturgical cycle is growing as the parish adjusts to its new building. In the early portion of its history, St. Matthew might have become a new model of the symbiosis between liturgy and architecture as the parish had integrated some aspects of the liturgical offices of New Skete Monastery, which promotes a reinvigorated cathedral rite for contemporary Orthodox Christianity.[40] St. Matthew primarily employs the received tradition of the Byzantine rite, so the symbiosis of liturgy and architecture is quite elementary. In other words, the architectural design provides an adequate space to celebrate the received liturgical tradition. One difference at St. Matthew is that the open architecture with its unique iconographic program might be conducive to organic local liturgical development; only time will tell.

St. Matthew's architecture is certainly not a cliché, though it is eclectic, as it draws from numerous cultural, artistic, and historical motifs. The most informative quality of St. Matthew's architecture is its reflection of the parish's commitment to find an ecclesial niche in the present, emphasizing mission and hospitality over the retention of ethnic heritage, while seeking to grow into the future. Contextual obstacles limit the parish's ability to achieve every aspiration in the present, as the community must share space with others and mute its exterior expression of Orthodox Christianity. The parish's energy in establishing a quality ecclesial niche within the limitations of its current context has the potential to become an archetype in the future of Orthodox architecture in America.

CHAPTER FOUR

HOLY VIRGIN CATHEDRAL

Holy Virgin Cathedral of the Russian Orthodox Church Outside of Russia (ROCOR) is located in San Francisco and has 180 families.[1] It was founded in 1927 by immigrants from Russia who initially worshiped in a store on Sacramento Street in San Francisco. The community purchased an Episcopalian church building on Fulton Street in 1930 and gathered there until 1965.[2] Holy Virgin Cathedral received a large influx of Russian immigrants from China, particularly from Shanghai and Harbin, in the 1950s who infused new life into the parish.[3] A city in northeast China, Harbin had Russians who labored as merchants on the railway beginning in the pre-revolutionary period.[4] Harbin's Russian population was large, approximating 22,000. The immigrants from Shanghai and Harbin who settled in San Francisco found refuge in the United States through the intercessions of their bishop and benefactor, Archbishop John Maximovich, who was glorified as a saint in 1996. The parish commenced the process of building a new church in San Francisco in 1961, with the consecration of the site and groundbreaking taking place that year. In 1962, the construction process was halted due to a painful rupture in the community concerning an allegation of misappropriation of funds. ROCOR appointed Archbishop John Maximovich as bishop of San Francisco in 1963, and under his leadership, construction continued, although he himself was caught in the crossfire of the enduring parish divisions. The cathedral's exterior work was completed in 1964 and included the blessing and raising of five large crosses to be placed on top of each of the five domes, which were covered in 24-karat gold leaf.[5] The first liturgy was celebrated on the Sunday of Orthodoxy in 1965, and the cathedral was dedicated in 1977.

The community also owns a sizable parish hall that hosts customary events of community gathering and is the location for two community schools—a high school and a school for small children. Holy Virgin Cathedral is an example of an Orthodox structure in America that coheres with patterns we have observed in previous chapters, including an emphasis on cultural retention and ministry to immigrants. Holy Virgin Cathedral's story offers new perspectives on the way architecture communicates an Orthodox community's particular story due to the following unique features: the cultivation of a traditional liturgical life, especially through excellent iconography and music; a complex local history shaped by two prominent figures of ROCOR, St. John Maximovich and Archbishop Anthony Medvedev; and the re-creation of the sacred space after the death and glorification of St. John Maximovich, which denoted the cathedral's transition from an immigrant community to a site of pilgrimage in global Orthodoxy.

ARCHITECTURAL FEATURES: CLICHÉS

Upon first glance, Holy Virgin Cathedral appears to be an architectural cliché. The current architectural structure was designed by Oleg Iwanitsky. The exterior is impressive, with five cupolas, including a vast and vertically imposing central cupola that enhances exterior visibility (fig. 4.1). The church is a basic square with five domes, four domes in each corner of the square and one dome in the center, clearly patterned after the Kremlin's Dormition Cathedral in Moscow.[6] The exterior coheres beautifully with San Francisco's rolling urban landscape. The central cupola appears to be disproportionately large, but its verticality draws the attention of an observant viewer in the general vicinity of the neighborhood. The cathedral's façade has six large icons, three on each

Figure 4.1 Holy Virgin Cathedral, exterior (photo by author)

side of the main entrance into the narthex with a large cross in the middle above the door. From left to right, the exterior icons depict Saints John Chrysostom, Basil the Great, and Gregory the Theologian (to the left of the cross), and Saints Spyridon (bishop of Trymithous), Cyril of Alexandria, and Athanasius the Great. The depiction of saints on the exterior who made substantial contributions to Christology, Trinitarian theology, and soteriology suggests that one will encounter a community of people who uphold conciliar tradition and worship the Triune God of the ecumenical councils upon entering the church.

Accessibility to the church from the exterior is limited. The church has only a few parking spots in front that are reserved for cathedral clergy, and parking is metered during the week. Recently, the cathedral has secured volunteers who open the church to receive visitors on weekdays, so the public has increased access to the community. Father Perekrestov noted that the cathedral receives mostly visitors who are coming to venerate the relics of St. John Maximovich and pray at his shrine.

Interior Space

The impressive exterior disguises a surprisingly intimate interior space. The height of the cupolas suggests vastness from an exterior view, but the cathedral's interior is quite cozy. The total square footage of the cathedral interior is 5,500. The narthex is 780 square feet; the sanctuary (altar and vestry), 1,380 square feet; and the nave, 3,360 square feet. The arrangement of space is also disproportionate inside. A typical narthex welcomes visitors with instructions on church decorum and announcements of forthcoming events posted in both English and Russian. The architectural design creates challenges, as the positioning of the iconostasis with the sanctuary does not allow for a hanging lamp. The interior is small but navigable, since the only seating is in the rear of the nave, with four benches, two on each side (fig. 4.2). The sanctuary is also surprisingly small. The cathedral has three altars: the chief altar is devoted to Mary Theotokos, the left altar to St. John of Kronstadt, and the right altar to St. Nicholas of Myra. The main altar contains a small table of oblation used for liturgies celebrated at each altar. A small office is behind the sanctuary, and a wall divides the sanctuary from a passageway connecting the northern and southern ends of the sanctuary. The rear area contains the vestry with a refrigerator and a microwave oven.

The west end of the church has two galleries that are designated for two of the cathedral's three choirs.[7] The nave has two notable fixtures: the bishop's cathedra in its center, and the shrine of St. John Maximovich on the southern wall of the church. The shrine contains the relics of St. John in a glass-encased tomb, and allows open access via two small steps (fig. 4.3). The shrine also contains several icons of St. John and a hanging vigil lamp. The room in the church that contained the sepulcher of St. John in the period between his death and glorification (1966–96) has become the Church of the Finding of St. John's Relics. After St. John's glorification, the cathedral transformed the sepulcher into a church and added an iconostasis designed by Archpriest Stefan Sabelnik.

In addition to St. John's shrine, the cathedral also has more than one hundred relics. Four relics are in a small reliquary lying on the altar

Figure 4.2   Holy Virgin Cathedral, interior (photo courtesy of Helen Sinelnikoff-Nowak)

table. The sanctuary also contains a large sixteenth-century Byzantine cross. Father Perekrestov mused that "every other icon" contains a relic. I took note of several relics, including a stone in the icon of Blessed Xenia of Petersburg and a Cossack hood under an icon of St. Nicholas Romanov. The cathedral has an icon of the Dormition of Mary Theotokos containing a stone from Gethsemane, the historical location and contemporary center of her Dormition and burial.[8] The relics are available to people for veneration, with the exception of those in the sanctuary. The relics also have a local flavor: Father Perekrestov stated that ten canonized saints walked the streets of San Francisco, and he is working on creating an icon of them.

Holy Virgin Cathedral has a vast and inviting exterior that stands out in the urban landscape of San Francisco. The exterior square design, modeled after Moscow's Kremlin Dormition Cathedral, boasts five cupolas, with the central dome disproportionately large and tall. The cathe-

Figure 4.3 Shrine of St. John Maximovich (photo courtesy of Helen Sinelnikoff-Nowak)

dral's interior is a mosaic of contrasts that narrates the story of salvation history with an emphasis on the Russian imperial period and the sufferings of immigrants. The challenges of positioning the required fixtures to promote an appropriate harmony of space are mitigated by the cathedral's fidelity to maintaining a regular liturgical cycle. One gains precious insights into the cathedral's story and current place in global Orthodoxy by attending to three areas that I explore in greater detail below: liturgical aesthetics, especially the iconography; the cathedral as a liturgical center; and the shrine and relics of St. John Maximovich.

INTERIOR ICONOGRAPHY: A LESSON IN TRADITION

In previous chapters, we have noted the role iconography plays in communicating community identity and facilitating local liturgical aesthetics. The iconography of Holy Virgin Cathedral stands out for its brilliance and is one of the two central contributors to the cathedral as a liturgical center of ROCOR on America's West Coast. The cathedral commissioned Archimandrite Kyprian (Pyzhov) of Jordanville to paint all of the cathedral's interior icons.[9] Archimandrite Kyprian, born in St. Petersburg in 1904, was one of the finest iconographers of the twentieth century. He received professional training in painting as a student at the Montparnasse School of Paris, and later was mentored by the matushka (wife) of Father Alexander Elchaninov in Nice. Archimandrite Kyprian designed the iconostasis and painted the icons of Holy Virgin Cathedral over the course of nine summers. Father Perekrestov aptly sums up the impact of the iconography on the faithful: "the iconography saved our cathedral."[10]

The iconographic program of Holy Virgin Cathedral conforms to the Middle Byzantine architectural paradigm by depicting salvation history in a hierarchical manner. An icon of the Ancient of Days, God the Father, adorns the central cupola, the highest-ranking component of the interior space (fig. 4.4). The apse has an icon of the Platytera, with an icon of the Mystical Supper immediately beneath (fig. 4.5). The northern wall has icons of Marian feasts, including the entrance of Mary into the temple, and the western wall has an icon of Elijah's ascension to heaven in a chariot of fire. The southern wall contains several icons of saints, including one of the few icons with an English inscription, depicting St. Ambrose of Milan. The cathedral's iconography is certainly awe-inspiring, and it attests to the cathedral's fidelity to excellence in liturgical aesthetics, communicating salvation history with a comprehensive pictorial representation of the Orthodox Church's festal and Paschal cycles, along with the communion of saints. In the

Figure 4.4 Icon of the Ancient of Days, painted by Archimandrite Kyprian Pyzhov (photo courtesy of Helen Sinelnikoff-Nowak)

Figure 4.5 Icon of the Mystical Supper (photo courtesy of Helen Sinelnikoff-Nowak)

interest of connecting the iconography to community identity, I focus on two notable icons: the central icon of the Ancient of Days in the central cupola and the icon of the Royal New Martyrs.

Icon of the Ancient of Days in the Central Cupola

Orthodox churches typically adorn the central dome over the nave with an icon of Christ Pantocrator, but this is not the case in Holy Virgin Cathedral. In gazing upward into the dome, one sees an icon of God the Father, the Ancient of Days, surrounded by angels. The following inscription defines the dome on a circular rim immediately below: "Holy, holy, holy, Lord of Sabaoth, heaven and earth are full of thy glory; Look down, Lord, from your holy heights on the people standing before you and awaiting your great mercy." The inscription underneath the dome, taken from Isaiah 6 and Psalm 102:19, clearly marks the icon as depicting the person of God the Father. Portraying God in an image has been controversial in Byzantine-Russo iconography for centuries. The Moscow Council in 1666–67 prohibited the painting of icons depicting the Father, but despite the authority of this plenary council, the question of portraying the unseen God as an icon remains controversial.[11] The cause of such controversy is the patristic sense of the utter "otherness" of God's nature, leading many church fathers to speak of God in an apophatic manner. The incomprehensibility of God's nature and the inability of humanity to apprehend it made depicting images of God the Father impossible. Some have attempted to legitimize icons of God as depicting the eternal Logos before the historical incarnation, interpreting the passage from Daniel 7 as a manifestation of the Logos, whose incarnation allows his iconic depiction. While the Moscow Council dismissed the legitimacy of painting icons of God (which was based on the privilege granted to prophets of the Old Testament to see God with human eyes), the practice of painting icons of God the Father persisted in the Church.[12]

The presence of this icon in the dome of Holy Virgin Cathedral attests to the parish's fidelity to the longstanding practice of Russian iconography in the Church. The implications of depicting God the Father to the liturgical assembly and visitors are noteworthy. Those who gaze upon this icon behold the divine godhead without any mediation, granting them direct access to God the Father, depicted in two dimensions. Additionally, the vast height of the central cupola enhances the sense of divine verticality with the icon of the Ancient of Days. In this vein, the interior iconography of Holy Virgin Cathedral conforms to iconographic tradition in maintaining a sense of verticality, recalling the theological typology popularized by Maximus the Confessor discussed in chapter 1. Furthermore, the interior iconography delivers the promise of the exterior icons on the cathedral's façade by communicating the Christology and Trinitarian theology of the church fathers of the fourth and fifth centuries.

In parish communities that do not have icons of God the Father, people partake of the divine nature by beholding numerous icons of Christ. Holy Virgin Cathedral has several icons of Christ, including two stunning icons near the altar of St. Nicholas of the Descent into Hades and the Crucifixion. The inclusion of an icon of God the Father holding the place of privilege in the central dome establishes the cathedral's iconographic depiction of the cosmos, God's kingdom. The icon of the Father provides a snapshot of the future life in God, in which all of humanity will be reconciled to the Father himself. The cathedral's iconography emphasizes the monarchy of God in Orthodox Trinitarian theology, both in the audacious depiction of God and through assigning this icon to the vertical apex of the cathedral's interior space. The celebration of liturgy in the present is directed toward the future, and life with God is the destiny for all. The assembly, then, experiences a prolepsis of the future life with God when it celebrates the liturgy in the present. Having noted the theological controversies surrounding icons of God the Father, the placement of this icon in the cathedral's central dome communicates a bold and robust Orthodox eschatology. The wall-to-wall nature of the iconography naturally draws the attention of the observer upward in an ascent: the final stop of this visual ascent is the icon of God the Father in the central dome.

Icon of the Royal New Martyrs

Holy Virgin Cathedral contains several icons and relics of the royal Romanov family, including a prominent icon of the Royal New Martyrs (commemorated on July 4/17) painted by Archbishop Alypy of

Chicago, a protégé of Archimandrite Kyprian.[13] The Royal New Martyrs icon depicts nineteen total figures. The central portion of the icon depicts the Holy Martyr Tsar Nicholas (on the left), the Holy Martyr Tsaritsa Alexandra (on the right), and the Holy Martyr Tsarevich Alexis (in the middle). Sixteen additional martyred members of the royal family are pictured on the periphery of the icon. A small icon of the Holy Virgin is embedded at the top, with the piece of the bloodied wall of the room in which the family was murdered over an image of the Ipatieff house at the bottom. The cathedral has another icon of Tsar Nicholas with a relic belonging to him, a Cossack hood underneath.

The presence of icons and relics of the Royal New Martyrs is not unusual at Holy Virgin Cathedral, given that ROCOR glorified the royal family in 1981. The Moscow Patriarchate followed suit, glorifying the Royal New Martyrs in 2000, the only difference being the Patriarchate's glorification of the tsar and his family as passion-bearers.[14] The presence of this icon and the relics it contains at Holy Virgin Cathedral is distinct because it bears witness to ROCOR's continuous preservation of the memory of the execution of the royal family and the persecution suffered by the Russian Orthodox Church. ROCOR's legacy is unashamedly monarchist, an ideal upheld by the most prominent archpastors of Holy Virgin Cathedral, including St. Maximovich and his successor, Archbishop Anthony Medvedev, who composed the texts for the liturgical services devoted to the royal family. The presence of the icon in the cathedral also symbolizes the mission advanced by ROCOR during the Soviet epoch. Despite opposition, ROCOR glorified the royal family and challenged the Moscow Patriarchate to respond. In this instance, the Patriarchate followed ROCOR's lead, and the decision to glorify the royal family in 2000 served to promote rapprochement between the divided bodies of the Russian Church, which occurred in 2007.[15]

The icon of the royal family is thus multifunctional. Besides identifying the royal family as members of the communion of saints, the icon and its relics remind beholders of imperial Russia's past, which developed into a tragic pattern of new martyrdom in the aftermath of the Bolshevik Revolution. But the icon also symbolizes the cathedral's mission of reconciliation in the present because it is a symbol of the cathedral's leadership in witnessing to modern Christian martyrdom and challenging the Moscow Patriarchate to honor the new martyrs. On account of the Patriarchate's decision in 2000, the icon is now also a symbol of reconciliation and forgiveness.

The icon of the Royal New Martyrs follows the lead of an earlier myrrh-streaming icon of the Tsar-Martyr Nicholas. An icon of the Tsar-Martyr Nicholas was painted by Ija Schmit, the founder of the Society Honoring Russian Nobility.[16] Forty-four thousand copies of the icon were printed for distribution in Russia, and one of these icons began to gush myrrh in 1998.[17] Writing in 2000, prior to the reconciliation of ROCOR with the Moscow Patriarchate, Richard Betts connected the pilgrimage of this myrrh-streaming icon to Russia to the repentance of Russians for the sin of regicide:

> This icon of Tsar-Martyr Nicholas has become a symbol of repentance for thousands of Russians who mourn the regicide of the Tsar and his family, and honor them as passion-bearers. Thousands of Orthodox Christians have venerated the icon. [Then] Metropolitan Kirill (Gundyaev) of Smolensk . . . stated "this occurrence, as an indication of God's grace, will be carefully reviewed by the Synodal Commission on the Canonization of Saints to determine whether it is of divine origin."[18]

Wendy Slater notes that "tales of miraculous interventions in Russians' lives by the martyred tsar and his family began to circulate during the 1990's," a phenomenon that persuaded the canonization commission of the Russian Orthodox Church to glorify Tsar Nicholas II and other members of the royal family as passion-bearers in 2000.[19] Slater's view challenges the Church's traditional stance on the saint as mediator by claiming that this icon, along with others depicting Nicholas II, is "profoundly ahistorical" because the icons model Nicholas II on Christ and St. Job, making him into a redemptive figure for contemporary Russia, which "disregards Nicholas' political role."[20] These two depictions of Nicholas II (by Betts and Slater) are irreconcilable and represent the collision of the hagiography of a saint who belongs to a local community and a historical assessment of a holy figure that refuses to discount his deficiencies.

The miraculous myrrh-streaming icon of Tsar Nicholas helps us to understand the significance of the icon of the Royal New Martyrs in Holy Virgin Cathedral. The cathedral's faithful devotion to the memory of the royal family is not necessarily a petition for the restoration of the monarchy in Russia. Instead, the Tsar and his family have a new divine mandate: to deliver healing and repentance to Russia so that it might become a contemporary manifestation of the Holy Rus' of the past. In this vein, Tsar Nicholas and the royal family are trans-locational saints, exercising the dual functions of interceding for the Orthodox faithful in America and promoting rapprochement and regeneration of the Orthodox Church in Russia. The presence of the icon of the Royal New Martyrs and the vibrant observation of their feast on July 4/17 at Holy Virgin Cathedral manifests the cathedral's role as a central catalyst for reconciliation and the rebuilding of Orthodox Russia.

CONTINUATION OF TRADITION: A LITURGICAL CENTER

Liturgical life at Holy Virgin Cathedral is the center of the community's life. Father Perekrestov noted that the cathedral is the only community in the United States that celebrates the Divine Liturgy every day of the year.[21] The cathedral clergy's chief pastoral task is liturgical celebration—Father Perekrestov noted that worship occupies most of his and the other clergy's time throughout the week. On weekends, the full liturgical schedule is maintained. Vigil on Saturday night is lengthy, lasting two to three hours, and there are two liturgies on Sunday mornings, each lasting more than two hours.[22] The cathedral offers a full cycle of liturgical offices, surpassing what one might expect in a typical Orthodox parish in America. The maximalist approach to liturgy maintained by the cathedral community coheres with the values of the liturgical heritage to which they belong. Father Perekrestov attributed the cathedral's sustenance of a full liturgical schedule to the legacy of its pastors. St. John Maximovich insisted on a full schedule and celebrated the Eucharistic liturgy daily, and Father Perekrestov stated that the cathedral clergy deeply value this liturgical heritage, passed from St. John to Archbishop Anthony, his successor, and the cathedral clergy.

Liturgical uniformity is alien to the history and mentality of the Orthodox Church, which has promoted limited freedom in the keeping of local liturgical customs throughout history. In response to my question on the coherence of the cathedral's liturgy with that of ROCOR, Father Perekrestov observed that ROCOR also has liturgical diversity. That said, I would describe Holy Virgin Cathedral as a liturgical center that cultivates and sustains a maximalist approach to liturgical celebration that one identifies with ROCOR.[23] By "maximalist," I mean fidelity to fulfilling the requirements of the Church order by observing the feasts of the liturgical year in all of its ranks and orders and promoting the frequent celebration of the Eucharist and Liturgy of the Hours without unnecessary abbreviation. In this vein, Holy Virgin Cathedral adheres to the liturgical legacy of Jordanville and exercises influence over the liturgical practices of ROCOR communities in the western region of the United States. Father Perekrestov stated that Archbishop Anthony in particular handpicked and appointed clergy throughout the diocese who would maintain and promote liturgical maximalism. The spirit of this liturgical style becomes generational, as men who are raised in such communities receive theological formation and are appointed to lead these communities in their lifecycles.

Compared to other Orthodox communities in this study, Holy Virgin Cathedral's maximalist liturgical approach is distinct. The cathedral's liturgical practice is useful for our purposes for two reasons: first, as a crucial comparator in examining the traditional paradigm of liturgy and architecture where form follows function, and second, as a clear manifestation of diverse and competing liturgical schools within America. Despite its own inner diversity, ROCOR has numerous parishes that follow a pattern of liturgical practice hearkening back to the influence of Metropolitan Antony Khrapovitsky. A good illustration of this liturgical philosophy was expressed by one of Metropolitan Antony's disciples, Father Michael Pomazansky, whose teaching and theological output has deeply influenced the interior life of ROCOR. Father Pomazansky wrote a critique of Alexander Schmemann's heralded study of liturgical theology, and in it, he explained the value of liturgical maximalism:

They tell us: no one keeps the Typicon, and besides, the theological key to understanding it has been lost. We answer: the difficulty in fully keeping the Typicon is connected with the idea of maximalism inherent in the Orthodox understanding of Christianity. This maximalism is found in relation to the moral standards of the Gospel, the strictness of church canons, the area of ascetic practice, of prayer and services based on the commandment, *pray without ceasing.* Only in monasteries do the church services approach the norm of perfection, and at that only relatively. Life in the world and parishes forces an unavoidable lessening of the norm, and therefore the parish practice cannot be viewed as the Orthodox model and ideal in the sphere of church services. Nonetheless, we cannot refer to the practice in parishes as a "distortion," in the theological sense, of the principles of Divine services. Even in the cases of "intolerable" shortening, the services retain a great amount of content and exalted meaning, and do not lose their intrinsic value. Such shortenings are "intolerable" because they bear witness to our self-indulgence, our laziness, our carelessness in our duty of prayer. One cannot objectively judge the value of the liturgical Rule according to the practice here in the diaspora. One cannot draw conclusions from this practice concerning the total loss of understanding of the spirit of the Rubrics.[24]

I have quoted Father Pomazansky at length here because his explanation of maximalism discloses the liturgical agenda of ROCOR, which is kept by Holy Virgin Cathedral. These communities view the Orthodox order of divine services outlined by the Typikon as an ideal that should be the norm for parish or monastic Orthodox worship. In the same article, Pomazansky offers a clarification on the state of the contemporary Typikon, noting that the Typikon has developed organically in history and is like a fully grown plant.[25] His appraisal of maximalist liturgy as the norm is quite positive, and he dismisses Schmemann's historical assessment of the Typikon's development as deficient because of Schmemann's employment of Western methods. Pomazansky, then, represents the liturgical school manifested by the liturgical ethos at Holy Virgin Cathedral, which differs significantly from Schmemann's school, which actively sought liturgical renewal in the Orthodox Churches.

The distinction between schools of Orthodox liturgical theology is crucial because of the longstanding relationship between liturgy and architecture. Many of the parishes I profile in this study have designed interior spaces that conform to the basic requirements of the Byzantine liturgy, and these parishes do not adopt a maximalist liturgical ethos. We have found that communities fine-tune the liturgy to make it suitable for the limitations of interior space, and in some cases, liturgy is one activity among many others that take place in the buildings on a community's property. Holy Virgin Cathedral's maximalist philosophy illustrates the diversity of liturgical approaches within Orthodox America by steadfastly adhering to a late nineteenth-century Russian imperial model that values the monastic liturgical norm and hierarchy.

Concerning the liturgy/architecture relationship, Holy Virgin Cathedral conforms to the new norm of liturgical adjustment in terms of the placement of architectural components. The sanctuary space merely suffices for the clergy, and the space of the nave is somewhat limited, which can become challenging when the cathedral is the location for a major feast or churchwide gathering. That said, the nave's openness promotes mobility and movement and facilitates ritual use of the body in worship, a staple of Byzantine liturgy. The cathedral's liturgical maximalism coheres with the architecture in two other significant ways. First, the cathedral's massive, tripartite iconostasis with three altars promotes the notion of the sanctuary as the holy space where the priest dialogues with God in prayer. The cathedral's massive iconostasis is not surprising as it is a cliché, a manifestation of the high iconostases that became popular in the Middle Byzantine period and were inherited and cultivated further by Russia.

The accommodation of two additional altars communicates the cathedral's sense of ongoing salvation history. The altars devoted to the Theotokos and St. Nicholas represent the community's veneration of antique Christianity, whereas the altar devoted to St. John of Kronstadt honors a modern saint whose life is consistent with the communion of saints. The iconostasis coheres with the iconographic program because the whole interior is an experience of the rich diversity of the communion of saints. The verticality of the iconostasis also symbolizes the liturgical maximalism, which is supported by the cathedral's adherence to sharply defined roles for the clergy. For example, ROCOR dismisses the possibility of reciting some of the priestly prayers aloud for the people to hear.[26] The rationale for maintaining the practice of reciting the prayers secretly depends on a hierarchical image of the Church's liturgy, attributed to St. Dionysius the Areopagite. The following short passage from an apology by Cyril Quatrone defines the priest as bearing the weight of pastoral responsibility to dialogue with God on behalf of the people:

> During the anaphora, the priest is the one vouchsafed with the privilege of being the instrument through which the bread and wine are changed into the body and blood of our resurrected Lord. He is the one who celebrates this awesome and terrible act. He is the one who has been prepared through the previous mystical prayers, as well as his own very extensive private prayers, which are canonically required before he serves. He is the one whom God has ordained for this function. Not us! . . . This is why the prayer of the anaphora is not for us.[27]

A vertical iconostasis that separates the clergy from the people shapes the experience of a liturgical participant. Essentially, Holy Virgin Cathedral sets a high liturgical bar for visitors and parishioners. The primary community gathering is at liturgy, there are limitless opportunities for worship, and the community observes the majority of the Typikon's order. A synthetic theme emerges from the interior sacred space. The liturgical participant is drawn vertically, to ascend upward toward God the Father, whose image resides in the central dome. The process of ascent is rigorous, requiring hard work in the liturgical assembly, literally several hours for one liturgical celebration. The primary event is the Eucharist, painted on the apse of the sanctuary, and the participant joins an incredibly diverse communion of saints in making the offering to God. The depiction of the communion of saints is strikingly vivid: dozens of relics throughout the church provide tangible encouragement of saintly presence, especially the community's most-revered saint, St. John Maximovich, whose incorrupt body is available for intercessory prayer. The liturgical act that gradually prepares one to join this communion of saints occurs with precise assignments: the people must trust the clergy who lead them in prayer because they do not have access to all of the clergy's petitions. At Holy Virgin Cathedral, liturgy and architecture promote a strong eschatology and invite participants to devote their lives to God. The invitation is appealing because of the cathedral's aesthetic beauty, and encouragement comes from the communion of saints. The liturgy itself reminds the participant that the task of ascent requires true devotion and much hard work.

Complicating this assessment of liturgy and architecture in Holy Virgin Cathedral is the local quality of the lives of its saints. The cathedral contains many icons of the royal family, and the community's patron, St. John Maximovich, was an avowed monarchist. Certainly, the memory of the royal family and the tsarist epoch of Russian history remain precious to the hearts of the cathedral's founders, benefactors, and the current faithful. Many of the faithful survived intense episodes of migration, forced to leave their places of settlement and find a new home in San Francisco. Given the character of migration, which was shaped by dangerous encounters with death, I hypothesize that the preference for a maximalist liturgical approach and the thunderous call to holiness coming from the communion of saints is attributable, at least in part, to a heightened apocalyptic sense originating from the community's legacy of immigration and confrontation with annihilation. All liturgy is apocalyptic, but the sacred space of Holy Virgin Cathedral communicates a higher decibel of apocalypticism through the sacred space and maximalist liturgy.

While there is diversity in Orthodoxy on the West Coast, I suggest that the cathedral's influence as a liturgical center has contributed to the shaping of liturgical practices in non-ROCOR churches, especially the Serbian Orthodox Church and the Orthodox Church in America (OCA). In America, this influence originates with figures such as St. John and Archbishop Anthony, although the liturgical maximalism itself probably originated in the monastic revival in imperial Russia, with Metropolitan Antony Khrapovitsky carrying this ethos into immigration and disseminating it to his close disciples, including St. John. The cathedral's status as a liturgical center is not limited to the duration of the services or adherence to the liturgical year. The cathedral also has a strong reputation for imparting spiritual direction. Father Perekrestov remarked that the clergy function as careful stewards of the spiritual life, especially with the recent influx of pilgrims who worship at the cathedral when they come to visit the relics of St. John. The cathedral's rule for receiving communion requires that everyone makes a formal confession prior to the liturgy, and the clergy discern preparedness in pilgrims who approach the chalice.[28] Father Perekrestov noted that Orthodox visitors have expressed their appreciation for the cathedral's attention to providing robust spiritual direction. An example of an instance of meaningful spiritual direction occurs when a priest takes as much time as needed to hear a confession, without hurrying so that the line of penitents would become shorter. My impression of Father Perekrestov's description of spiritual direction is that the cathedral strongly encourages people to partake of confession, though the clergy do not require the faithful to engage in the spiritual practice of govenie.[29]

In some ways, Holy Virgin Cathedral fits the traditional paradigm of liturgy and architecture shaping one another. The community makes the interior sacred space suitable for liturgical celebration, though there are no distinguishing architectural components that correspond directly with a particular liturgical function, with the exception of the shrine of St. John. However, a sense of pious gravitas accompanies the frequency of the community's liturgical celebration. The clergy reinforce and emphasize this gravitas by encouraging all to repent of their sins before they partake of the Eucharistic banquet, a sacramental discipline that is strictly enforced. In this vein, the liturgy shapes the architectural theology: a full participant in this communion must strive for the type of holy life epitomized by the countless saints who worship God from icons on the cathedral's walls and interior. If the community of saints values humility, repentance, and the avoidance of sin, then the living community must strive with them, in search of the same goal: union with the Father, who is depicted in the cathedral's central dome.

ST. JOHN MAXIMOVICH

The history of Holy Virgin Cathedral took an important turn with the arrival of Archbishop John Maximovich in 1962. Archbishop John's tenure in San Francisco was brief—only four years until his unexpected and untimely death in 1966. His arrival in San Francisco was the catalyst for a major turning point in the life of the community, and after his death and glorification, he has proven to be the most influential figure shaping the community's present and future. ROCOR's synod sent Archbishop John to Holy Virgin Cathedral to oversee the completion of the church's construction that had been halted due to severe divisions within the church community. He effectively rebooted the cathedral's construction despite his own sufferings through the process. I illustrate the magnitude of his influence in shaping the cathedral's identity by briefly surveying his legacy before and after his tenure in San Francisco. I then analyze how the shrine devoted to his memory has become the new cornerstone of the cathedral's present life that is also shaping its future.

St. John before San Francisco: Shanghai, Tubabao, and Western Europe

Numerous sources present the narrative story of St. John Maximovich.[30] Here I present a synthesis of the stories that contribute directly to our exploration of Holy Virgin Cathedral. My presentation focuses on the following elements: St. John's patronage of Russian Orthodox communities in Shanghai and Harbin, harboring a critical mass of immigrants from these locations to safe refuge in Holy Virgin Cathedral in San Francisco; St. John as a disciple of Metropolitan Antony Khrapovitsky and his cultivation of the Synodal-era Russian liturgical ethos; St. John's devotion to the Russian imperial heritage and his prophetic condemnation of the Soviet Union; and St. John's posthumous ministry of reconciling ROCOR with global Orthodoxy.

St. John was particularly beloved in San Francisco by the immigrants who arrived there from Shanghai and Harbin. After his ordination to the episcopacy in 1934, he was assigned bishop of Shanghai and arrived there in 1935.[31] His ministry was energetic, beginning by resolving conflicts and brokering peace between immigrant Serbs, Greeks, and Ukrainians.[32] He devoted special energies toward helping children and making frequent hospital visits. Protopresbyter Elias Wan stated that St. John founded an orphanage and prioritized visiting people: "because Vladika John was very busy from morning till night, he was almost always late to services. He ran about all day long, visiting hospitals and homes. He had no concept of time; he didn't even wear a watch."[33]

St. John oversaw the evacuation of his flock from Shanghai in 1949, when it became apparent that the communist revolution would overtake all of China.[34] He successfully shepherded the movement of five thousand people into Tubabao in the Philippines in 1949, though living conditions for the community were exceedingly harsh.[35] In his biography of St. John, Father Perekrestov chronicles St. John's tireless endeavor to arrange for the immigration of his flock in Tubabao to San Francisco, a process that achieved fruition in mid-1951.[36] Recognizing the completion of this process, the Synod of ROCOR appointed St. John as archbishop of the Western European Eparchy in 1950.[37]

Two elements of St. John's narrative from his pastoral care for his flock in Shanghai are noteworthy for their contribution to Holy Virgin Cathedral. First, he provided courageous pastoral care for his flock in overseeing their transition from Shanghai to San Francisco, via Tubabao. One cannot understate the difficulties of this period. St. John traveled broadly during this period despite his own abject poverty and that of his people. Second, St. John established a pattern of liturgical and ascetical austerity. Wan offered a precious glimpse into St. John's devotion to maintaining the order of divine services:

> Vladika John served Liturgy every day, all year round. Different priests would assist him in rotation. The services were very long. With his arrival, Vespers took place in the evening together with Compline. During Compline, at the very beginning of the service, there were always readings from one of the three canons to the saints. At six o'clock in the morning was the Midnight Office, followed by Matins and Liturgy. Vladika John . . . insisted that all verses appointed to be sung, be sung and not read. . . . He was very strict with the clergy. . . . Many people didn't like the fact that the services lasted so long. . . . In Shanghai there were pastoral meetings every Thursday. If someone was absent, he demanded a full explanation. At these meetings, most of the time was spent on questions of how to serve. Vladika would ask the priests about certain unique aspects of some of the upcoming services, testing their knowledge.[38]

St. John's emphasis on preserving the fullness of the liturgical cycle is remarkable for an émigré Orthodox community and testifies to his liturgical ethos. His strictness was not limited to the clergy. Perekrestov explains a dilemma St. John confronted while in San Francisco in 1949 when the Russian community organized a concert on the eve of the Sunday of All Saints.[39] St. John admonished the people to refrain from attending the concert and instead attend the Vigil for this important feast of the liturgical year. The following morning, during the course of his homily, he admonished those who had attended the concert and refused to permit them to receive Holy Communion until they repented. St. John read the prayer of absolution over them himself. Zealous advocacy for a longsuffering flock and liturgical maximalism shape the narrative of St. John's life before he became bishop of San Francisco, and the arrival of thousands of immigrants from Shanghai to San Francisco bridges this gap.

Portrait of St. John during His Tenure in San Francisco

In many ways, the narrative of St. John's tenure in San Francisco is a continuation of the themes presented above. At the request of the faithful in San Francisco who knew St. John from his tenure in Shanghai, ROCOR's Synod sent him to San Francisco to deliver peace in the turbulence of a quarrel over the use of church funds for building of the new cathedral.[40] Archbishop Tikhon was the ruling hierarch at the time, and he died in 1963.[41] After the Synod appointed St. John as the ruling hierarch of the western diocese, he resumed the construction of the cathedral. Perekrestov and others note that many opposed his decision, and that he responded to them by requesting that they join him in dialogue.[42] The sources state that St. John endured suffering during this period of tension and division, exacerbated by some parishioners involving him in a lawsuit.[43] While the municipal court stated its incompetence to rule in ecclesial matters and the Synod of Bishops confirmed and supported St. John, many of his opponents continued to accuse him with ill-will. In response, he refused to blame them, even when they attempted to tarnish his reputation by sending accusatory letters and documents to the Synod.[44] Other witnesses state that St.

John avoided conversation about the unpleasant events in San Francisco, and often "fell asleep" when asked about this period of strife.[45] On the one occasion St. John blamed someone for the community divisions, it was the devil.[46]

After the cathedral was erected, St. John again directed his attention toward promoting education, establishing required theological courses for clergy and laity, arguing that the laity must be acquainted with Orthodoxy in order to teach it to their children.[47] He was also consistent in exhorting the people to sustain a rigorous liturgical life. During his lifetime, he issued several liturgical directives. For example, on Pascha, he exhorted the people to receive Holy Communion, which required them to stay for the full duration of a long order of services.[48] He also issued a directive prohibiting the faithful from enjoying entertainment on the eves of feast days: "those who attend a dance or similar form of entertainment and diversion may not participate in the choir the next day, may not serve in the altar, enter the altar or stand on the kliros."[49] He created a rule for all acolytes on proper behavior and disposition during church services, and the twentieth rule stated that those who "violate the 'Church rule for acolytes' will stand on the left kliros until the conclusion of the divine service," meaning that they would be prohibited from serving.[50] In his remembrance of St. John, Archimandrite Ambrose stated that St. John "could be very strict and very forbearing at the same time," and was especially strict about the divine order of services.[51] But St. John occasionally contradicted his own liturgical maximalism: another witness spoke of St. John's refusal to chastise a priest who abbreviated a Vigil so that it would last only forty-five minutes.[52]

St. John was a loyal monarchist and thus consistent with the legacy of ROCOR, but while his sermons condemned the Bolsheviks for the destruction they wrought in Russia, he interpreted the situation as an opportunity for repentance and the emergence of a new Russia out of the ashes of destruction. He predicted divine punishment for the Bolsheviks, who were guilty of regicide: "How many times more grave and sinful was the murder of the Orthodox monarch anointed by God; how many times greater must the punishment be for the murderers of Tsar Nicholas II and his family?"[53] In a thoughtful homily on the spiritual condition of Russians abroad, St. John lamented the divisions among Russians outside Russia, and pointed to proponents of sophiology as exemplifying immigrant intelligentsia who preferred the worship of man to the worship of God.[54] He also asserted that a multitude of Russians were to blame for the calamity that befell Russia:

> Until now, there has been no real repentance; the crimes that were committed have not been openly condemned, and many active participants in the Revolution continue even now to assert that at the time it was impossible to act otherwise. By not voicing an outright condemnation of the February Revolution, of the uprising of the Anointed One of God, the Russian people continue to participate in the sin.[55]

St. John made many other assertions vigorously criticizing the Revolution and the communist government, but he also made two notable predictions. First, he believed that the blood of the New Russian Martyrs would "regenerate Russia and make it radiant with new glory."[56] Second, he outlined the potential contribution of Russians living abroad in spreading Orthodoxy and contributing to Russia's regeneration, though he appeared to expect that they would eventually return to Russia.[57]

In summary, St. John imparted a variegated legacy to his successors at Holy Virgin Cathedral in San Francisco. His liturgical austerity echoes the maximalism we explored above, a landmark for this study because Father Perekrestov considers Holy Virgin Cathedral to be cultivating a culture of liturgical strictness. Father Perekrestov states that the current cathedral clergy assiduously attempt to maintain the same liturgical ethos St. John imparted to them, symbolized by the daily celebration of the Divine Liturgy.[58] St. John also passed on a legacy of sensitive archpastoral ministry defined by the burden of unjust personal suffering and co-suffering with one's flock. Finally, he handed down a legacy of cultivating a strong Russian Orthodox community abroad to sustain the ideals torn down by the communists, a legacy that rests on ongoing repentance. In the following section, I demonstrate how the cathedral's shrine of St. John furthers his legacy and applies it to the contemporary life of the cathedral in a new way.

PARADIGM SHIFT: GLORIFICATION OF ST. JOHN

A paradigm shift occurred at Holy Virgin Cathedral in 1993, when the cathedral clergy examined the remains of Archbishop John, which were located in a sepulcher beneath the church. After much effort, they discovered that his relics were incorrupt.[59] St. John's glorification occurred on June 19, 1994. This date marks the final turning point in the narrative story of Holy Virgin Cathedral, which is communicated by the most important component of its sacred space: the shrine of St. John Maximovich.

Cliché: Shrine of Incorrupt Relics

Most people visit Holy Virgin Cathedral to venerate the relics of St. John Maximovich, which are enshrined on the southern wall of the church. The shrine is a small fixture with an ornate roof, containing the relics of St. John in a glass-enclosed tomb.[60] The cathedral's cozy interior space makes St. John's shrine easy to find—it is immediately visible upon walking into the nave of the cathedral. Above the tomb is an icon of St. John, who holds Holy Virgin Cathedral in his left hand, a sign of his eternal advocacy of the cathedral community (fig. 4.6). The shrine draws numerous visitors from around the globe, and anyone can come forward to venerate the relics and pray to St. John. The shrine's design is classical Russian, quite similar to that of dozens of shrines containing incorrupt relics throughout Russia, which were a special source of devotion in the late imperial and early Soviet periods of Russian history.[61] On the annual anniversary of St. John's glorification, the cathedral moves the tomb containing St. John's relics to the middle of the nave, before the central analogion. Recently, the cathedral has opened every day (after the daily liturgy) for pilgrims and visitors. During my visit on a typical Friday, all of the visitors came to venerate St. John's relics and pray at his tomb. The daily flow of pilgrims and visitors, the online and e-mail requests for prayers to be offered at St. John's tomb, and the growing popularity of his memory is shaping Holy Virgin Cathedral into a church devoted to the memory of a living saint. Moreover, his shrine is a powerful symbol bringing ROCOR's

Figure 4.6　Icon of St. John Maximovich (photo courtesy of Helen
Sinelnikoff-Nowak)

and the cathedral's past and the global Orthodox community into the present, making the cathedral an edifice of pilgrimage and reconciliation. I now analyze the service to St. John and the presence of his incorrupt body to illuminate the cathedral as a temple that communicates the Orthodox Church's notion of the Paschal Mystery in a powerful and tangible manner, intimately connected with the history of the cathedral's faithful and ROCOR.

The Service to St. John: Bringing the Past and the Future into the Present

The service to St. John defines him as a faithful successor and defender of Orthodoxy, exuding many familiar marks of holiness exemplified in the Eastern communion of saints.[62] The first sticheron on Lord, I Have Cried at Vespers (Psalm 141) depicts St. John as an ascetic, a promoter of liturgical maximalism, a loving pastor, and a possessor of spiritual gifts:

> Let us hymn John, the holy hierarch of Christ, the advocate given us by God, who applying himself to unceasing prayer, and strengthened by the serving of the Liturgy and communion of the most holy mysteries, went forth bravely to his labor, hastening to the homes of the suffering and to those treated in hospitals . . . he was vouchsafed from on high the gifts of healing and clairvoyance.[63]

Another sticheron on Lord, I Have Cried (in Tone 3) attests to St. John's defeat of the atheist communists in his pastoral labors: "O good minister of the Gospel of Christ, who didst gird thyself about with the truth of Orthodoxy, with the sling of thy words thou didst drive away the ravenous wolves who do not confess Christ to be the true Wisdom of God, and who seek after alien wisdom."[64] By coupling this sticheron with St. John's critique of the peoples of the Russian diaspora, one could also interpret the "wolves" to be Russians in the diaspora who lapsed from fidelity to the Orthodox Church.[65] The hymns from the service honor St. John's labors in Shanghai and Western Europe, as expressed by his troparion (the chief hymn of his feast): "Lo, thy care for thy flock in its sojourn prefigured the supplications which thou dost ever offer up for the whole world."[66] The sessional hymn sung after the

Polyeleos (in Tone 4) offers a brief reminder of St. John's restoration of several pre-schism saints to the Orthodox Church calendar during his tenure as bishop of Western Europe: "O excellent lover of the glory of the ancient saints unknown to the East and neglected in the West, thou didst follow in their steps."[67] The troparion expresses a basic tenet about St. John: his labor for a community of pilgrims in this world is remembered in the liturgy (as the past) and prepares the assembly to celebrate him as an advocate of the whole world today (in the present). In other words, the lessons the assembly learns from hearing the hymns about St. John in the past shape them into viewing him as a universal saint, an advocate for the globe today. Father Perekrestov's description of pilgrims who come to venerate his relics today confirms this dogmatic assertion from the hymnography of his feast. A sticheron from Lord, I Have Cried exhorts the globe to come to Holy Virgin Cathedral to venerate St. John's memory and follow his example:

> Join chorus, ye East and West, ye North and South, celebrating the memory of the holy hierarch and wonderworker. Rejoice, o heavens, receiving the new angel, the divinely inspired man of prayer and unmercenary pastor, the gracious healer, prophet and herald, John, our merciful helper, the mighty surety for us at the judgment.[68]

When one compares the kind of people who come to venerate St. John with this sticheron from his service, the coherence between liturgical exhortation and reality is striking. The flow of pilgrims to venerate his relics and pray at his shrine is global, and this phenomenon is gradually transforming Holy Virgin Cathedral from a complex émigré community into a global cloud of witnesses praising God for their wonderworker, St. John.

ST. JOHN: A REPOSITORY OF ORTHODOX HAGIOGRAPHY

The hymnography expresses every aspect of St. John's wonderworking life. In Orthodox hagiology, saints are categorized as martyrs, confessors, passion-bearers, ascetics, monastics, hierarchs, and holy fools, among others. St. John was a hierarch who could be assigned to several of these hagiological categories. The service to St. John expresses the multivalent manifestation of his sanctity. He was an exemplary ascetic, as expressed by a sticheron from Lord, I Have Cried: "How can we not marvel at thy sleepless vigilance, and how can we not hymn thine ascetic life?"[69] His life evokes the legacy of the great ascetics of the Egyptian and Palestinian deserts, an image of St. John presented by the sessional hymn at the second chanting of the Psalter: "With faith and love do we all honor thy memory today, O heavenly man and earthly-angel; for thou wast a true desert-dweller amid this greatly turbulent world."[70]

St. John is both a local and universal saint, as the doxastikon on Lord, I Have Cried refers to him as "the luminary of the Russian diaspora, the teacher of diverse nations."[71] The local quality of his sainthood is amplified in kontakion no. 8 of the Akathist Hymn: "Here wast thou called to suffer persecution and, by thy patience, righteousness and instruction, to guide the flock, and didst erect the church of the Mother of God, the Joy of All Who Sorrow."[72] He was also a healer: several of the hymns refer to the unmercenaries praising St. John and celebrate the eternal quality of his healing ministry, as we see on the second troparion on Ode 5 of the canon chanted at Matins: "The gift of healing was given thee even when thou wast a priest, and thou didst increase it in the days of thine episcopate; and thou dost perfect it in the life which is eternal."[73]

Among the most powerful statements appearing in the service to St. John are two hymns that establish his legitimacy in the communion of saints, whose sanctity is equal to models who blazed trails of holiness in the past. First, the Ikos at the Canon (at Matins) envisions a cosmic celebration of St. John's life and ongoing advocacy for the Church:

> The heavens rejoice with us now, and the choirs of the saints receive a new and all-glorious adornment. The apostles greet a universal preacher; the ancient martyrs praise one who wondrously glorified their memory; holy hierarchs converse with their peer in eloquence and wisdom; the venerable marvel at a vigilant ascetic; holy kings honor an advocate for the restoration of Orthodox kingship; and the unmercenaries share their incorrupt and unapportioned reward with

an unmercenary healer. As all-glorious as thy ministry was, o father John, so great was the multitude of wreaths fashioned for thee. Wherefore, with the choirs of the saints pray to Christ God in behalf of us who fall down before thy precious relics, that our souls may be saved in peace.[74]

Another example of St. John as a legitimate participant in the communion of saints comes from the Akathist Hymn composed in his honor, particularly Ikos 7:

We see thee as a new chosen one of God, who wast manifest in the latter times as one of the holy hierarchs of Gaul, exhorting thy flock to preserve the same Orthodox faith that they confessed, and astonishing the peoples of the West by this holy life. . . . Rejoice, thou who wast a new Martin by the miracles and ascetic feats. Rejoice, thou who wast a new Germanus by thy confession of the Orthodox faith. Rejoice, thou who wast a new Hilary by thy divine theology. Rejoice, thou who wast a new Gregory by thy love and glorification of God's saints. Rejoice, thou who wast a new Faustus by thy monastic fervor. Rejoice, thou who wast a new Caesarius by thy steadfast love for the canons of the Church of God.[75]

ANALYSIS: A PROPHETIC SHRINE

The shrine of St. John Maximovich and the service sung in his honor manifest him as the primary symbol defining Holy Virgin Cathedral and the narrative history of ROCOR. At first glance, it would seem that the hymnography sung in his honor represents the story of his life that culminated in his glorification. An attentive liturgical participant would learn not only about St. John from this service, but also about Holy Virgin Cathedral and ROCOR. I analyze how St. John's shrine and service shape Holy Virgin Cathedral's sacred space in the present in this section.

St. John's shrine is a holy place exercising theological and prophetic ministries. The shrine's theological ministry occurs in the simplicity of its existence. Each day, dozens of pilgrims enter Holy Virgin Cathedral to venerate the relics and invoke St. John to aid them. St. John's reputation for granting prayer requests through healings and other wonders is legendary, and is probably the main attraction for the pilgrims. The desire to enter into the sacred space of the saint himself adds an additional layer of intimacy. People who were previously unfamiliar with St. John can enter the shrine and call upon him for aid, the only degree of separation between saint and believer being a layer of glass in the saint's tomb. The hagiographical narratives attest to St. John's performance of countless wonders of healing, protection, deliverance from danger and sin, and the protection of the Church. This aspect of his narrative conforms to the paradigm of the cult of the saints that has existed for almost two thousand years in Christian tradition.[76] From this perspective, the only outstanding feature of St. John's shrine is its brazen existence, proudly proclaiming an ancient tradition through bodily presence in an age of religious iconoclasm and doubt in the ability of saints to perform miracles.

I propose that St. John's shrine is a theologically dense symbol surpassing the common denominators of the cult of the saints on account of the specific history of Holy Virgin Cathedral and ROCOR. As the descendant of Russia's Orthodox Church in the imperial era, ROCOR was an outspoken critic of the Soviet regime for the majority of its history. Metropolitan Antony Khrapovitsky, ROCOR's leader in exile and the chief figure who shaped its history, was also St. John's mentor. Metropolitan Antony cultivated a vibrant Church devoted to sustaining the monastic model popularized by the monastery of St. Job in Pochaev (in contemporary Ukraine) and remained steadfast in the exiles' condemnation of the Soviet regime. This steadfastness included a painful rupture with the Moscow Patriarchate in 1927 due to the decision of Metropolitan Sergius Stragorodsky, Patriarch Tikhon's successor, to pledge the Orthodox Church's support for the Soviet state.[77] ROCOR's rejection of this fatuous attempt to enslave the Orthodox Church by the Soviet state was painful, in part because Metropolitan Antony was one of the most vocal supporters of the restoration of the Patriarchate.

The rupture of ROCOR from the Patriarchate and the gradual realization that exile from Russia was going to last much longer than originally anticipated resulted in the slow but sure growth of an ecclesial identity that condemned not only the Soviet regime, but also many other symbols of a dark age. Besides the murder of clergy and laity, perhaps the most offensive act of the Soviet regime against the Russian Orthodox Church in the early period of Bolshevik rule was the state's organized attempt to discredit the Church by exhuming relics of saints throughout the country. Such relic inspections were performed throughout Russia and Ukraine in an attempt to expose relic fraud and liberate the people from the false idea that the bodies of the saints were preserved in a state of perfect incorruption.[78] The Church faithful considered such acts to be blasphemous, and Soviet authorities were frustrated by the people's resilient faith in their country's wonderworking saints, even if their holy remains had slowly turned to dust over hundreds of years. Robert Greene offers an insightful description of the conflict in the early stages of relics inspections:

> After nearly a year of Soviet power, the Revolution had not managed to sweep the saints and their relics into the dustbin of history, and while symbols of sanctity remained visible fixtures on the political and cultural landscape of Russia during the first years of Soviet power, the hotly contested issues of sacrality and sainthood soon became ideological fault lines along which the Orthodox Church and the Soviet state were visibly divided. . . . The Bolshevik elite sought to bring this conflict to a speedy conclusion by confronting the material dimension of sanctity head-on, launching a campaign to shake the Orthodox Church to its foundations by striking a double blow against the very notion of bodily incorruptibility and against the miracles on which the cults of the holy dead were founded.[79]

The reaction of the faithful to the Soviet campaign was startlingly resilient, and the Soviet quest to purge the cult of wonderworking saints from the faithful's consciousness not only failed, but also contributed to their steadfastness in promoting the communion of saints.[80] The Church did not relinquish its claim to saints working wonders, but its officials did have to explain the meaning of incorruption, especially when the exhumations produced limited relics of saints consisting of a few bones, with other materials added to produce the appearance of a complete body, incorrupt and intact.[81] When granted an opportunity to explain the Church's position, officials stated that complete incorruptibility was not an absolute criterion for recognizing sanctity, and that remains of saints that had completely decomposed did not reflect negatively on their degree of sanctity.[82]

ROCOR celebrates St. John Maximovich and narrates in great detail the finding of his relics, which were incorrupt.[83] The erection of a shrine in his memory, with the incorrupt relics in full view for all to venerate, offers a profound theological gift in light of the sordid Soviet history of exhuming relics to disenfranchise and delegitimize the Orthodox Church. Theologically, when one draws near to St. John's relics and observes him, one views an inanimate body. His bronze hands are visible through the glass, but even if one appraises his relics with piety, he is dead. His bodily presence in the shrine at Holy Virgin Cathedral is a stark, human confrontation with the problem of death. A dispassionate and detached observer might be entirely unimpressed with the display at the shrine, in spite of its marvelous decoration and evocative iconography. Yet it is precisely because of his inanimate body lying in a tomb for all to behold that his shrine offers those who approach an opportunity to confront death. Death, its sting and finality, collides with the rich narrative describing St. John as a wonderworker whose advocacy for the Church before God's throne is immeasurably gracious and powerful. In this vein, the shrine differs from the cemeteries and mausoleums containing the bodies of the dead throughout the world, and in a certain sense, even surpasses the Orthodox Church's erection of tombs memorializing Jesus's death and burial on Holy Friday and Mary's death and burial on the feast of her Dormition on August 15.

St. John's shrine is theologically rich because it tangibilizes the reality of death in motion. The beholder must process the reality of a body lying before him who is proclaimed as a live and energetic patron of the Church before the divine throne. St. John's shrine, then, unveils the complex mystery of Pascha before one's eyes and allows one to enter into the Church's mystery of Pascha through the life—and death—of one of those belonging to the communion of saints. The exaposteilarion of the service to St. John communicates this paradox of death and life coming together in the present, a collision of past and future viewed through the memory of a beloved church father: "'Even though I have died, yet I am alive! Grieve not, O ye people!' Thus thou hast proclaimed after thy repose, illumining with mystic light those who hymn thee, O father John, all-wondrous and holy hierarch."[84] People will continue to visit Holy Virgin Cathedral to venerate the relics of St. John Maximovich, and as this practice endures in the life of this community and similar sister Orthodox communities throughout the world, the stories of the wonders he works will similarly circulate. That said, one cannot understate the potentially ecstatic experience awaiting those who behold the presence of the dead. St. John's shrine offers all an opportunity to enter the Paschal Mystery by confronting the reality of death at any given time outside the liturgical year and also outside official liturgical celebrations. The background story of the Bolshevik challenge to the tenets of sanctity resulted in clarification on the part of Church officials, a clarification that is insightful for one who desires to view and embrace the life that Jesus promised after the grave.[85] The process of embracing this life begins at tombs, and the narrative story of St. John provides an informative context to facilitate this entrance into mystery.

The background story of the defilement of relics leads us to the prophetic ministry of St. John. His ministry was one of advocacy and deliverance from danger, including the condemnation of the Bolshevik state that launched a brutal assault on the Church. Caught in the crossfire of this epic and tragic war between the state and the Church were the clergy and the faithful of the Russian Orthodox Church. ROCOR's refusal to accept the Moscow Patriarchate's tepid alliance with the Soviet state caused painful ruptures within the global community of Russian Orthodoxy. St. John died long before the collapse of the Soviet Union and the emergence of the Russian Federation. His desire for the restoration of the monarchy has not come to pass, but it has been vindicated, and I argue that his shrine is a symbol of the Orthodox Church's victory over the Bolsheviks' atheistic assault.

In this vein, St. John's shrine functions as another instance of a tangible memorial symbolizing the violence of the recent past described by Amy Papalexandrou (see chapter 1).[86] In chapter 2, I described St. Katherine's exterior design and interior iconography as an implicit symbol of a community's memory of a violent past. St. John's shrine is an explicit symbol of this memory because of the Soviet regime's attempt to discredit the Russian Church through relic fraud.

The erection of a shrine containing the incorrupt relics of a saint who condemned the Soviets, protected his flock from danger, and healed divisions within the wounded Russian Orthodox émigré community became an enduring symbol of the Church's victory over the state in a costly war.[87] St. John's attempts to build up a strong émigré community that could contribute to the restoration of Russia seem to have been fulfilled in his glorification, and his shrine is a symbol of the life-giving activity of Holy Virgin Cathedral and ROCOR.

The shrine of St. John is also the most powerful and enduring symbol of the life of today's Holy Virgin Cathedral. The community's context has shifted drastically, from providing refuge to the faithful fleeing from civil war in China, to embracing a new era of rapprochement with the Orthodox community. For most of its history, ROCOR found itself on the periphery of global Orthodoxy because of its conflict with the Moscow Patriarchate. ROCOR was canonically legitimate, but enjoyed close relations with only some Orthodox Churches (especially the Church of Serbia), largely because the Serbs supported ROCOR and forged close ties with its leaders in the early stages of ROCOR history. The fissures between ROCOR and other Orthodox communities in immigration are not imagined. One eyewitness told me that it was customary for ROCOR clergy and the faithful to remain in the narthex of then-Metropolia churches (now the OCA; the Metropolia was part of the Moscow Patriarchate until 1970) when entering the church.[88] The eyewitness states that St. John crossed that line by walking into the nave of a Metropolia parish, though he did not know if St. John went into the sanctuary. The narthex represents an important threshold in the design of Orthodox interior sacred space.

In 2007, following a heated and tumultuous process, ROCOR reestablished communion with the Moscow Patriarchate; rapprochement was realized.[89] The restoration of communion opened floodgates for the reconciliation of ROCOR with the rest of global Orthodoxy. Father Perekrestov noted that this process is in a honeymoon period, especially in this era of cultural wars, since ROCOR's traditionally strict approach to Church life differs from the approaches of other Orthodox Churches. As one of the most recent saints to be glorified in America while simultaneously representing Orthodox of Russia, China, and Western Europe, St. John has become a global figure and universal saint. As a global figure, he draws pilgrims from varying regions of the globe, and they come to know the narrative story of Holy Virgin Cathedral and ROCOR through him. Naturally, the influx of pilgrims throughout the world brings a global audience into the sacred space of Holy Virgin Cathedral. When they visit, they become familiar with the cathedral and its community, and reconciliation continues. This process of the global rapprochement between world Orthodoxy and ROCOR is heavily localized because of St. John's presence at Holy Virgin Cathedral in San Francisco. Holy Virgin Cathedral is in a state of evolution; this community is becoming a space that provides a home, both temporary and permanent, for an increasingly diverse global population. This paradigm shift accords with the narrative of St. John's life: a holy man encounters the people of the globe and seeks to unite them with God and each other. Thus, in worldly death, yet alive in Christ, St. John brings people into communion with ROCOR through Holy Virgin Cathedral. Consequently, the cathedral has experienced a paradigm shift: it is no longer a home for immigrants where culture and resilient sustenance of national identity is maintained, but it has become a sacred space of reconciliation among Orthodox people. For this reason, St. John's tomb and shrine are the most potent symbols shaping the sacred space of Holy Virgin Cathedral.

SAINTS CYRIL AND METHODIUS HIGH SCHOOL AND THE SAINT JOHN OF SAN FRANCISCO ORTHODOX ACADEMY

Liturgy is at the center of community life at Holy Virgin Cathedral, and so this chapter has focused on the church. The community also owns a large hall in which annual festivities occur, including the annual Russian Yolka celebration and other community gatherings and banquets. A final product of the legacy that St. John contributes to the community's self-identity is the cathedral's two schools.

Saints Cyril and Methodius High School was founded in 1927 and functions as a high school that meets two afternoons each week.[90] The school provides instruction in Russian language and culture and the

Orthodox faith for children to the age of sixteen. The existence of an afternoon school that meets periodically is not unusual for an Orthodox émigré community: one finds such models in similar émigré communities of numerous ethnic groups in America.

The Saint John of San Francisco Orthodox Academy is an accredited K–12 school founded in 1994 and currently has approximately seventy students. The academy offers a complete curriculum, including a basic core curriculum for all grades in the humanities, sciences, and mathematics, with specialties in language (including instruction in Latin and Russian). The cathedral founded the school to provide families an opportunity to educate their children in an Orthodox environment. The Saint John of San Francisco Orthodox Academy captures St. John's vision of a global Church, manifested by two important statements in a brief narrative designed to appeal to parents who are weighing school options for their children:

> Our students are prepared to be active, contributing members of society. Their studies foster skills that enable them to take part in the world around them, dedicated to learning, service and leadership. By fostering elements of a child's education that are often left out of secular curricula (such as a strong sense of morality, ethical decision making, practical and devoted piety, a sense of authentic Christian identity in the world), our graduates are able to engage with the world and society more robustly, more wholesomely, and more fruitfully than many others.

> St. John's Academy is the only school of its kind in North America. Our students live in the embrace of the Orthodox Church and encounter its full dimensions: the Russian Orthodox heritage of the Cathedral under whose domes it is situated; the Greek, Antiochian, American, Palestinian, Serbian and other Orthodox heritages represented by its teachers, students, and Board of Directors; and indeed the universal community of Orthodox Christians whose devotion to our patron, St. John the Wonderworker of Shanghai and San Francisco, incorporates every ethnic, local, cultural and jurisdictional tradition of the Orthodox Church.[91]

These passages demonstrate the community's desire to enrich a typical humanities curriculum by adding courses and a learning environment emphasizing Orthodox Christian values, which include participation in the cathedral's liturgies. The second statement, though, constitutes a new development in the cathedral's history: the academy desires to form citizens who might find a home for themselves in the global Orthodox community. The academy captures St. John's current ministry of rapprochement among the Orthodox of the world. The community's devotion to creating a school on its property that promotes Russian culture and history and a humanities curriculum with a global Orthodox theme is unique in Orthodoxy. In terms of the architecture, the cathedral simply uses its existing facility to offer instruction. However, the existence of the two schools and their priorities illuminates a stronger reciprocity between the parish hall and the cathedral temple.

The community is forming its children in the building adjacent to the church to become strong and frequent participants in the life of the cathedral, a ritual the children rehearse not only on Sundays, but also in school. The Saint John of San Francisco Orthodox Academy's curriculum reveals the cathedral's mirror image of community self-identity. The academy forms children to become knowledgeable and responsible citizens of a global Orthodox community, which is the cathedral's current station on account of its patron, St. John Maximovich. St. John's vision, then, holds the two communities together and removes the physical space between the cathedral and the parish hall since the children learning in the hall are being prepared to confront the challenges the world brings to the shrine of St. John.

CONCLUSION

In this chapter, we have surveyed the life of a unique émigré Orthodox community. Our investigation has yielded some results that are similar to those of the architectural models profiled in previous chapters. In many ways, Holy Virgin Cathedral is a cliché. The cathedral's basic design, following the pattern of the Kremlin's Dormition Cathedral, offers aesthetic appeal but is not particularly practical. The interior space has some challenges for the harmony of liturgical fixtures. The central cupola is disproportionately large; the iconostasis was set too close to the apse, making the sanctuary too small and causing challenges for a cathedral that receives numerous visitors and is the host for many churchwide events. The interior sacred space is smallish and cannot accommodate a large crowd.

The interior challenges are mitigated by brilliant iconography, and the community boasts superlative liturgical arts. Its choir is the envy of choral conductors, and the walls were painted by a master iconographer. The iconographic program communicates a fascinating mosaic of the communion of saints, embracing fathers and mothers of the Old and New Testaments and depicting many new martyrs who represent the community's collective memory of the Russian imperial era. In the presence of more than one hundred saintly relics, especially the shrine of St. John Maximovich, the visitor or liturgical participant beholds a privileged vision of the cosmos, crowned with the icon of God himself in the central dome. The rigorous liturgical maximalism revered by the cathedral's leaders shapes their understanding of the sacred space: askesis is required to join this sacred communion, and one experiences such askesis in this life, aided by the memory of the saints proclaimed in narrative and depicted in image. In this vein, the cathedral constitutes not merely a cliché, but a group of the faithful who value the entirety of their Christian history and strive to make the ideal—Christian holiness—the norm.

Holy Virgin Cathedral offers an additional layer that distinguishes it from other Orthodox parishes in America. The community experienced several waves of immigration, and each episode of moving involved persecutions from regimes hostile to Christianity and the real threat of death. Intense persecution unveils the immediacy and imminence of God's reign, and the cathedral's liturgical maximalism and iconography present a tangible and proximate eschatology, one heightened by the presence of the bodily remains and relics of St. John Maximovich.

St. John, however, has allowed the cathedral to continue to live in motion. The finding of his relics and the celebration of his glorification reshaped the cathedral's interior sacred space and oriented it toward its present mission: rapprochement with and promotion of global Orthodoxy. The cathedral's reception of Orthodox pilgrims from diverse regions of the world has introduced people to the historical narrative and theological treasures of ROCOR in Holy Virgin Cathedral. Father Perekrestov's observation of a paradigm shift in motion, where the cathedral's primary ministry is care for pilgrims, confirms the reshaping of sacred space. I propose that St. John offers a second equally substantial contribution through the reshaping of the sacred space. St. John's legacy and the texts of his service suggest that his relics proclaim the community's victory over the scandalous Bolshevik persecution of the Orthodox Church symbolized by their campaign against relic fraud.

St. John's shrine and bodily remains make the Orthodox teaching on Pascha tangible to the visitor. Observers see the faithful standing before a dead and incorrupt body, calling on a wonderworking saint to intercede on their behalf before God's throne. The presence of the dead is no horror show or pagan ritual: it is a celebration of the Christian message of bodily resurrection. The heavy and imminent eschatology communicated through the iconography makes sense in the presence of saintly remains: together, they communicate the Orthodox Church's confidence in eternal life with the triune God. St. John's shrine and the veneration of his relics communicate a partially realized eschatology: the future has come, but not completely, because God's final consummation of his Paschal Mystery will be accomplished in the next life, with Christ's second coming. Holy Virgin Cathedral might appear to be a cliché, but like the parishes of preceding chapters, it inscribes its self-identity on its sacred space. In this case, the relationship between liturgy and architecture is imperfect, but comes close to fulfilling the traditional Orthodox paradigm we are testing throughout this study. The addition of the shrine of St. John and the conversion of the crypt into the church commemorating the finding of his relics illustrates the phenomenon of architecture in motion. In this instance, we see a fixed edifice that has no real room for addition evolving and becoming something new. With the addition of the shrine of St. John, the cathedral was also becoming a community that was deepening its communion with global Orthodoxy. In other words, architecture and local ecclesiology enjoyed a particular symbiosis in this case study, which confirms the multivalence of architecture as a symbol communicating self-identity.

CHAPTER FIVE

ANNUNCIATION GREEK ORTHODOX CHURCH

Annunciation Greek Orthodox Church in Milwaukee is famous on account of its renowned architect, Frank Lloyd Wright. The parish community, established in 1904, is one of two Greek Orthodox parishes in Wauwatosa, a suburb on the west side of Milwaukee. The parish owns the following properties: the church (with a seating capacity of one thousand), the James W. Pihos Cultural Center, the Greek Orthodox Manor (a home for senior citizens), and a parking lot. This chapter analyzes Annunciation's architecture by exploring how the design emerged in conjunction with the community's evolution from immigration to Americanization. The chapter also discusses how particular architectural features might be suitable for liturgical innovation.[1]

PARISH HISTORY

A helpful resource on Annunciation parish's history was published in 1986 by Milwaukee native John Gurda.[2] This book guides the reader through the parish's formative stages and focuses on the deliberations of the building committee, the hiring of Wright as architect, and the construction of the church.

Annunciation's story follows a reasonably typical pattern of Orthodox communities in America. The Greeks who arrived in America at the end of the nineteenth and beginning of the twentieth centuries established churches, which functioned as centers of immigrant community life. Annunciation was established in 1904 and became legal in 1906, initially worshiping in a series of rented buildings and then building a church in Milwaukee in 1914.[3] The first building was designed by Carl Barkhausen, which Gurda describes as "an imposing brick edifice built into the side of a west-facing hill."[4] The church was more than a temple of worship—it was also the center of community gathering, a place that cultivated the retention and sustenance of ethnic identity.[5]

Annunciation was a picture of an immigrant community; Gurda describes the neighborhood as essentially Greek, with families able to raise their children in a Greek subculture, reinforced by a Greek school that taught youth Greek culture and language after regular school.[6] Immigrant patterns affected the Annunciation community in less favorable ways. Immigrants had arrived in America with the memory of Greek independence fresh. The appointment of the Annunciation as the parish patronal feast was no accident since Greek Independence day and the Annunciation feast fall on the same date, March 25.[7] Greek immigrants initially believed that their sojourn in America would be temporary, and they followed the political course of events in Greece closely. As political tensions increased in Greece, immigrants tended to coalesce around particular figures, and tensions within the parish led to a permanent fracture in 1922, with the dissidents forming Saints Constantine and Helen parish.[8]

Annunciation was characterized as an assimilationist parish, and its chief internal organization was the American Hellenic Educational Progressive Association (AHEPA). The building of the first church symbolized the beginnings of recognizing America as a permanent home, and since the immigrants would not return to Greece, they sought ways to blend in with their new surroundings. Assimilation introduced a complete American experience, and the Greeks were not immune to their environmental conditions. The Great Depression impacted the community, and Greeks who fought defending the United States in World War II realized that their fellow soldiers were likewise fellow citizens, contributing to a stronger sense of solidarity with other Americans in the parish.[9] The Greek civil war was a considerable source of angst for the immigrants, who came together to offer support to Greeks and mitigate suffering. After World War II, more signs of assimilation appeared as the community became more affluent with numerous professionals in the community.[10]

The gradual process of Americanization was also evident in the liturgical evolution of the parish. The original church did not have pews and integrated byzantinisms into the decoration through stone and terra cotta work along with icons imported from Mount Athos.[11] In 1923, the parish installed pews and hired Dr. Canell Cornell, a gifted layman, to assist the rector; Cornell founded a youth choir and set music to four-part harmony to continue the updating of the parish's life.[12] Some parishioners protested this Americanization: one parishioner recalled the women banging against the brass rail upstairs, disrupting the services in protest on account of the installation of the pews.[13] Adding pews was a natural move for the parish because it demonstrated its acceptance of American religious traditions, which included pews, youth choirs, and polyphonic music.

The immigrant community encountered an important threshold after World War II when increasingly affluent families sought to "better themselves" by becoming homeowners in the suburbs.[14] The parish's initial response was to establish a building committee to raise funds for a community hall, but the committee's deliberations concluded that the neighborhood was no longer adequate for the community, so in 1952, the parish shifted course by seeking to build a new church. The composition of the building committee symbolized the community's transition from an immigrant community to one becoming more firmly ensconced in American society: the committee had thirty-eight members; of those, exactly half were immigrants and half were American-born.[15]

This initial review of Annunciation's parish history is relevant to our analysis because it exhibits important patterns that shape Orthodox architecture in America. The first pattern is the selection of a building: the Greeks settled in a building they could afford that functioned as the epicenter of community life and was suitable for the liturgical rite that had accompanied them to America. As the community evolved, the architecture did not develop with them, and the community's values impacted both the liturgy and its expressed need for a new home. The community recognized a need for an auxiliary building for general community gatherings and education, which the existing church structure could not provide. The community's commitment to American assimilation led to minor but noticeable liturgical changes: pews were installed to make the interior blend with the standard American worship space, and a youth choir was created to sing in four-part harmony, again corresponding to the prevailing cultural environment. The creation of a building committee and the decision to build a new church structure that was most suitable for the majority of the community's constituents correspond to the pattern of adjustment: the community went to the suburbs as a confirmation of its arrival in and acceptance by America. The following section of the parish history concentrates on the architectural features of the church and the parish's interaction with the architect, Wright. In this section, we will see that the pattern of assimilation is disrupted by architectural innovation that suggested new and creative possibilities for liturgy while simultaneously departing from architectural tradition and causing the community to reflect on its objectives and mission.

ARCHITECTURAL INNOVATION: FRANK LLOYD WRIGHT

Annunciation's building committee took up the task of interviewing several architects for the design of the new church. By 1955, the committee was searching for a local architect, and experience with Orthodox architecture was not necessarily required. The specifications for the property were as follows: a church seating 700, a Sunday school for 300, a social hall for 500, and a space within the church for a large choir, with a projected budget of $500,000.[16] Originally, Wright was not among the selected finalists, but it was an influential member of the community (Christ Seraphim) who enthusiastically suggested Wright.[17] Only a small majority carried the motion to hire Wright for the church's design, which illuminates the community's rather tepid initial response to the possibility of hiring a top-drawer architect.[18] Annunciation's less-than-enthusiastic response characterized much of the experience of the process of designing, constructing, and renovating the church property. The parish's post-Wright history is complicated, as Gurda's account witnesses to some distance between the community's sense of comfort in its building and the reputation and international platform Wright infused into the building and, by association, the community. The present parish community is ardently loyal to Wright's design, a disposition that has created some tensions within the parish and also complicates its decision-making progress for renovations and additions.

The actual design of the church presents features beginning with the prominent dome, which is essentially the church. Upon approaching the parish property from West Congress Street, one sees three buildings across a broad and expansive front lawn (fig. 5.1). A large cross greets vehicles entering the property, and it provides a direct visual line to the entrance of the church. The first building one greets is Greek Orthodox Manor on the left, with the James W. Pihos Cultural Center to the immediate north of the church itself, with the parking lot in the rear of the church (fig. 5.2). The prevailing design motif is a shallow dome that rests on a gently curved bowl, with a cross inscribed in a circle, a fusion of two ancient theological concepts.[19] A blue fountain is at the front of the church, mimicking the church's blue roof, a copy of the life-giving spring of the Theotokos in Constantinople and evoking the theme of Mary as the window to heaven (fig. 5.3).[20] A narrow sidewalk encircles the church's exterior for processions, and several trees add to the landscaping on the exterior. Currently, a cross, added in the 1990s, adorns the roof.

Gurda suggests that Wright's design was aided by his wife, Olgivanna, who hailed from Montenegro and was raised in the Orthodox Church.[21] Gurda's collection of reminiscences of Wright's creative process indicates that Wright was well versed in the basics of Byzantine architecture and had received a general overview of the requirements of the Orthodox liturgy. Besides the dome functioning as the chief design motif, the architecture was also marked by arches and the appearance of the dome resting on windows that maximized natural lighting.[22] Wright's addition of the spherical windows that ringed the

Figure 5.1 Annunciation Greek Orthodox Church, exterior (photo by author)

Figure 5.2 Greek Orthodox Manor (photo by author)

Figure 5.3   Annunciation Greek Orthodox Church, fountain (photo by author)

edge of the dome had the appearance of a "string of pearls," according to Gurda.[23] Wright added lightrees for the interior stairwells, and his design carried two additional features that are noteworthy: the dome shape of the church itself was designed to facilitate maximal interior visual access, to remove visual obstructions for the laity (fig. 5.4).[24] Equally significant to the features but subtle to the untrained eye are the four piers supporting the building, visible on the exterior, described by Anthony Cutler:

> One [of its subtleties] is the changing role of the four great "piers" when seen from a distance and when approached more nearly. In distant view they serve to support the shallow ellipse formed by the dome and its subordinate counterpart. But in immediate proximity they act as firmly grounded, rectilinear forms in which are resolved the broad sweeping planes of the overall design. As such they constitute stabilizing anchors in the flowing system of convexities and concavities.[25]

Figure 5.4   Annunciation Greek Orthodox Church, lightree (photo by author)

The narthex has two large candleboxes shaped in a circle (fig. 5.5). The circle shape repeats the dominant circular shape of the dome on the interior, a deliberate design by Wright, who also added an efficient disposal system: a removable cap allows one to dispose of the candles through a chute going directly into a waste bin in the lowest level of the church.[26] The narthex includes an iconostasis, prefiguring the liturgy one will enter. The narthex eschews a typical entrance into the church as the entrance is from the south instead of the west, which means that there is no center aisle connecting a western entrance to church oriented to the east. Seating is on benches with the original blue cushions, again integrating the color scheme of the dome and fountain. Three lightrees contain white and blue lights and direct attention to the ceiling while also promoting a sense of verticality. Two of the lightrees flank the iconostasis and the third is in the rear by a staircase ascending into a gallery.

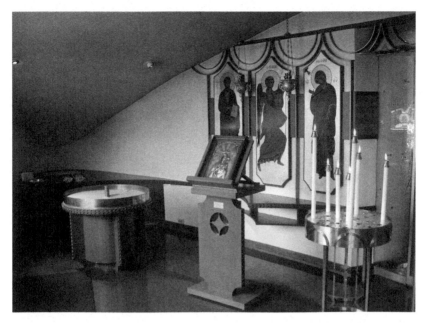

Figure 5.5   Annunciation Greek Orthodox Church, narthex (photo by author)

The sanctuary is quite small, with a utility room containing vestments and other liturgical items (fig. 5.6). There is no high place, though there is an oval carved into the wall that gives the appearance of a modest apse; another small oval with a shelf is on the right (facing east), and an equally sized oval shelf functions as the table of oblation where the prothesis is celebrated. The sanctuary is designed for one celebrant, and concelebration is difficult because of the cramped space.

Wright's design included an iconostasis that provided visual access from the nave into the sanctuary, an innovation at the time (fig. 5.7).[27] The iconostasis integrates 1,800 crosses. The secretary to Archbishop Iakovos, Eugene Masselink, was commissioned to paint the icons, and he attempted to paint them in contemporary forms.[28] In the 1990s, Annunciation commissioned new icons for the iconostasis in two levels, and added a large panel of the Theotokos (Platytera) in the second gallery behind the iconostasis (fig. 5.8).[29] The icon of the Theotokos

Figure 5.6 Annunciation Greek Orthodox Church, sanctuary (photo by author)

Figure 5.7   Annunciation Greek Orthodox Church, interior (photo by author)

currently blocks visual access to an original interior fountain, which is no longer in use. The ambo and bishop's cathedra stand on a large solea and include the cross motif that defines the iconostasis (fig. 5.9). The height of the cathedra blocks visual access to the right side of the iconostasis, so that it is difficult to see the icons of St. John the Baptist and the Archangel Gabriel. The interior seating is circular on the lower level and the floor is leveled, descending toward a center point where the ambo meets the floor of the nave at its most narrow point. The upper gallery has several stained glass windows, and the dome and walls of the interior have no iconography.

The upper gallery encircles the church. Wright designed it to include two choirs, which are on the east walls and optimize antiphonal singing. Annunciation's choir director is able to communicate directly with the clergy because the podium literally looks down into the sanctuary, a visual point of access available to participants who stand in the

Figure 5.8   Platytera Theotokos icon (photo by author)

parts of the gallery adjacent to the sanctuary. The cross-in-circle motif is difficult to identify in the interior until one notices the four crosses and circles that are placed in the four corners of the interior cross; these circles conceal Annunciation's ventilation system.

Wright designed the church but neglected to add a social hall, chapel, and offices, which were all part of the architectural program. He attempted to resolve this issue by adding a wing to the building that was below ground level, to avoid the appearance of severe disproportion on the exterior while adding the necessary space for community activities.[30] The banquet hall was in the basement of the church. The second noteworthy feature of the original design was Wright's inclusion of a sunken garden: this provided a glimpse into the natural environment and allowed the congregation to view the greenery, a deliberate integration of Wright's topographical preference for buildings that blend in with their natural surroundings.[31] The current lower level has a functioning kitchen, a gathering space, offices, a classroom, and a

Figure 5.9 Annunciation Greek Orthodox Church, bishop's cathedra (photo by author)

Figure 5.10   Annunciation Greek Orthodox Church, chapel in basement (photo by author)

chapel. The chapel has two white globes that stream exterior light for illumination, and the icons and altar of the original church of Annunciation constructed in 1904 are in the chapel in accordance with Wright's wishes to honor Annunciation's history (fig. 5.10).[32] The ceiling of the chapel is slightly elevated so that the chapel is identifiable on the exterior.

The groundbreaking ceremony for Annunciation's new church occurred in 1959, a little more than a month following Wright's death.[33] The committee managed to find craftsmen who were able to construct the edifice in accordance with Wright's design.[34] The church was dedicated in 1961 by Archbishop Iakovos and consecrated in 1971. The Greek Orthodox Manor was added in 1984 after the parish received a federal subsidy for the building, and the cultural center was erected in 2004, even though the community had outgrown the basement space for the banquet hall in the mid-1980s.[35]

AN ASSESSMENT OF THE ARCHITECTURE

The prevailing perception of Annunciation's church is that it was an incredible achievement of the Greek Orthodox community and an announcement of their arrival in the sea of Americanization that swallows each immigrant group. Gurda's prose echoes this perception—referring to Annunciation's decision to hire Wright, Gurda noted that "a Wright building would be an unmistakable statement that Milwaukee's Greeks were a group to be recognized and respected."[36] The church structure was proclaimed a national landmark in 1974, and since its erection, it has attracted visitors and pilgrims. An examination of the evidence suggests that the distance between the community and the architectural design that emerged at the very beginning of the hiring process has always remained. The distance between the architecture and the community has many sources, including the architect's creation of a structure that anticipated a concurrent liturgical evolution that has not come to pass. Despite this distance, Annunciation's parishioners are fiercely loyal to Wright's design and tend to resist renovations, replacements, and additions.

Architectural historians have diagnosed the structure's eccentricities. Anthony Cutler's analysis (written in 1972) treats the general pattern of Greek Orthodox communities as over-investing in Justinian's sixth-century Hagia Sophia.[37] Cutler identifies architectural features of Annunciation that integrate Hagia Sophia's motifs into the design, including the crown of windows upon which the dome appears to rest, which evokes an intensity similar to that of Hagia Sophia's dome.[38] Cutler concludes that Wright's church is a reduction of the Hagia Sophia, relying heavily on the ancient cathedral's main cupola as a dominant motif of the contemporary plan.[39] Cutler is quite critical of Annunciation's blend with the surrounding environment and also suggests that the structure of the church lacks a proper relationship with the ecclesiastical diocesan structure since Milwaukee is essentially a provincial church adorned with the architectural form of a supreme metropolis: "Wright's luminous flying saucer, his last church, came to rest not on the prairie but in a field; around it, if at a respectful distance, have clustered the dismal duplexes of suburban Wauwatosa."[40]

Kostis Kourelis and Vaseilios Marinis caricature Annunciation as a "futuristic spaceship."[41] They dismiss Wright's Annunciation as a Unitarian space, cohering with Wright's own religious background.[42] They also offer a curious critique of Annunciation's interior space:

> Wright conceived of the naos as an auditorium in the round. . . . Although the altar is marked by a sanctuary barrier, this screen is a translucent, decorative surface, in contrast to the traditional Byzantine opaque sanctuary. Such dissolution of the barriers between altar and naos is evident in many Midwestern churches.

Kourelis and Marinis address the issue of parish autonomy in designing and constructing church edifices with greater vigor than Cutler, who, to his credit, distinguished between provincial and metropolitan structures. Kourelis and Marinis identify three periods of Greek Orthodox architecture in America. Phase 1 is the formative century when immigrants began to blend in with the American population and found themselves renovating the interior space of structures belonging to radically different liturgical traditions. Phase 2 encompasses the 1950s to the 1980s, which corresponds with the Greek community's entrance into the middle class and assimilation: "This generation of American-born Greeks wished to prove their progressive achievements and to highlight the social distance from their lower-class parents and the miseries of their experiences."[43] The prevailing architectural styles were high modernism, and the autonomy of parishes in the Greek Orthodox archdiocese of America permitted building committees to adopt architectural trends from other American denominations. Kourelis and Marinis also refer to the Greek adoption of Vatican II attitudes toward sacred architecture, which liberated Catholic churches from historical prototypes and precipitated an explosion of wild designs.[44] Their periodization of Greek Orthodox architecture in America is immensely helpful and clearly establishes Wright's design of Annunciation as occurring in phase 2, though the reader should note that Annunciation's community spans all three phases (as a living parish community).

When we examine the internal evidence from Annunciation's history, it becomes clear that the community fits Kourelis and Marinis's paradigm to a point, but that their selection of Wright's design was paradoxically fateful and opportunistic. Numerous examples verify Annunciation's attempt to celebrate its arrival on the American scene. Gurda refers to Annunciation's history as an odyssey, and he is correct since the parish community has settled, moved, built, and expanded through the initial stages of immigration and assimilation into American culture. As we have seen in earlier chapters, Orthodox communities in America adhere to ethnic identity and resiliently cultivate and sustain it through their architectural structures. In this vein, the selection of Wright's design was both faithful to tradition while departing from it. Cutler is correct in stating that the design focuses on the dome as the dominant structural motif. The adoption of a modified dome as the chief cornerstone of the building seemingly verifies Cutler's thesis that Greek American churches honor the tyranny of Hagia Sophia, which would make Annunciation a cliché. But Wright's explanation of his project and its relationship to Hagia Sophia in his own words is worth citing here, at least in part, for clarification:

> This Greek Orthodox edifice with its Byzantine background as inheritance seems particularly delightful as its heritage—Saint Sophia of Constantinople—was so close to the nature of great architecture. It is never necessary to cling slavishly to a tradition. The spirit of religion is all that is really significant as life changes and emerges. The temple of worship for the citizens of Milwaukee of Greek ancestry is conceived in that religious spirit according to changes already in sight. The building is therefore not a copy of Byzantine architecture—but better than a copy, it is in the proper scale and feeling to reflect the beauty of the architectural heritage of that ancient period without copying a single feature.[45]

At the surface level, Wright's comments might seem to confirm the meeting of reality with perception: the structure retains tradition while adapting to the community's evolving circumstances. In this vein, Annunciation's architectural motif conforms to Amy Papalexandrou's notion of memory inscribed on architecture, though to a lesser degree than St. Katherine and Holy Virgin Cathedral.[46] The domed structure presents a potent reminder of Hagia Sophia's influence, but there is no particular reference to violence in the community's recent past.

Annunciation's selection of a celebrity American architect confirmed Greek Americans as legitimate players in broader American society. But it seems in some ways that the architect's vision differed from that of the community's. For example, when the parish requested a chapel, a cultural hall, and classrooms, the architect delivered a massive church with the auxiliary architectural features severely minimized. A good example is the wing Wright added to accommodate the need for a Sunday school: by placing the wing at ground level, he delivered the lowest level of community need without compromising the church's exterior grandeur. Gurda's book suggests that Wright did not design the structures according to the community's specifications, which is true, since the community added a cultural hall in 2004. But we might also consider the possibility that Wright's prognostication of the community's evolution and development was erroneous.

Several episodes from the parish's life appear to confirm the differences between Annunciation's and Wright's visions. Gurda reflected on the aura cast by Wright: clergy and parishioners were in awe of him and his stature, and the relationship between Church and architect was formal and distant.[47] In the years following the church's construction and dedication, some members struggled with structural problems in the dome and wondered aloud if the church was actually a "burden imposed on the parish by an impractical architect who exalted himself, not Orthodoxy, in the unusual design."[48] In the same post-construction parish period, Father Angelo Kasemeotes concluded that "the psychology of the parish did not match the building. They were conservative and friendly, just regular Midwesterners."[49]

The best illustration of the distance between the Greek community and their edifice comes from the muted reactions of Archbishop Iakovos to the architectural design. Gurda notes that he stated that he would not have approved the design had he been the ruling bishop in 1959.[50] Archbishop Iakovos's remarks on the eve of the consecration reveal his difficulty in finding a positive way to describe the new building: "This church is a complete departure from traditional Greek Orthodox architecture, and at the same time it suggests a new element in our life."[51] Gurda suggested that Iakovos struggled with the design because it had no clear feature identifying it as a church. Iakovos used metaphors to describe the church, comparing it to a "miniscule opera house" worthy of a good choir and a priest who was a skilled homilist; he also compared the church to an ancient Greek theater that simultaneously educates and introduces participants to "understand deity and divinity."[52] Iakovos's effort to articulate the church's features in a praiseworthy tone should not be surprising because the edifice's structure and interior environment caused an adjustment period for the community. The design and the stature of the designer created dilemmas for the community, and some of them are irresolvable.[53] Annunciation has adapted to this situation by resolving some of these problems on its own, by building a new cultural center that completes the requirements of the original specifications submitted to Wright in 1956.

Kourelis and Marinis attribute the construction of Annunciation's church to the inevitable assimilation of Greek émigré communities into American society, which resulted in the adoption of American styles and practices.[54] In many ways, Wright's design of Annunciation coheres with the evolution of church becoming theater, as presented by Jeanne Kilde.[55] Wright's building contains many of the features Kilde attributes to the nineteenth-century American architectural milieu, which included audience rooms that were "large and broad to bring large numbers of people within the sound of the preacher's voice," and were "usually square, circular, or octagonal in plan."[56] Especially prominent is Annunciation's large gallery that attempts to optimize visual access to the center of the church's worship plan, which was another staple feature of nineteenth-century American evangelical architecture (fig. 5.11).[57] Kilde's presentation of architectural features of nineteenth-century evangelical congregations is valuable for our analysis, as a comparison suggests that Wright founded his design on these chief features and simply made adjustments for Orthodox worship: the preaching stage was modified to accommodate an altar and a simple iconostasis.

Cutler asserts that Annunciation is an example of an attempted Byzantine revival that professes a love for history while failing to explore its fullness.[58] Our examination of the building process to this point shows that perception and reality intersect in these three assertions, to a

Figure 5.11   Annunciation Greek Orthodox Church, gallery (photo by author)

certain degree. But I argue that it is insufficient to lay this matter to rest; instead, we need to realize that this was a phase in the history of Greek architecture in America and that Annunciation is a living community that transcends Kourelis and Marinis's helpful periodization of architectural history. Annunciation's history manifests small episodes that indicate a slow but gradual process of adaptation to the American environment in the liturgy before Wright ever agreed to design the new church, exemplified by the installation of pews in the original church built in 1914 and the formation of a choir with four-part harmony. The decision to build the church in the suburbs also evinces the community's adaptation to realities.

Wright's design promoted a different kind of liturgical participation. For example, Cutler notes that there is a considerable contrast between the ample upper story of the church and the confined space below in the nave, the chief gathering area of the assembly.[59] Wright's stairwells also promoted gender intermixture in the liturgy, an innovation since women and men stood on opposite sides of the church in the liturgy of the native countries. Cutler observes that the disproportion between the upper story and the cozy nave actually appeals to the worshipers, who have a sense of full liturgical participation without obstructions.[60]

The conversion of the dome from a dominant motif to the shape forming the interior space changed the liturgical experience of the faithful at Annunciation. This is the only plausible explanation for the uncertain responses parishioners had to Wright's initial design: they had to acclimate to their new worship environment, as did their clergy, as shown by Archbishop Iakovos's struggle to explain the liturgical significance of the interior. It appears that Wright had anticipated further liturgical development on the part of the worshiping community that would reduce the visible barriers between nave and sanctuary and promote more lay liturgical participation. Wright likely recognized the shift of power from the clergy to the laity prevailing in the American Christian environment of his time.[61] The entire worship environment occurs in a circle, and since access to the sanctuary is granted to all by the circle, the separation between the holy space of the sanctuary and the nave is diminished. In reality, there is a handful of points in the upper gallery where one has limited access to the sanctuary. Depending on where people sit in the church, one's visual orientation is not necessarily centered on the liturgy celebrated in the sanctuary, but might be directed to people seated on the opposite side of the gallery.

Furthermore, in some points of the building, one must labor to gain an optimal view of the liturgy. The actual impact of the design is thus mixed: some participants have unusual direct access to the sanctuary, whereas others have no access or are oriented toward some other point in the building. The reduction of lines of separation between nave and sanctuary is also manifest in the translucent iconostasis at Annunciation, which Kourelis and Marinis call a "dissolution of barriers" known in other midwestern churches.[62]

We should also note the sparse interior iconography. While Annunciation has an iconostasis and three icons in the sanctuary, there is no iconography on the walls; most unusual is the absence of a Pantocrator and accompanying icons on the ceiling of the dome, which seems particularly odd given the architectural promotion of verticality. The absence of iconography is another symbol of the parish's fidelity to Wright: he insisted that worshipers would be drawn into the ceiling of the dome, and the parish has resisted adding a Pantocrator despite encouragement from clergy and diocesan bishops.[63] In all likelihood, the fact that Annunciation shares many features with nineteenth-century American evangelical architecture might also explain the sparse iconography since evangelical spaces would not designate wall space for an iconographic program. In summary, Wright's design preceded Vatican II and its declarations on sacred space, so we can only conclude that the relationship between his design and an anticipation of increasing lay participation in the liturgy was either coincidental or representative of his feel for the nature of American sacred spaces.

Cutler's remarks on the trajectory of architecture contemporaneous with the construction of Annunciation are informative. He addresses the matter directly when he asks why Annunciation opted for a motif evoking Hagia Sophia despite the liturgical changes occurring in America.[64] Cutler asserts that sentiment drove the design motifs since the Greek Orthodox were not experiencing a liturgical revival in America.[65] I believe that it is possible that Wright conceived his design in anticipation of a liturgical revival because such a renewal would occur as a by-product of assimilation into American culture. Since the Greeks had truly arrived on the American scene, their worship would adopt distinctly American flavors and values, including the active participation of the people in the liturgy. Furthermore, the move toward active liturgical participation was gaining momentum in the ecumenical and liturgical movements, and Wright's design preceded the privileging of active participation by a mere seven years. Marinis's suggestion that Greek architects were influenced by the teachings and styles of Vatican II is insightful, but the process of cross-pollination between Orthodox and other Christians did not begin with Vatican II. This process was in motion for several decades of Orthodox-Catholic and Orthodox-Anglican encounters, and Catholics had also commenced liturgical reforms that Orthodox would know about before Vatican II.[66] Wright's design placed the Greek Orthodox of Annunciation into a liturgical environment that was only beginning to emerge in the mid-

1950s for churches adhering to high liturgical traditions, and one that such churches never completely embraced, especially since churches like Annunciation contained features belonging to evangelical communities in America.

Our analysis of the worship space does not depend on Wright's intentions for Annunciation's liturgy, however. The analysis has disclosed a different variant of the symbiosis of architecture and liturgy. The architectural form adheres to the Byzantine heritage of the community by including a dome, but it reforms that heritage by attempting to make it correspond to the new environment of the liturgical community. The liturgy envisioned by the design was highly participatory, and elements of increased participation were evident in Annunciation's history. There is no evidence that suggests that the architectural form follows the Orthodox liturgical function, and in this instance, Annunciation follows the general pattern established by the other parish profiles of this study. Annunciation occasionally fine-tuned its liturgical practices in its history (the installation of pews and permitting gender intermixture), but the liturgy remained essentially the same in its order and structure, with some changes in its style. Annunciation is like St. Katherine and Holy Virgin Cathedral in that the community observes the basic liturgical requirements of the Orthodox Church and builds a structure capable of maintaining a basic liturgy. In this instance, however, the form envisioned more rapid liturgical development that would be presumably shaped by the surrounding American environment. The form failed to complete the shaping of the function: parishioners generally enjoyed more visual access and a cozy internal environment, but there was some distance between liturgical function and architectural form.

We can understand the distance between form and function when we revisit the community's specifications submitted to Wright in 1956, which included a chapel, a Sunday school, and a parish center. From the outset, Annunciation parish was more than a liturgical assembly: it was also a community desiring to sustain its heritage and preserve it in the generations that followed. The community's ministry to all its generations is manifested by the building of the Greek Orthodox Manor and the cultural center. By 2004, the specifications of the original plan were finally actualized, and the result reconfigured the architectural program of the community. Wright sought to mute the exterior features of non-liturgical space, and Annunciation's adjustments to its environment and ministry to its people led to new constructions. Ironically, the construction of the cultural center encountered internal resistance from those who were fiercely loyal to Wright, and some parishioners left Annunciation on two occasions: first, when the new icons were installed on the iconostasis, and second, when funds were raised for the cultural center and the parish built it.[67] Pilgrims will still visit Annunciation to see the church, but they will discover a community of people who are not only liturgical but also gather in and express themselves through the other buildings on the property.

CONCLUSION

Annunciation parish provides an excellent profile for this study that helps us understand the multidimensionality of contemporary Orthodox architecture. Annunciation presents a hybrid architectural form that is a paradox because it simultaneously integrates tradition while departing from it by reshaping the dome into a church. The community's employment of a celebrity architect distracted it from a more complete immersion into American culture since Annunciation had to content itself with a magnificent church with deficient meeting and gathering spaces for a vibrant community that prioritizes cultural cultivation. The first question Annunciation's profile poses to the future of Orthodox architecture in America concerns permanence. To my knowledge, Annunciation's design did not inspire copies within the Greek community in America, and while this is probably due to the architect's uniqueness, models tend to inspire copying.

Throughout this chapter, we have detected a generally consistent internal tension at Annunciation concerning the community's reception of its architectural form, thanks largely to Gurda's comprehensive narrative. While a large constituency of parishioners remains faithful to Wright's design, others, including bishops and priests, have encouraged updating the interior design to integrate more traditional elements of Orthodox sacred space, beginning with the iconography. The desire to accord with the Orthodox norm in architecture, art, and music coheres with the Greek Archdiocese's requirement that parishes construct edifices that meet the approval of the diocesan hierarch. A deeper theological meaning lies underneath the layer of this rule: the perception of uniformity in sacred architecture commonly held by Orthodox clergy and laity. The new iconographic program at Annunciation is designed to achieve the Orthodox norm, but its addition does not complement Wright's overarching vision of the interior's design and decoration. Given its history and loyalty to Wright's legacy, it is likely that Annunciation will find the process of negotiating a return to aesthetic tradition to be challenging in Wright's space.

Annunciation, like most medium- to large-sized Orthodox parishes, performs community planning for the future. It is quite possible that the parish's constituency will evolve so that the present facilities are no longer suitable at some point in the future, though that date lies far ahead, given the recent construction of the cultural center. Outside of the parish's immediate future, the story of the church's construction challenges contemporary pastors and communities to carefully consider their priorities and be both realistic and deliberate about expectations when they submit proposals to architects. Annunciation's recognition as a national landmark brought it notoriety, but it did not change the internal challenge of Orthodox pastoral ministry, nor did it mitigate the community's need to add facilities to its property. The unique architectural style of Annunciation will probably remain an exception in the American Orthodox community for the foreseeable future, but its creative and deliberative process should be informative for other Orthodox seeking to develop an architectural program.

Annunciation's architectural form invites vibrant liturgical participation, and our analysis concludes that Annunciation fits the paradigm where architectural form and liturgical function have a weak relationship, especially since the Orthodox liturgy is celebrated in a space originally designed for evangelicals. Annunciation's example leaves us with one final question that I would like to pose to the reader: should Annunciation have become a community that adjusted its liturgy to conform to the architecture? It seems that the opportunity to permit the architectural form to shape the actual liturgy has always been present at

Annunciation; it remains to be seen whether or not the community will become a liturgical center with the freedom to fine-tune the liturgy so it expresses the worship suggested by the form. Cutler's remark that Annunciation is a provincial community is helpful here since liturgical centers are usually in a metropolis. That said, Annunciation poses a larger question about the dynamic between architectural form and liturgical function because the innovative architectural form did not result in the anticipated liturgical function. This confirms my hypothesis that contemporary parish life in American Orthodoxy has long evolved past the architecture/liturgy, form/function paradigm, so that form and function can only develop in new ways together, cross-pollinating one another throughout an organic process of development.

CHAPTER SIX

ST. VLADIMIR'S SEMINARY AND NEW SKETE MONASTERY

This chapter discusses Three Hierarchs Chapel of St. Vladimir's Seminary in Yonkers, New York, and the Church of the Holy Wisdom at New Skete Monastery. I have selected these two structures because they differ from the parishes profiled in previous chapters in that they exercise special influence within Orthodoxy in America. St. Vladimir's Seminary was the center of a Eucharistic revival attributed to Father Alexander Schmemann, who disseminated his teachings through the hundreds of disciples who sat at his feet in the classroom.[1] The construction and dedication of Three Hierarchs Chapel in 1983—the year of Schmemann's death—was an architectural culmination of his contribution to liturgical theology in American Orthodoxy. The construction of the Church of the Holy Wisdom at New Skete Monastery in 1982–83 occurred after a series of rigorous consultations with liturgical historians and their work, including Juan Mateos, Thomas Mathews, and Robert Taft, among others.[2] The Church of the Holy Wisdom was constructed to accommodate the reinvigorated cathedral office New Skete adopted and adapted to conform to the realities of contemporary monastic life.

THREE HIERARCHS CHAPEL AT
ST. VLADIMIR'S SEMINARY

This chapter begins with an examination of Three Hierarchs Chapel at St. Vladimir's. St. Vladimir's community worshiped in a small room at General Seminary in New York from 1938 to 1947.[3] When St. Vladimir's moved to Crestwood in 1962, the community constructed a small chapel, which was the center for daily services and all other liturgical offices. The growth of the seminary community necessitated expansion of the chapel. The planning for Three Hierarchs Chapel occurred during the course of several conversations involving seminary faculty.[4] The principal contributors to the architectural scheme were Fathers Alexander Schmemann and John Meyendorff, David Drillock, and Father Alexis Vinogradov. Vinogradov is a trained architect and had written his master's thesis on Orthodox architecture so he is the most important figure in the design of Three Hierarchs Chapel.[5] In this section, we will see that the design of Three Hierarchs Chapel is innovative, a departure from some of the traditional samples profiled above. Essentially, the design is an attempt to create a new architectural paradigm for Orthodox worship space that could be modular, with necessary adaptations, for parish communities.

During the process of envisioning the chapel design, contributors voiced their personal opinions, and ultimately Vinogradov was granted broad leeway in completing the design. The most important factors that shaped the finished product were economic constraints, the desire to eschew copying predominant models (Greek and Russian), and the creation of an interior worship space that eliminated faux distinctions between clergy and laity. The chapel's groundbreaking occurred on May 16, 1981, with the seminary worshiping in two common rooms for daily services while celebrating Sunday and festal liturgies in the crypt church of nearby Annunciation Catholic Church. On September 14, 1981, the old chapel was dismantled. On December 24, 1982, the assembly moved to Three Hierarchs Chapel during the singing of the Nativity troparion, with Schmemann presiding at the blessing of the temple for the first service. Three Hierarchs Chapel was dedicated on May 13, 1983.[6] Schmemann described the dedication of the chapel as a pivotal moment in the life of the seminary, like "passing an examination."[7]

Vinogradov described the design process as collaborative. He was invited to propose several models, and his preference was a stone building that did not have an onion dome and did not incorporate stereotypical Orthodox features. Vinogradov recommended a building that would cohere with contemporary domestic architecture. He explains his approach to designing contemporary Orthodox churches:

> An Orthodox temple is a cosmic icon that begins from the inside out. It is first and foremost not a pretty jewel. . . . As any proper Orthodox icon reveals the cosmological nature of man's salvation by being set outside (an icon of an interior scene is still set outside, with a curtain draped across buildings to indicate that it is inside), so the church interior gathers the world inside to offer it up to God. That is why its exterior aspect is unconcerned with style—it is emphatically not a particular building, but in reality every building, as it draws the world into itself.[8]

The rationale for eschewing traditional Orthodox features on the exterior of Three Hierarchs Chapel was twofold: first, a chapel styled after domestic architecture would retrieve the liturgical experience of the pre-Nicene and pre-imperial Church, where communities gathered to worship in homes, in small gatherings. Second, a new architectural design would establish an architectural pattern free from the predominant models of the mother churches abroad. One can see the influence of Fathers Schmemann and Meyendorff on Vinogradov here, especially given the milieu of the chapel's design and building. Schmemann and Meyendorff were the principal figures promoting an authentically autocephalous Orthodox Church in America, a vision that became reality when the Moscow Patriarchate granted the Metropolia autocephaly in 1970.[9] But much of global Orthodoxy rejected the newly founded Orthodox Church in America (OCA) on the basis of an absence of canonical authority for Moscow to give autocephaly, a privilege traditionally reserved for the Ecumenical Patriarchate of Constantinople. During the formative years of the OCA, St. Vladimir's Seminary was a central location of theological reflection and formation of a generation of clergy who would implement the vision of a genuinely local Church in America. With liturgy and architecture providing the most proximate environment for experiencing Church, a new architectural design that privileged contemporary motifs over the models preferred in Eastern Europe, the Middle East, and the Balkans would have the capacity to communicate an Orthodox identity in America capable of self-sustenance.

The exterior of Three Hierarchs Chapel does not conform to the Middle Byzantine models we have viewed elsewhere in this study (fig. 6.1). Economic and spatial constraints prohibited a long, axial plan, and Vinogradov created a drum shape that accommodates a small dome on the interior, with the appearance of pointed, pitched roof on the exterior. His design permitted an infrastructure for regular framing, and the pointed roof was a deliberate nod to the Slavic roots of the seminary's history.[10] The chapel's exterior is brick, a deviation from Vinogradov's recommendation of a stone chapel; the seminary opted for brick for economic reasons. Dominant exterior features include a large entryway before the chapel's doors (the main entrance), with an icon of the Three Hierarchs (Saints Basil the Great, Gregory the Theologian, and John Chrysostom) greeting the faithful. The entryway was deliberately large to facilitate a sense of entrance on feast days and to promote liturgical processions, especially for Paschal Orthros, when the assembly gathers at the main entrance to begin the festive celebrations. The chapel sits atop a hill facing west, so the natural landscape emphasizes exterior verticality that the pointed pitched roof, the icon of the Three Hierarchs and large entry space, and the gold tent of the roof amplify. The gold tent is an example of innovative design that offers the false appearance of exuberance. The tent actually performs an economic and functional purpose, as it conceals an exhaust fan that is vented out—the fan sucks the incense and hot air out of the chapel and blows it outside.

Three Hierarchs Chapel faces west, which caused some concern during the planning process, given the Byzantine preference for churches facing east (paradise). The reasons for the westward orientation vary. First, the seminary campus had limited options for a chapel. Placing the chapel on the lower end of the campus near Scarsdale Road was a possibility, but the current position of the chapel essentially makes it the focal point of the campus—its natural height and central location draws students, faculty, staff, and visitors to worship. Both Vinogradov and Paul Meyendorff commented on the tension created by the chapel's occidental orientation. Building the chapel on the lawn that runs parallel

Figure 6.1   Three Hierarchs Chapel (photo by author)

to Scarsdale Road in Crestwood would have afforded two advantages: the elderly and infirm would not have to ascend a hill to enter the worship space, and the chapel would be properly oriented. Making the chapel the focal point of the seminary's life superseded the desire to have an eastward orientation. Vinogradov noted the existence of numerous models of churches that did not face east. He emphasized a theological opportunity with the chapel's westward orientation: the chapel would accentuate the eschatological telos of the body of Christ and would not privilege any particular orientation since the destiny of each worshiping assembly is the New Jerusalem, not a particular city of this world. He elaborates the theology underpinning the architectural style:

> Theologically, the kingdom of God does not de facto translate architecturally into physical grandeur. Despite massive literature to the contrary the Gothic cathedral or the Hagia Sophia are not the summa of liturgical expression and achievement. . . . Orthodox architecture

strived to allow the material to find its natural form, to distribute loads and weights without tormenting the senses. The vertical architectural lines do not vanish into a spatial abyss, the residence of a scary and distant God, but rather these lines fold over in space, converging on a bright domical heaven in which God comes in his incarnate Son to encounter his creation and to share its life and fate.[11]

St. Vladimir's Seminary enjoys a unique benefit among Orthodox theological schools in America: the institution's reputation as the premier academy of Orthodox theology affords it the privilege of pilgrims. The seminary's proximity to New York City and institutions offering complementary academic programs in religion and theology, such as Fordham, Columbia, and Union Theological Seminary, enhances St. Vladimir's public stature. The tenure of renowned professors Alexander Schmemann and John Meyendorff contributed to the seminary's stature, and the institution hosts several annual public events that draw large crowds of academics representing a variety of traditions along with Orthodox clergy and laity.[12] In addition to annual events such as the Father Alexander Schmemann Memorial Lecture and Orthodox Education Day, St. Vladimir's now hosts a public event in honor of John Meyendorff and frequently participates in events of significant public stature.[13] St. Vladimir's integrates liturgy into the programs of such events so that much of the public is exposed to worship at Three Hierarchs Chapel. The chapel's location on the hill and away from Scarsdale Road is not a hindrance in this instance because Three Hierarchs Chapel's height draws one's vision toward the chapel upon entering the small campus. On Orthodox Education Day, the seminary sets up a large outdoor tent for the hierarchical liturgy to provide more space for the larger crowds.

The combined elements of the seminary's stature in Orthodox academia and its role as the frequent host of public events reminds us of the role of liturgy in the public square explored in chapter 1. Some principles of John Baldovin's presentation on stational liturgy apply here, especially the frequent liturgical engagement of the seminary community with the larger public.[14] The seminary's liturgy is not stational by definition, and the institutional quality of the community lends itself to increased public engagement. That said, the chapel's visibility on the small Crestwood campus and the community's commitment to bringing the liturgy into public view—at least occasionally—is outstanding among the parishes in this study and is a notable quality of the architecture/liturgy symbiosis.

The interior space of Three Hierarchs Chapel illuminates the deliberate intention of drawing clergy and laity together. The narthex is in direct contrast to the exterior entrance to the church, as the narthex is small.[15] The rationale for the minimal narthex was to encourage people to be in church—the seminary community did not want a crying room, so children would be encouraged to participate in the liturgy. In the original seminary chapel, there was no upper-level loft for the choir, and the seminary had one choir that stood on the left side of the chapel. The interior of Three Hierarchs Chapel has the simple cross shape—it is small and maximizes space in the middle portion of the nave. Vinogradov stated that the design discouraged worshipers from standing in the back of the chapel and facilitated a natural movement toward the altar. When the chapel was constructed, the seminary had one choir. During the academic year, two choirs often sang in the chapel, a male choir and a mixed choir. Currently, the seminary has only one choir singing the responses for liturgy.[16] The space occupied by one or both choirs was large enough to accommodate worshipers who were not singing in the choir. The position of the choirs toward the front of the chapel was conducive to encourage assembly singing, as the conductors would often turn and lead the assembly, especially for liturgical responses such as acclamations and responsorial psalmody. The addition of the second choir introduced a regular rhythm of antiphonal singing. This practice was purposefully established to demonstrate how a cathedral liturgical style could inspire liturgical participation by the whole assembly.[17] Vinogradov adds that the original nave had no seating at all, to promote standing during worship and maximize the limited interior space. Since the chapel's consecration in 1983, chairs have been placed in the back portion of the nave.

The design for the sanctuary and the installation of the original iconostasis supported the notion of an ordered assembly worshiping together. The iconostasis originally consisted of four new panels with

Figure 6.2 Three Hierarchs Chapel, original iconostasis (photo courtesy of Georges Florovsky Library at St. Vladimir's Seminary)

low deacons' doors (fig. 6.2). The iconostasis design conformed to the priority of maximizing natural light and interior visibility. Paul Meyendorff described the visual effect as encouraging unimpeded access to the Lord's Supper, depicted by the fresco painted in the apse. For liturgical celebration, the small size of the sanctuary permitted one presbyteral celebrant assisted by a deacon. The rest of the clergy would join the faithful in the nave, a deliberate attempt to blur any distinctions between clergy and laity within the community. Two additional panels were affixed to the four simple panels constituting the new iconostasis in homage to the seminary's history: the two panels were used in the original chapel and migrated to Three Hierarchs Chapel. Vinogradov notes that his original plan called for a vestry to be placed beneath the chapel. The clergy would vest downstairs and come up for the liturgy, prepared to liturgize. This notion coheres with the strategy of mini-

Figure 6.3   Three Hierarchs Chapel, diakonikon (skeuophylakion) (photo by author)

mizing the distinction between clergy and laity. A large vestry encourages numerous clergy to congregate in the sanctuary, which encourages them to be away from the laity in the nave.

The original architectural scheme minimizing the sanctuary was modified in the 1980s and 1990s. The seminary administration expanded the sanctuary area, mostly on account of the frequent hierarchical liturgies celebrated at Three Hierarchs Chapel. Arches were added to the iconostasis, which increased its vertical dimension and compromised the priority of maximizing access to the Mystical Supper.

The sanctuary's smallness was mitigated by a rather large diakonikon (fig. 6.3).[18] The diakonikon is a large, separate room to the left of the sanctuary where the presider celebrates the prothesis rite. During the Divine Liturgy at St. Vladimir's, the clergy and servers gather in the skeuophylakion and literally enter the nave and proceed with the gifts to the altar. Given the small size of the chapel, this was a modest innovation, but effective, since the customary Great Entrance is a brief movement from a small table of the sanctuary to the altar, requiring only a few small steps. The presence of a diakonikon created real liturgical motion, so the gifts were truly being carried from a separate room to the altar in an authentic procession. Consequently, the creation of the diakonikon is an instance of retrieving liturgical history and revising the interior space of the church to make more sense of the liturgical requirements.

The original iconographic plan for Three Hierarchs Chapel was simple. According to Vinogradov, Schmemann was not keen on murals and panels and favored painting the sanctuary, which would contribute to encouraging the assembly to draw toward the altar as the focal point of worship. The limited height of the iconostasis enhanced interior visibility, and much of the iconography was painted by Elizabeth Ozouline, a protégé of Leonid Ouspensky and iconographic master at St. Serge Institute in Paris. Given the original minimalist approach to interior iconography and the generally small size of the chapel, the icon of the Mystical Supper in the apse became the chief image of the chapel and communicated the centrality of Eucharistic celebration and theology in the community's life. Besides the Mystical Supper icon in the apse, the program was quite simple: a Pantocrator in the dome and icons for the four panels of the iconostasis (fig. 6.4). The minimalist iconographic approach was a source of internal disagreement, so over the course of the chapel's existence since 1983, many new icons have been added.

The seminary retained the heritage of its recent past by including the panels from the old chapel that were affixed to each end of the iconostasis; these icons were painted by Nikita Struve. The Pantocrator of the dome is surrounded by four large icon panels ascending upward like triangles, which I will describe in relationship to the iconostasis: an icon of the Theotokos Oranta with the Risen Lord and the Apostles immediately above the iconostasis; the Pentecost icon to the immediate right of the iconostasis; an icon of the Crucifixion opposite the iconostasis (immediately above the narthex on the chapel interior); and the icon of the Myrrh-bearing Women at the Tomb on the left of the iconostasis. These four icons surrounding the Pantocrator in the dome

Figure 6.4   Three Hierarchs Chapel, Pantocrator in the dome (photo by author)

highlight Pascha as the fulfillment of salvation history. Jesus's death and the announcement of the resurrection at the empty tomb result in a praying Church living in the new time of the kingdom, described by Schmemann as the time of the Church. The chapel has no stained glass windows, which speaks to its iconographic program but also accentuates the desire to maximize natural lighting. The dome allows light to flow in from all four sides, and the interior illumination was impressive during my visit on a dark, cloudy, and rainy day in June 2014.

LITURGY AT THREE HIERARCHS CHAPEL

St. Vladimir's Seminary is a complex community consisting of students, faculty, staff, and Orthodox Christians who live in the region.[19] As an institution of higher learning, the seminary experiences frequent turnover as students graduate and new students join the community. The seminary community generally retains its cycle of divine services in spite of the ever-changing community composition. For each student, liturgy in the chapel is the focal point of community life, which the seminary communicates to prospective students.[20] Architecture and liturgy are core components of a student's learning experience at St. Vladimir's, and consequently they constitute a model students can adopt when they engage in pastoral ministry in the parish.

During the academic year, the seminary has a robust schedule of services. Matins and Vespers are celebrated Monday through Friday, with Compline added during Great Lent. The Epistle and Gospel appointed in the lectionary are added to the daily offices, which provide students with an opportunity to practice preaching.[21] The seminary community observes the twelve feasts of the liturgical year; for most feasts, a Vigil is celebrated on the eve and Divine Liturgy on the morning of the feast. Liturgy is frequently celebrated on the sanctoral cycle as well, though not always preceded by a Vigil.[22] Vigil (Vespers and Matins) is celebrated every Saturday evening, and Divine Liturgy on Sundays.[23]

The Lenten and Holy Week cycle of services is observed with greater rigor at St. Vladimir's. During the first two days of Clean Week (the first week of Lent), students are excused from classes and follow the Liturgy of the Hours in chapel. The services include the singing of the biblical canticles and a series of homilies and exhortations from St. Theodore the Studite, and culminate with the canon of St. Andrew of Crete and Great Compline. Clean Week presents a maximal liturgical schedule, as does Holy Week, which entails the reading of the entirety of one Gospel through the course of the Liturgy of the Hours and the Liturgy of Presanctified Gifts, not to mention the popular evening services.[24]

ANALYSIS OF THE ARCHITECTURE

Three Hierarchs Chapel at St. Vladimir's Seminary is an innovative architectural model that attempts to cohere with Orthodox community life in America. Vinogradov's design of the chapel embraces the spirit of architectural innovation that does not slavishly copy a particular historical style, but instead engages the architectural priorities of the community's environment. Three Hierarchs Chapel is not a cliché of any particular style, yet it retains fidelity to tradition by privileging theological motifs that have been secondary in Byzantine architecture. Also, the chapel's utilitarian quality has contributed to its becoming a model that has been copied by other communities in the United States.

Three Hierarchs Chapel facilitates the frequent liturgical celebration of a small seminary community whose size is expected to remain stable, with the actual people changing as cohorts of students enroll and graduate. The interior design emphasizes a large common space in which everyone gathers, and there are limited features separating the clergy from the laity. The large open space toward the front of the nave near the sanctuary promotes mobility and brings everyone together since the assembly literally shares the same space with the choir. The small sanctuary discourages clergy from congregating there, so noncelebrating clergy worship together with the assembly and the choir in the same cozy space. The absence of separation between the orders of the assembly promotes a sense of everyone gathering at the same altar. The low iconostasis provides visual access to the sanctuary, another contribution to facilitating corporate worship where "they [are] all in one place together" (Acts 2:1, NAB). The limited iconography of the sacred space and the pointed, pitched roof containing a modest interior dome are examples of attempts to remain faithful to tradition without slavishly copying particular models.

This brief summary of the architectural features leads to a conclusion on the two most salient points pertaining to the larger thesis of this study: the architecture was designed to cohere with the liturgical renewal cultivated at St. Vladimir's by Alexander Schmemann and his disciples, and the design also provided an implicit preview of the ecclesial landscape of Orthodoxy in America. Three Hierarchs Chapel was essentially the laboratory for the liturgical renewal promoted by Schmemann. St. Vladimir's students rehearsed this model of renewal in chapel liturgy for three years, with the students representing the OCA and the Antiochian and Serbian Churches in America, among others. The active participation of the laity in the liturgy and Eucharistic renewal are the chief cornerstones of the renewal attributed to Schmemann.[25]

One example of corporate participation is the assembly joining the choir in singing refrains and responses. The interior design joining the assembly with the choirs occasionally transformed the assembly into a choir. It was customary for chapel conductors to face and lead the assembly in singing refrains, acclamations, and responses during liturgical offices. Furthermore, St. Vladimir's modeled the practice of reading orations aloud for all to hear and encouraging people to receive communion frequently during Schmemann's tenure and afterward. Graduates of St. Vladimir's certainly adopted the liturgical practices learned at the seminary in the parishes they were called to shepherd, resulting in the permeation of liturgical renewal into parish life. There is no doubt that in select cases, the architectural innovation played an important role in promoting liturgical renewal in the parish.[26] This study has looked at two other instances where the increased emphasis on the priesthood of the laity shaped the interior architectural design, at St. Matthew Orthodox Church and Annunciation Greek Orthodox Church. In the case of Three Hierarchs Chapel, the ressourcement theology of the laity promoted by Schmemann was the primary factor influencing architectural design. Furthermore, the architecture of Three Hierarchs Chapel represents the shift of social power from the clergy to the laity mentioned by Jeanne Kilde.[27]

The second element is the anticipation of the development of an authentically indigenous Orthodoxy on the North American continent. Churches tend to develop in dialogue with the cultural and demographic environment, as we saw with Annunciation Greek Orthodox Church in chapter 5. The design of Three Hierarchs Chapel is sensitive to North American architectural priorities, which include blending with the local architectural styles, employing materials available locally, attending to energy efficiency, and erecting structures that correspond to community realities.[28] Three Hierarchs Chapel was a model for other Orthodox parishes, including St. Gregory in Wappingers Falls, St. Nicholas in Portland, Oregon, Christ the Savior in Southbury, Connecticut, Saints Cyril and Methodius in Terryville, Connecticut, Holy Trinity Church in Elmira Heights, New York, and Christ the Savior Church in Harrisburg, Pennsylvania.[29] Each structure has architectural features similar to those of Three Hierarchs Chapel with minor differences. For example, St. Gregory has a minimal iconostasis and large open nave area with the choir positioned in the rear and more extensive interior iconography; St. Nicholas has a large baptismal font at the entrance and features big wood beams on the interior and the exterior representing the region; and Christ the Savior in Southbury has a slightly taller iconostasis and a vast nave. Each of these structures has a small interior with limited seating capacity. Vinogradov designed these smaller interiors intentionally, with the goal of preventing community sizes from becoming too large. He explained this decision by stating that a community that has surpassed one hundred people indicates the need for planting a new community in the region.[30]

One might view a preference for a smaller community size as odd and countercultural, but it presents certain advantages. Pastorally, a smaller parish encourages a more intimate relationship between the rector and the community. A rector would not be overextended or need assistants to manage his pastoral responsibilities. The community's people would also come to know one another, a potential opportunity to build community from within and maximize fellowship. Smaller communities are also advantageous from a property management perspective. A smaller community is suitable for an energy-efficient, utilitarian structure that would presumably require minimal maintenance and reduce property management burdens on succeeding parish generations.

One can also identify potential disadvantages to limiting community size. No one would oppose building community from within, but networks of close relationships can become obstacles to welcoming new people into the community if internal parish groups have intimate relationships. A similar pitfall could be posed to the rector, whose ministry might become too focused on intra-parish issues. One must also account for diversity in the profile of a prospective parishioner: some Christians want to belong to an intimate community of fellowship, whereas others are more comfortable with the anonymity provided by larger communities. North American Orthodoxy should not limit itself to medium- and small-sized communities, just as Roman Catholic and evangelicals need not be exclusively mega-sized.

All discussion of community size and advantages aside, it is clear that Vinogradov's parish model fits the prevailing North American profile; in this vein, the Vinogradov model is both suitable and realistic since approximately 42% of all parishes have one hundred people or less attending church on a typical Sunday.[31] Barring the unexpected arrival of large numbers of immigrants, North American Orthodoxy is experiencing a downward trend in growth. A parish community consisting of approximately one hundred people generally represents stability and health, and Vinogradov's preferred model of an affordable and energy-efficient structure with an intimate interior is suitable for the current situation. That some communities have adopted the Vinogradov model and others have hired him as a consultant for design speaks to his influence, at least within the OCA.

In conclusion, it is essential to highlight the relationship between architecture and liturgy at St. Vladimir's Seminary as a product of liturgical renewal. The priority of corporate worship, "all together in the same place" (Acts 2:1), is manifest in the design of Three Hierarchs Chapel and similar Vinogradov structures in America. We should also note that the purpose of liturgical renewal at St. Vladimir's was ultimately ecclesiological. What one experienced in the liturgy at Three Hierarchs Chapel was a preview of *possible* Orthodox Church life in North America: a relatively small church designed to unify and animate the assembly to continue the liturgy after the liturgy without reference to aesthetic museum artifacts of the past such as grandiose domes, enormously vertical interiors, and wall-to-wall iconography. The architecture of Three Hierarchs Chapel speaks to a vision of Orthodoxy that blends in with society while transfiguring it; the architecture represents a vision of Church in the world if not of it, one that is not sectarian. The architecture's simplicity and utilitarianism represents not only North American architectural precepts, but also an honest appraisal of Orthodoxy's role in America, one that is not messianic (e.g., Orthodoxy must save America), but modestly and courageously witnesses to the culturally transcendent message of the gospel. Three Hierarchs Chapel, then, is not a cliché, but is an original architectural innovation that communicates the heritage of St. Vladimir's liturgical renewal and a vision for pastoral ministry in smaller communities. This architectural profile differs from examples in earlier chapters that feature immigrant communities sustaining the models of the past in the present.

NEW SKETE MONASTERY

New Skete Monastery in Cambridge, New York, began as a community of Byzantine Franciscans in 1966.[32] The community desired to live an "authentic Eastern Christian monasticism for our day, inspired by the vision of the early monastic fathers."[33] The monks express their vision for community life in their own words:

> [The monks] also had a passion for liturgy, seeking to infuse new life into Eastern Catholic worship. In that spirit, they took the name "New Skete," after one of the first Christian monastic settlements in northern Egypt, in the desert of Skete. From the very beginning, their intention was to incarnate the simplicity of the original principles of monastic life, unencumbered by the institutionalized accretions of the centuries, and to do this in a way that made sense for twentieth-century America.[34]

Several episodes in the life of the community, especially encounters with key figures, shaped the future course of New Skete Monastery. Dom Damasus, a Benedictine prior at Mount Saviour in Pennsylvania and a pioneer in monastic and liturgical renewal, provided lodging for the community.[35] After searching for a suitable location, they ended up in Cambridge, New York, and were firmly established in an idyllic setting on three hundred plus acres of dense woodland on Two Top Mountain, performing the heavy manual work of building the community themselves.[36] The community expanded with the addition of a community of contemplative nuns in 1969; the nuns occupied a space on a hilly pasture across the road from the monastery, and the community "acquired the unusual characteristic of being a modern male and female monastic community."[37] A married couples' community that embraced the life and vision of New Skete began in 1982. New Skete concluded its journey through Eastern Christianity by being received into the OCA in 1979.

As a community devoted to principles of ressourcement and aggiornamento and in search of the authentic spirit of Eastern liturgy, New Skete exercised the freedom traditionally belonging to Eastern monastic communities in creating a suitable liturgical ordo. Several members of the community remarked that their experience of the liturgical movement and the energy surrounding the liturgical reforms authorized by Vatican II contributed to their motivations to adopt a liturgical ordo that would be suitable for their community. The ordo they adopted is grounded in the desire to live an authentic Eastern Christian life in the contemporary conditions of the world. Another key figure who contributed to the shaping of New Skete liturgy was the Jesuit liturgical historian Juan Mateos.[38] In 1965, Mateos led a seminar on Eastern liturgy at New Skete, which resulted in additional consultations with him. The monastic community researched ancient models of the liturgy that would be suitable for their realities. New Skete is a working monastery: the monks raise and train German shepherd dogs and market gourmet foods, and the sisters support themselves by baking cheesecakes.[39]

New Skete's selection of principles that serve as the foundation for its liturgical scheme likewise shapes its architecture. The devotion of members of New Skete to their work, necessary for their financial stability, limits the number of liturgical offices they can pray in community each day. They gather for Matins before the workday begins and Vespers in the evenings, which renders the Athonite monastic liturgical model ill-suited for their life.[40] Instead, they have turned to the now-extinct cathedral offices of Jerusalem and Constantinople, revising them into modern forms suitable for monastic life in contemporary America.[41]

I will offer a more comprehensive analysis of their liturgical reforms below, but the adaptation of the cathedral offices shaped their architecture. For New Skete, architectural form needed to follow liturgical function. Its first temple (Holy Transfiguration Church), devoted to the commemoration of the Transfiguration feast, was dedicated in 1970 (fig. 6.5). In implementing an adapted liturgical ethos rooted in renewal, New Skete built a new central temple of worship, the Church of the Holy Wisdom, in 1982–83 (fig. 6.6). The church was dedicated on the feast of Mid-Pentecost in 1983. The temple's name suggests that it is a cliché of Hagia Sophia, and the church contains several architectural features belonging to Constantinopolitan provenance, but the church is actually designed for efficiency. The monks built the church so they could celebrate a modified cathedral liturgy that was conducive to their contemporary monastic setting.

If Mateos was the key academic figure who helped them shape their liturgy, Thomas Mathews's historical studies of Constantinopolitan architecture and liturgy inspired the design of the Church of the Holy Wisdom. In the following section, I describe the complex of buildings at New Skete. I then discuss the iconographic program, followed by an overview of several liturgical principles adopted by New Skete that shaped the architecture. One of the liturgical principles underpinning New Skete's life is the restoration of the proper relationships in the dialogues of euchology and the Liturgy of the Word. Such dialogues include a designated space for the clergy to be seated during the Liturgy of the Word, the restoration of the office of antiphons sung on the way to liturgy, and the reinvigoration of ministries performing the duties assigned to them.

BUILDINGS AT NEW SKETE

As a community encompassing religious men and women and married couples, New Skete's community lives in three distinct parts of the

Figure 6.5 Holy Transfiguration Church, New Skete Monastery (photo by author)

Figure 6.6   Church of the Holy Wisdom, New Skete Monastery (photo by author)

property. The main section of the monastery contains a building with cells for the men, a few guest rooms, offices, a library, and a dining room; this main building connects to the current temple, the Church of the Holy Wisdom. Holy Transfiguration Church is separate but very close to the main structure; a bell tower in the midst of the outdoor area announces worship. The women's quarters are 3.4 miles west, about a 10-minute drive from the main area of the monastery. The monastery's property also includes Emmaus House, quarters for the married couples who belong to the community, and a large structure for the dogs raised by the monks.

As a monastery, the community's life revolves around work and worship. A spirit of self-sustenance defines the community's ethos; the members' livelihood depends on their work, and they built the monastery's buildings themselves. The realities of their working schedule permit them to meet twice a day for community prayer in the Liturgy of the Hours, for Matins and Vespers. On Saturday evenings, they celebrate Vespers, with Matins on Sunday morning followed by the Divine Liturgy. When I requested reflections on the significance of their particular ordo, one monk mused that the structure of the Liturgy of the Hours enjoyed a symbiosis with their work. Matins provided the necessary food to begin the workday, and the labors of the day naturally concluded with community prayer. The most salient feature of the worship was the necessity of gathering with the community, to join in doxological praise and petition with the same people with whom one has labored, eaten, quarreled, and rejoiced.

Holy Transfiguration Church

Before describing the program of buildings, a few words about the environmental setting of the monastery are in order. In introducing this section, I mentioned that the setting is idyllic because of the naturally beautiful landscape. The monastery's setting against a small mountain pairs the buildings of the property with the vast height of the mountain and the numerous trees, bushes, and wildlife constituting the landscape. In this vein, New Skete follows the Eastern monastic tradition by worshiping in the temple designed and constructed by God: nature. Even during divine services in the stunning Church of the Holy Wisdom, one's attention is drawn to God's temple outside, especially since the monastery's moments of liturgical silence permit nature to sing its doxology.

New Skete originally prayed in the small Holy Transfiguration Church, an edifice that conforms to the Middle Byzantine synthesis of this study. Small onion domes adorn the roof of the church. The interior is small with ample space for gathering in the nave, suitable for a small monastic community. The wooden structure with onion domes offers an attractive exterior. The interior has one predominant feature: icons depicting the Gospel lessons from the Sundays of Pascha, encompassing the period of Pentecost. The icons were painted by Constantine Youssis, who had a studio in New York.[42] The experience of gathering in the interior is one of taking in the various perspectives on the Risen Lord: it is a confession of faith in Christ as the giver of resurrection, best described by Alexander Schmemann as the new time of the Church living in the Holy Spirit, inaugurated by the resurrection. Following the construction of the Church of the Holy Wisdom, Holy Transfiguration Church became a stop in New Skete's modified stational liturgy, and it is also a gathering for occasional service such as terce and sext from the old Constantinopolitan cathedral rite.

Church of the Holy Wisdom

The highlight of the monastery's properties is the Church of the Holy Wisdom. The building was designed collaboratively by the monks and nuns of New Skete, who also constructed it themselves. Constantinopolitan and hagiopolite cathedral liturgy inspired the interior design. The building faces east, and since the western end of the church connects to the library, offices, and cells, the main entrance of the building is at the southern wall. On the exterior, a gentle slope goes down from the main entrance to a suitable gathering place marked by a fountain, immediately adjacent to Holy Transfiguration Church. The interior is cruciform, a functional approach to offer structural support on the northern and southern walls. Worshipers enter the south entrance into a large narthex with a Golgotha, the site of many liturgical offices such as Baptism. The nave is vast with large chairs creating an ambo shaped as a semicircle; there is one seat for the presider in the center, the choir standing toward the north in the rear (fig. 6.7). The inspiration of Constantinople's Hagia Sophia is inscribed in the floor, as a piece of marble from Hagia Sophia (tessera) was given as a gift to New Skete. A spacious solea leads to the sanctuary, which is surrounded by a chancel barrier as a three-sided templon with low walls containing two-sided icons (on the sanctuary's interior and exterior) (fig. 6.8). The panels, columns, and architrave were done by Paul Mozes, with English oak.[43] Participants have ample visual access into the sanctuary, which has doors on the front and two sets of opposing deacons' doors on the northern and southern ends of the structure, thus not adjacent to the typical royal doors as one experiences in the Middle Byzantine synthesis. The central icon of the sanctuary is a Deisis with church fathers covering the east wall above the synthronon, painted by Brother Sergius Giroux.

Figure 6.7 Church of the Holy Wisdom, New Skete Monastery, nave (photo by author)

THE ICONOGRAPHIC PROGRAM

The walls above connecting the ceiling to the nave contain icons of dozens of figures central to New Skete's identity. In this section, I present and analyze the significance of the iconography in some detail since the program communicates New Skete's ecclesial identity. The walls depict holy figures in groups of two to five, a procession of saints painted by Deacon Iakov Ferencz adorning the walls in accordance with the following order, from the west end of the southern wall to the east end; the holy prophets Isaiah and Elijah; Saints Hildegard of Bingen, Nectarios, Elizabeth of Moscow, Ephraim the Syrian, and Silouan of Mount Athos; Father Alexander Men, Archbishop Michael Ramsey, Patriarch Athenagoras, and Pope Paul VI (without halos) (fig. 6.9); Saints Theresa Benedicta, Catherine, Barbara, Agnes, and Cecelia; Saints Timothy, Barnabas, Mark, and Paul; Saints Matthias, Nathaniel,

Figure 6.8   Church of the Holy Wisdom, New Skete Monastery, sanctuary templon (photo by author)

Jude Thaddeus, Simon the Zealot, James Alpheus, and Matthew. These figures adorn the southern wall from east to west: Saints Peter, Andrew, John, James, Philip, and Thomas; Saints Mary Magdalene, Martha, Mary, Johanna, and Mary; Saints Irenaeus of Lyons, Ambrose, Gregory of Nyssa, and Gregory the Great; Mother Maria Skobtsova, Dorothy Day, Father Lev Gillet, Mother Teresa of Calcutta, and Father Alexander Schmemann (without halos) (fig. 6.10); Saints Patrick of Ireland, Augustine of Hippo, Andronicus, Athanasia, and Maximos the Greek; and the prophets Moses and David.

The iconostasis also has a broad selection of saints. Here are the icons adorning the chancel barrier on the sanctuary's exterior from the northern to the southern ends: Saints Nil Sura, Melanie, Stephen, John Climacus, John Cassian, and Pachomius. Mary Mother of God and Jesus are in their customary positions on both ends of the doors. The final icon on the front of the iconostasis is Saint Sarah, followed by

Figure 6.9   Church of the Holy Wisdom, New Skete Monastery, nave, frescoes of Father Alexander Men, Archbishop Michael Ramsey, Patriarch Athenagoras, and Pope Paul VI (without halos), painted by Deacon Iakov Ferencz (photo by author)

Saints Benedict, Macrina, Laurence, Cassiana, and Nicholas Cabasilas on the southern exterior of the iconostasis. On the interior, from the high place on the south wall are Saints Scholastica, Theodosius of the Kyivan Caves, Tatiana, John Damascene, Moses, Archangels Uriel, Gabriel, Michael, and Raphael (on the interior of the front), and Saints Columban, Seraphim of Sarov, Phoebe, Antony, and Macarius.

The icons adorning the nave and sanctuary portray a wide variety of saints processing toward the Deisis and are notable because they convey the following features worthy of analysis: an unusual balance of men and women; a strong mixture of saints from East and West; and a local veneration of saints integral to New Skete's history who have not been received as saints in the universal Orthodox Church. The iconographic program thus honors the shared past of East and West and

Figure 6.10   Church of the Holy Wisdom, New Skete Monastery, nave, frescoes of Mother Maria Skobtsova, Dorothy Day, Father Lev Gillet, Mother Teresa of Calcutta, and Father Alexander Schmemann (without halos), painted by Deacon Iakov Ferencz (photo by author)

anticipates the restoration of union to the Churches. The saints also represent the present status of New Skete's community.

The monastery's ecumenical background is obvious when one beholds the saints and notes the balance between East and West, with Western figures such as Gregory the Great, Augustine, Benedicta, Scholastica, and Hildegard, among many others, prominently portrayed on the walls. The iconostasis communicates the same ecumenical dimension by including saints such as Columban, Benedict, and Laurence alongside more stereotypically Orthodox saints such as Seraphim of Sarov and Theodosius of the Kyivan Caves. The inclusion of numerous Western saints honors New Skete's origins in the Franciscan order of the Western Church. This depiction of the past points to the future in the collection of figures who are not yet canonized in the

Orthodox Church but are venerated locally by New Skete, with the absence of halos denoting their interim status.[44] The depiction of Patriarch Athenagoras and Pope Paul VI together on the northern wall honors the kiss of peace exchanged by the two bishops in 1964 in Jerusalem. Likewise, the depiction of people such as Maria Skobtsova and Lev Gillet honors the labors of twentieth-century figures who literally bridged East and West and contributed to ecumenical rapprochement through their actions. The inclusion of Alexander Schmemann indicates the monastery's homage to a figure who contributed to the community's formation. Partaking of worship in the nave exposes New Skete's powerful ecumenical ethos. The nave's iconographic program highlights the period of Christian history when East and West were united and anticipates that the assembly worshiping in the nave will share these values and promote the same ecumenical ethos. The eclectic collection of saints offers a hopeful picture for the contemporary worshiper: the communion of saints includes men and women, along with monks and married saints, emphasizing the universality of the call to holiness in the Church.

The symbiosis of iconography in the sanctuary communicates similar theological motifs. For example, the northern deacons' door, which depicts Saint Phoebe on the interior and Saint Stephen on the exterior, and the southern door portraying Saint Tatiana on the interior and Saint Laurence on the exterior honor the period in Church history when both men and women offered diaconal service in the Church. Essentially, the monastery's life is depicted in the sanctuary: the religious who work and offer worship in the same day find inspiration and advocates in predecessors such as Benedict, Columban, and Nicholas Cabasilas. The depiction of four archangels on the interior of the front end of the iconostasis is deliberate, conveying the message that those who preside and assist in the sanctuary join the highest ranks of angels in serving God and providing refuge for God's people.

Thus, the iconographic program at New Skete is unparalleled in American Orthodoxy due to its creative mixture of ranks of saints, the inclusion of numerous women, and the depiction of several Western saints. This program symbolizes a crucial aspect of New Skete's identity: having been received into Orthodoxy in 1979, it continues to honor its past in the Roman Catholic Church and view its present ministry as one of promoting ecumenical dialogue and cooperation modeled by prominent twentieth-century figures. The openness of the interior and the broad visual access to all participants make it impossible not to notice the monastery's ecumenical mission and desire to promote vocations for both men and women. The equal weight given to women is a unique feature in the monastery's iconography. The monastery's decision to publish liturgical texts with inclusive language manifests consistency in the community's policy of honoring the image of God given equally to men and women.[45] In summary, New Skete simultaneously honors the present, as a community of men and women, and anticipates a future where men and women of East and West—and presumably North and South—will worship God at the same table without canonical impediments.[46]

THE OFFICE OF ANTIPHONS AND THE AMBO

If the iconographic scheme of the Church of the Holy Wisdom communicates New Skete's ecclesial identity, the liturgical celebration illustrates the axiom of architectural form following liturgical function. In the current liturgies of St. John Chrysostom and St. Basil, the three antiphons are sung after the beginning of the liturgy and the Great Litany.[47] In Constantinopolitan liturgy, the office of the antiphons depended on the stational schedule, with stops at intermediary churches or the Forum.[48] Upon arriving at the appointed church (in a stational liturgy), the people would gather outside the main entrance before the nave and at six other doors on the side, and the patriarch would recite the entrance prayer.[49] The people would then sing the introit hymn (Psalm 94) with its refrain. The people would enter the church through Hagia Sophia's numerous entrances as the liturgy progressed to the next chief element, the proclamation of the word with the Epistle and Gospel proclaimed from the church's immense ambo.[50]

New Skete's liturgy has restored these elements of the cathedral rite to the Eucharistic liturgy. New Skete has three variants of the Liturgy of the Word: in version 1, the antiphons are sung in procession outside; in version 2, the antiphons are sung in the narthex; and in version 3, the community gathers outside the doors of the temple for the entrance prayer, which is taken from the earliest extant Constantinopolitan euchologion, Codex Barberini 336.[51] The architecture facilitates a sense of liturgical progression in the Eucharistic liturgy. In New Skete's restoration, the church sings the psalmody outside the nave in front of the small fountain: upon entering, everyone takes their proper place, with the presider and assistants in the center of the ambo, the assembly in the seats, and the choir positioned to the left. The architecture facilitates a sense of communal prayer, as everyone is gathered in the nave with the clergy on the ambo. The ambo is not a replica of the impressive structure of Hagia Sophia. At New Skete, it is a bema under the large carpet in the nave, and it contains the lectern for proclaiming the Scriptures and seats for the presiding clergy. The clergy remain on the ambo until it is time for the Great Entrance. The ambo leads to the solea and provides a natural point of movement to the sanctuary, mimicking the progression of the liturgy from the proclamation of the word (performed at the ambo) to the sanctuary to present the offering. The architecture gently promotes an important liturgical restoration: at New Skete, the prayer of accession is recited at the solea (evoking a sense of movement to the sanctuary) while the deacon performs the duties originally appointed to his order: he prepares the holy table, incenses, and fetches the gifts from the holy table.

These focal points of New Skete's sacred space are held together by a temple shaped like a basilica, with a U-shaped open templon. The large open space of the nave with its appointed seating arrangements and orientation facilitating a progressive Eucharistic liturgy promotes one of New Skete's central liturgical principles: the participation of the people in the liturgy. In this vein, New Skete shares the same priority of liturgical renewal promulgated by St. Vladimir's, namely, corporate worship, the participation of the people in the liturgy. At New Skete, the clergy's and laity's coming together is even more manifest than at St. Vladimir's because of the architectural design. The bema is large enough to hold the celebrating clergy, and New Skete's preference for Constantinopolitan and hagiopolite cathedral models of liturgy keeps all the orders of the Church together in one place for a greater portion of the liturgy.[52] Because the divine offices are celebrated daily at New Skete, the experience of an assembly in the same place is much more profound. At Vespers on Saturday evening, the presider enters the sanctuary only for the censing; everything else is done from the ambo. The assembly moves to the Golgotha in the narthex for the Canticle of Simeon and the troparia, returning to the ambo for the dismissal.

Two examples from the Divine Liturgy persuasively illustrate the notion of the assembly as a priestly order offering the liturgy in unity: the procession with antiphons on the way to church and the performance of the rite of the entrance with the gifts. New Skete has three options for the entrance into the church; in each case, the assembly and clergy gather together (either outside or in the narthex) and enter the church together. The priest and deacon go to the ambo with the Gospel book while the rest of the community takes its place alongside the clergy. The Liturgy of the Word, which contains an Old Testament lection, is proclaimed from the ambo. In sum, the church is mobile, assembling in the church at a station for hearing the word. The next movement occurs at the entrance of the gifts: before the entrance, the priest recited the prayer of accession from the solea. At this time, the deacon prepares the holy table, incenses, and goes to the prothesis to bring in the gifts. The clergy's activity in the sanctuary is functional: the presider proclaims the anaphora and begins the rite of Holy Communion there, but the clergy leave the sanctuary for the nave to exchange the kiss of peace with the entire assembly, accentuating the unity of the priestly order, which includes clergy and laity.

These two movements from the Divine Liturgy manifest a symbiosis of liturgy and architecture. The ambo is designed to create sufficient space for the proclamation of the word of God with everyone gathered together in the same space. The clergy remain with the religious and the laity until it is time to deposit the gifts on the holy table. New Skete's low iconostasis encourages visual access for all. The movement of the celebrating clergy into the sanctuary is purely functional: for most of the liturgy, they are with the people, and there are few barriers separating them from the rest of the assembly. The elevation of the role of the laity in New Skete's liturgy and its inscription on the architecture testify to the community's reception of the ressourcement theology of the lay priesthood and provides another manifestation of Kilde's hypothesis on architectural shifts occurring as a consequence of increased lay participation in the life of the Church.

The architecture of the Church of the Holy Wisdom at New Skete serves the needs of the liturgy. New Skete's liturgy differs from the other examples we have observed in this study. New Skete retrieved the cathedral office of Constantinople to a high degree, subverting the contemporary Byzantine paradigm of parishes celebrating hybrid cathedral-monastic offices that privilege the monastic since New Skete Monastery favors the cathedral rite. Oddly enough, New Skete's adaptation of the liturgy could be construed as both antiquarian and cliché through a particular heuristic lens. The form of the liturgy is strikingly faithful to the Constantinopolitan antecedents, and one can easily see the impact of the Mateos-Taft school of liturgiology in New Skete's contemporary worship. Three features are outstanding: the inclusion of the clergy in the assembly; the increased weight on the proclamation and hearing of the word of God on the large ambo; and the restoration of ritual acts to their original ministries.

REINVIGORATION OF MINISTRIES

Having presented the first two features above, I turn to the ministries in the examples we have observed here. New Skete's Euchologion consistently calls on the presider to pray: his chief role is to lead the assembly in prayer, for all to hear.[53] The deacon's ministry is expanded: quite literally, he waits tables. In the received Byzantine practice, the deacon cannot do anything without the priest initiating the action. Here, the deacon exercises the office of preparing the table and fetching the gifts to be offered, restoring the original liturgical precedent of the Great Church in Constantinople.[54] Furthermore, at communion, no one administers communion, but everyone receives communion from the hand of another, even if the one imparting communion is of a lower rank in the clergy.[55]

From a certain perspective, New Skete's liturgy is indeed antiquarian because it retrieves the medieval cathedral liturgy of Constantinople and reinvigorates it in contemporary North American Church practice. It is also a cliché because it is strikingly faithful to the precepts and order of the cathedral liturgy. New Skete obviously adapted certain aspects of the ancient liturgy to make it suitable for contemporary purposes, which is most evident in the options for the antiphons and entrance into the church.

Underneath this assessment of New Skete's architecture and liturgy lies the profound contribution of the academic to the pastoral. Liturgical historians insist that the role of the historian is to inform, not reform, to show the Church what is possible. In this instance, someone in the Church was actually listening to the academy. New Skete invited Juan Mateos and Alexander Schmemann to demonstrate what is possible, and the result is a reinvigorated Constantinopolitan liturgy that has the capacity to renew Church life in America. In the final analysis, this liturgy is not at all antiquarian because it is not a museum piece, but alive. New Skete's purpose was to reinvigorate not only Church life, and not only to invite the laity to participate in the liturgy, but to make the orders of the Church viable, evidenced in particular by the return of certain liturgical functions to the diaconate. We also see that New Skete referred to Hagia Sophia as a model for architecture, which coheres with the examples of St. Katherine and Annunciation parishes in this study. But unlike these parishes, there is no tyranny of Hagia Sophia, as New Skete's adaptation was designed to reinvigorate the Great Church cathedral liturgy, and not to sustain cultural identity by importing a structural model from one's native homeland into the diaspora.

In New Skete's model, we see a rare appearance of liturgical function actually shaping the architectural form. New Skete's adaptation of Constantinopolitan forms permits it to celebrate the modified cathedral liturgy. The most important contribution is the impetus for this architectural-liturgical restoration: to identify a liturgy suitable to the conditions of contemporary Christianity. New Skete's impact on Orthodox liturgy remains uncertain, though. Many parishes have implemented elements of New Skete's liturgy, but the breadth of their impact is limited.

CONCLUSION

Of all the Orthodox communities I have profiled in this study, St. Vladimir's Seminary and New Skete Monastery stand out on account of the close relationship each community's architecture has with the liturgy. On the surface, these two communities fulfill the axiom of architectural form following liturgical function. Three Hierarchs Chapel was designed by Alexis Vinogradov, a pupil of Alexander Schmemann. Because he is a disciple of St. Vladimir's Eucharistic revival and liturgical renewal, Vinogradov's Three Hierarchs Chapel facilitates many of the chief precepts of liturgical renewal in Orthodoxy, including corporate liturgy that blurs the distinction between clergy and laity, an experience of the liturgy as the eighth day of God's reign, and full sensory participation in the Eucharist, where the laity sees and hears all elements of the Eucharist. Vinogradov's design anticipated Orthodox Church life in America by modeling a suitable space for the parish, the smallest cell of Church life. Vinogradov's creative retrieval of theological principles that did not slavishly copy architectural paradigms from traditionally Orthodox countries is an instance of faithful innovation. Three Hierarchs Chapel's iconography communicates a symbiosis of past, present, and future in the interior iconography, with the Paschal icon over the narthex inaugurating the events of salvation history that situate the Church in the present, joining Mary and the apostles in worshiping the Risen Lord while anticipating the future, dining at his banquet table (depicted by the Mystical Supper on the apse), which the Church experiences as a foretaste at the Divine Liturgy.

The influence of liturgical renewal on the architectural structure is implicit at Three Hierarchs Chapel, whereas it is explicit at the Church of the Holy Wisdom at New Skete. New Skete consulted liturgical historians such as Juan Mateos and Thomas Mathews and based its design of the Church of the Holy Wisdom on featured principles from historical studies. The final result is an adapted form following a modified liturgical function suitable for contemporary communities. While New Skete referred to Hagia Sophia as a model, the modified structure does not attempt to copy the original salient exterior and interior features with precision, but instead privileges an efficient worship space. The

interior iconography of New Skete's Church of the Holy Wisdom depicts a similar sensitivity for liturgical time with the prevalent fresco of
the Lord's Supper adorning the rear wall of the sanctuary. New Skete's
chief feature is its ecumenical hope, blending numerous saints of East
and West, men and women, including a local veneration of holy people
who are not yet canonized (and thus without halos), but represent the
community's Roman origins. In summary, for New Skete Monastery
and Three Hierarchs Chapel, architecture is doing its job by creating a
suitable worship space that communicates the telos of an inclusive
kingdom of God where all join Mary and the apostles in worshiping
the Lamb of God.

Because Three Hierarchs Chapel and the Church of the Holy Wisdom represent the architecture/liturgy relationship, the fate of the architectural model is connected with the legacy of liturgical renewal. St.
Vladimir's Seminary has produced hundreds of graduates who studied
the principles of liturgical renewal and experienced them at Three Hierarchs Chapel. In most instances, graduates assigned to parishes
would conceivably implement liturgical renewal in their parishes' existing edifices, where the architectural design might not fit the modified
liturgy. Attempting to serve a renewed liturgy in a structure that was
not designed with that liturgy in mind requires adjustment. Parish pastors also must adjust to the liturgical heritage of an individual parish
and the legacy of its community. An existing structure emphasizing
interior verticality with a large iconostasis will inevitably clash with the
ecclesiological vision of a temple containing clergy and laity together,
where everyone focuses on the journey's destination—the Lord's Supper depicted on the wall of the apse (as it is at Three Hierarchs Chapel).

Diocesan rules, parish traditions, and an existing architectural
structure inevitably modify the celebrant's approach to liturgical ministry. Some communities will accommodate pastors who can shape an
internal liturgical ethos and make architectural adjustments that facilitate the liturgy, but often, pastors must adapt to established parish practices to minimize internal tensions. Furthermore, established communities consist of people who bring their liturgical dispositions to the
liturgy. These existing attitudes shape the participant's perception of
the liturgy, and while there are frequently multiple understandings of

liturgy in a given community, established communities often have a prevailing narrative. The profiles of previous chapters demonstrate this hypothesis, as communities tend to inscribe their structures with their cultural memories and values, which include theological presuppositions. Three Hierarchs Chapel and the Church of the Holy Wisdom thus represent attempts at a paradigm shift. The two communities consulted the fruits of academic research in an attempt to shape the pastoral, and the respective paradigms have points of intersection and divergence.

Three Hierarchs and the Church of the Holy Wisdom share the priority of mitigating the traditional division between clergy and laity in the liturgy to emphasize active participation of all in one place. The influence of liturgical renewal was more implicit at Three Hierarchs Chapel because the process was driven by a liturgical ecclesiology. To be sure, the lowered iconostasis, open nave, and reduced verticality and iconography were inspired by the fruits of academic research at Three Hierarchs Chapel. The Church of the Holy Wisdom is more explicitly liturgically based due to the direct relationship between principles from Thomas Mathews's studies of Constantinopolitan cathedral liturgy and the interior design of the temple. Simply put, New Skete's Euchologion shaped the interior design of the temple.

Attentive readers will ask about the impact of these two models, especially since they represent a paradigm shift. In my estimation, it is too early to present a final assessment of their impact because the schools inspiring the paradigm shifts are relatively young. Presently, it is clear that the impact of both paradigms is quite limited for several reasons. First, not all Orthodox in North America adhere to the ethos of liturgical renewal cultivated at St. Vladimir's and New Skete. Competing liturgical theologies representing alternative ecclesiologies exist throughout North America, many of which are cultivated at other theological schools. Second, not all disciples of these liturgical schools have the freedom or resources to implement a liturgical ethos in existing parishes due to diocesan liturgical regulations, established parish customs, the limits of existing architectural structures, and the preexisting understanding of liturgy prevailing in communities. Pastors assigned to communities without existing structures might enjoy more freedom in charting a future course for liturgical renewal and, along with it, architectural form. These facts represent the current status of Orthodox community life in North America. Orthodoxy in North America is not only multiethnic, but it is also theologically, culturally, and ecclesiologically pluralistic. Some might view this internal diversity as healthy with room for coexistence, whereas others might interpret it as facilitating division and competition among Orthodox. If the Schmemann and New Skete schools of liturgical renewal were to prevail in North America, a strong minority of Orthodox belonging to a more conservative school of liturgics would remain. Ultimately, the limited impact of the architectural models at St. Vladimir's and New Skete discloses Orthodox identity in North America as plurivocal and in an early stage of its evolution. It is possible that the pastoral architectural and liturgical forms will catch up with the models presented by the academic at St. Vladimir's and New Skete; it is equally possible that the pluralistic status quo will continue to prevail in North American architecture.

CHAPTER SEVEN

JOY OF ALL WHO SORROW ORTHODOX CHURCH (JOY) MISSION

This chapter profiles Joy of All Who Sorrow Orthodox Church (JOY) mission, located in Culver City, California. JOY belongs to the Diocese of the West of the Orthodox Church in America (OCA). The purpose of this chapter is to examine architecture and liturgy through the lens of a modern phenomenon in American Orthodoxy: the planting of missions, a process traced to the origins of American Orthodoxy in 1794 that became quite popular in the final quarter of the twentieth century. The chapter focuses on the particular challenges of architecture in mission communities given their small size, limited financial resources, dependence on rented or loaned assembly space, and interim status. I begin with an overview of missions in American Orthodoxy to foreground the analysis and situate JOY within American Orthodoxy's mission environment.

MISSIONS IN AMERICAN ORTHODOXY

The process of planting missions began to take shape in American Orthodoxy around 1970, occurring in part as a response to the new orientation of mission in the OCA, which received autocephaly from the Moscow Patriarchate in the same year. The OCA established a Department of Missions in 1974, and the work of the department centered on obtaining funds for new missions.[1] The theological rationale for establishing mission parishes is evangelization.[2] The OCA's guidelines for missions established four chronological levels of community status: mission station, provisional mission, mission status, and parish status.[3] Briefly, a mission station is an "outreach ministry of a single parish, group of parishes, deanery or diocese to a group of faithful," consisting of less than twenty-five pledging individuals; mission stations are established on account of a critical mass of the faithful who live too far from a parish, or because of the legitimate need for a new community.[4] Provisional mission status lasts for as long as three years. A mission "is a local church community of more than 25 pledging individuals, which is served by its own pastor."[5] Technically, a community cannot remain a mission for more than three years (according to these guidelines). After three years, a mission should graduate to parish status or revert to a provisional mission. A parish consists of at least fifty pledging individuals: "it worships in its own facilities, has housing available for its pastor, is able to compensate its pastor fully without his having to resort to outside employment, and is able to meet its own expenses and financial obligations to the diocese and the OCA without outside assistance from a sponsoring body."[6] Presumably, the parish's facilities are actually owned by the community.

The OCA provides a missions handbook that defines the purpose of missions and provides how-to steps on planting and establishing them.[7] Part 3 of the handbook presents a "mission start-up strategy" that outlines four distinct periods of growth in the mission's life: preparatory, pioneer, growth and organization, and reproduction.[8] The preparatory period consists of identifying a need for a mission, which could be inspired by a cluster of people in a particular area or outreach in a non-churched area.[9]

Once a mission is established, a target area is chosen based on a socio-religious study. The selection of the target area depends on criteria such as area growth, the stability of the economic situation, residential construction, and the existence of Orthodox communities. Other aspects of establishing a mission include identifying a core group of people; establishing a budget; initiating a liturgical cycle; starting outreach and catechesis; and, once a base community seems to be established, searching for a permanent meeting place, which includes the creation of a land or building fund.

The section of the missions handbook most relevant to this study is the how-to section on facilities. A list of suggestions attests to the interim status of missions and includes office-warehouse space, storefronts, funeral home and hospital chapels, and halls belonging to veterans' groups and fraternal organizations. In considering a property, the handbook prioritizes cleanliness, aesthetics, and signage, along with an easily accessible location.[10] Miscellaneous considerations include acoustics, the ability to set up for services, storage on site, and use of incense and candles.

The missions handbook provides basic guidelines for support in a mission. The following excerpt on funding details the expectations for income at various stages of the mission's life:

> An initial core group might need about $400–$500 a month to pay a priest for occasional services, modest rent, liturgical items, advertising. . . . When the mission group has liturgies on a bi-weekly basis, the mission may need around $600–$900 a month. When the mission group has liturgies on a weekly basis, the mission may need about $1,200 a month. . . . A mission on the way to becoming a full parish would have up to $5,000/month income. This presumes a minimum of about 30 families with a total of 50 adult members.[11]

The handbook contains some suggestions for seeking financial support within the OCA, including the OCA church-planting grant. The purpose of the planting grant program is "to make it possible for a mission served by a visiting priest who is also secularly employed to become a mission with a priest-in-residence whose time is exclusively devoted to building up and expanding the work and witness of the mission community."[12] Missions must apply for the grant and eligibility is determined by the support of the diocesan bishop. In the first year, a mission can receive up to $24,000, and reapplication for a total of three years is possible with $20,000 granted in year 2 and $16,000 in year 3. The grant stipulates that funds may be used only to provide salary and benefits for the priest.[13]

ANALYSIS

This introductory section is designed to articulate the rationale for missions within the OCA, which includes JOY. Given the history and significance of missions in the American Orthodox culture, a more exhaustive study of the theological rationale for missions and analyses of their narrative histories is both welcome and much needed. The OCA is not the only Orthodox entity in America to encourage the building of missions. The Greek Orthodox Archdiocese of America encourages the creation of new missions and offers resources and support through the Home Mission Parish Program under the aegis of its Department of Outreach and Evangelism.[14] The self-ruled Antiochian Archdiocese of America established a Department of Missions and Evangelism in 1988 to "make America Orthodox."[15] The Antiochian Archdiocese boasts the creation of 108 missions since 1988, with 55 of those becoming full-fledged parishes.[16] Clearly, the time for an assessment of missions in Orthodox America has arrived.

For our purposes, the material provided by the OCA offers a framework for analyzing the relationship of liturgy and architecture and the inscription of ecclesial identity on architecture at JOY. First, we should note the theological rationale for establishing missions in the OCA. The Church's encouragement of planting new missions comes from a paradigm shift in ministry, from maintaining and sustaining communities largely consisting of immigrants to evangelizing people who are seeking a church home. The missionary priority in American Orthodoxy experienced a resurgence in the final quarter of the twentieth century and its goals included Church growth, both qualitative and quantitative. Missionary activity is directed toward the unchurched, though the documents do not define this group with precision. In this vein, the term "unchurched" refers not only to non-Christians, but also to Christians who belong to a non-Orthodox denomination.

Second, the tangible telos of mission is an established parish with its own facilities as an end-product. The documents distinguish between the church as a community of people and a building, but the stages of mission status and development conclude with the same tangible result: a community with a minimum of fifty people that has its own building. Despite the emphasis on the church as a community of God's people, the building is an essential element of community life since it provides the requisite space for liturgy and fellowship. The description of liturgy in these documents is telling: the expectation is that a mission community will develop to a point where it can sustain a full liturgical life in accordance with global Orthodoxy, consisting of the full observance of Sunday liturgy (including Vigil and Divine Liturgy) along with the various festal, Lenten, and Paschal cycles. The documents do not envision a liturgy modified for a mission.

For example, in identifying a suitable assembly space, communities are expected to inquire about the use of incense and candles, and should anticipate building in time for setting up and tearing down. The set-up process refers to the standard Byzantine liturgy, which requires an altar, a table of preparation (prothesis), and some kind of iconographic arrangement. The vision of liturgy is fixed and uniform with the full expectation that missions will grow into the standard Byzantine liturgy. The only possible exception to this paradigm is the adoption of the Western rite, a model once pursued with greater vigor and interest in Orthodox mission, but now largely limited to a few instances in the Antiochian Archdiocese.[17] This vision of liturgy is quite narrow: there is no room granted for an indigenous and organic liturgical development conforming to the language, idioms, and symbols of American culture. The expectation is strict adherence to a variant of the Byzantine liturgical paradigm. The guidelines for missions envision a worship space that facilitates the basic observance of the fixed Byzantine cycle. In fact, the ultimate definition of a parish is reduced to liturgical observance, in a sense, since the privilege of mission funding and primary symbol of growth is manifest in the presence of a priest who is free from the financial responsibility of secular employment and can thus devote himself to serving a full cycle of divine offices.[18] The architecture of a mission, then, is minimalist by necessity: the goal is to develop the community so that it can fulfill the objective of achieving parish status, which presumes property ownership and either renovating a purchased building or developing plans for constructing an edifice. Missions also emphasize non-liturgical activity, especially catechesis and fellowship, as central means of building up the community. In the how-to section on facilities, the handbook recommends devoting space for fellowship:

> 50–75% of those present at a service stay for fellowship, and a minimum of 10 to 15 square feet per person is needed. A rule might be to have the fellowship hall size equal the size of the nave. Do not neglect the importance of adequate fellowship space. A great deal of ministry is done during coffee hour. This is the time we reach out to visitors and inquirers.[19]

A separate space is needed for fellowship and catechesis; the comparison of the fellowship space to the nave is telling, which illustrates the principles of proportionality and the weight given to liturgy.

The most substantial aspect of this review of rationales and how-tos for missions is their liminal existence. Missions are temporary: the original vision was for missions to become full-fledged parishes owning their own property, with new missions planted when existing parishes became overpopulated. The threshold for growth was three years, and the mission's status would be adjusted accordingly if the thresholds of the guidelines were achieved. The documents articulating the vision for missions and outreach anticipated that some missions would fail, but did not foresee missions that plateau and become semi-permanent communities with a lifecycle longer than three years, but unable to grow into a typical parish. The end-result of the mission process was the existing parish that observed a full cycle of the Byzantine rite and owned a building designed to accommodate that structure. The interim structures were minimal by design. Some missions have become semi-permanent communities that remain in the interim status in between mission and parish. This unexpected development has important implications for the landscape of Orthodoxy in America, in particular, the relationship between architecture and liturgy and the inscription of ecclesial identity on the interim architectural space.

JOY OF ALL WHO SORROW ORTHODOX CHURCH (JOY) MISSION

JOY began as a mission outreach in 1996. The current rector, Father John Tomasi, promoted Orthodox Christianity on the Venice Strand. In 2000, JOY joined the OCA as a mission. The small mission occupied a part of a building on Washington Boulevard for $7,000 a month in rent, which proved prohibitive. In 2009, JOY occupied its current space on Sepulveda Boulevard (a main thoroughfare of West Los Angeles, running parallel to the 405 freeway and connecting the urban centers constituting Los Angeles). As one might expect, JOY is one of numerous Orthodox parishes in the greater Los Angeles area, one of two OCA parishes on the west side of Los Angeles. The parish currently pays $3,600 per month in rent for its portion of the building. Income is very tight, and the rector makes only a very small stipend (less than $1,000 per month) since the parish lost two of its greatest financial contributors. Thus, JOY has been a mission for fourteen years, exceeding the three-year threshold for mission status. JOY exemplifies the Orthodox mission that has become semi-permanent: the journey to full parish status is elongated, and while the community continues to strive for permanence, it is too well established to dissolve.

JOY currently counts a total of 16 official members with average Sunday Divine Liturgy attendance at approximately 25 to 30, which has remained largely unchanged since 2008.[20] JOY is one of 19 missions in the OCA's Diocese of the West. Since 2008, the diocesan missions collectively grew by 13%. The highest rate of growth is in Chico, California (at 55%), whereas the steepest rate of decline was recorded in Bozeman, Montana (at minus 23%).[21] Community growth at JOY is inconsistent, as the parish reported 12 baptisms in 2011, zero in 2012, and 3 in 2013. JOY faces formidable financial challenges, evidenced by its identification of covering monthly expenses and increasing the priest's salary and housing allowance as its major challenges.[22]

Upon occupying the space on Sepulveda Boulevard, the people of the mission significantly renovated the worship space to make it suitable for Orthodox liturgy. JOY proudly follows the Julian calendar and draws heavily on monastic liturgical traditions in its practices.

Under the leadership of a parishioner with contracting experience, the mission renovated the storefront space into a basic rectangle. The total space is humble, 2,800 square feet that include the church, an entrance, a bookstore, a fellowship area, a kitchen, and a restroom. The worship space accommodates seventy people on Pascha, and owns six parking spaces behind the building (on Sunday mornings, parking is available on Sepulveda Boulevard). In short, "limitation" defines the liturgical context of JOY. Financial resources and meeting space are very limited, and on the surface, these limitations might seem prohibitive for community growth and development.

EXTERIOR DESCRIPTION

The architecture and iconographic design of the mission represents the community's composition and attempt to navigate its limitations. The location of the parish has both advantages and disadvantages. Its urban setting on a main thoroughfare fits a common Orthodox American context, but because it is located in a strip mall, it is hard to find the church and then secure parking once located.[23] Only people familiar with the location or determined to reach it can secure parking because the six allotted spaces are in the back of the building and are not well marked. A blue-on-white background sign states "Orthodox Church" in large letters, flanked by an icon of St. George and the Hospitality of Abraham (fig. 7.1). In the absence of a freestanding structure on property owned by the community, there is little more JOY can do to distinguish its exterior features. In this vein, JOY differs from independent parishes that own their own property and yet represents Orthodox mission communities. The mission's ability to decorate the exterior to attract visual attention is limited. In fact, JOY's decoration of the exterior fulfills Vinogradov's ideal for an Orthodox church design: the exterior blends with the rest of the eclectic and busy neighborhood, and is part of the remainder of the building by definition. The primary advantage lies in the constant flow of traffic on Sepulveda Boulevard: a multitude of drivers, passengers, and pedestrians walk by JOY every day.

Figure 7.1   Joy of All Who Sorrow Orthodox Church (JOY) mission (photo by author)

INTERIOR DESCRIPTION

Upon entering the building from the front entrance on Sepulveda Boulevard, participants can turn left and enter the parish bookstore, go straight into a small gathering area, or turn right and enter the church. Head coverings are available for women, symbolizing the community's preference for adhering to conservative Orthodox traditions; the rector openly describes the parish as an adherent of the traditions of the Russian Orthodox Church Outside of Russia (ROCOR) within the OCA, with the entirety of the liturgy performed in English. Parishioners renovated the rented liturgical space constituting the church. The space has two public entrances: one from the front door on Sepulveda Boulevard, and another on the side, separated from the fellowship area by a simple curtain. The parish's small choir stands in the rear, separated from the rest of the assembly by a short wall. The parish values

Figure 7.2   Joy of All Who Sorrow Orthodox Church (JOY) mission, iconostasis (photo by author)

good singing; besides intimacy, one of the space's advantages is its 3.5 second acoustical delay, which the renovators enhanced in finalizing the space renovation. The premium on quality Orthodox singing is evident on the parish's web site, which offers examples of video and audio clips from divine services. More substantial is the mission's publishing of a professional recording featuring its choir, which sings the Lamentations of Holy and Great Saturday.[24]

A simple, floor-to-ceiling iconostasis separates the sanctuary from the nave (fig. 7.2). The iconostasis contains the following icons, from north to south: Joy of All Who Sorrow, Theotokos, Christ, St. George, and St. John the Forerunner. Festal icons of the liturgical year flank the highest icon of the Mystical Supper. The deacons' doors open, and when clergy and servers enter and exit, they must be careful to take the appropriate steps up and down as the drop is steeper than one would expect. The sanctuary is small but serviceable, containing all the required components of Orthodox liturgy; a large icon of the Theotokos Orans hangs from chains, with light streaming in from the window behind.

INTERIOR ICONOGRAPHY

The iconographic arrangement of the church is the most interesting aspect of JOY because it effectively captures the community's mission context. The mission has no preordained and selected style of iconography and decorates the interior by following the principles of the presence of saints. The parish has collected a variety of relics and icons given to the rector and parishioners as gifts throughout the years. The icons are arranged everywhere, and faithful parishioners know their locations and history. Relics come from saints such as John Chrysostom, John of Damascus, Lucia, Bartholomew, Nicholas (from Rome), a stone from Patrona, a rock from St. Paul Monastery, earth from the Holy Sepulcher, earth from Gethsemane Skete (in Gethsemane), secondary relics of the Optina elders (a gift from the retired former diocesan bishop Tikhon Fitzgerald), and a piece of a cassock belonging to St. John Maximovich (fig. 7.3). According to Father Tomasi, the parish's most beloved icons and relics belong to Saints Nicholas and John Maximovich. The space limitation forces the community to place the icons where they are able: all over a column supporting the ceiling, and on the walls and ceiling. Despite the absence of stereotypical vertical dimensions, the worship space contains a false dome depicting the Pantocrator (fig. 7.4).

JOY thus attempts to add icons to the worship space with no deliberate organization; there is a slight preference for the "Byzantine" iconographic style (probably due to the rector's frequent visits to Mount Athos), with the art happily received as a gift. Father Tomasi links the parish's collection and arrangement of icons and relics as a representation of the following idea: a prayer that saints would come to the parish and want to dwell there. The parish's hope is that the people who join the parish in worship would represent the eclectic collection of saints who depict the small interior of the worship space: diverse in history and background, people who value the ascetical life, a living presence

Figure 7.3   Joy of All Who Sorrow Orthodox Church (JOY) mission, relics (photo by author)

Figure 7.4   Joy of All Who Sorrow Orthodox Church (JOY) mission, Pantocrator (photo by author)

of saints rejoicing in the community of intercessors who worship God with them.

Liturgical life at JOY is quite rigorous, which is mildly surprising since the rector holds a full-time position outside the parish. The parish web site offers the following regularly scheduled weekly services: Friday Vespers, Divine Liturgy and Vigil on Saturday, and Divine Liturgy on Sunday. A glance at any given monthly calendar exhibits the mission's faithful observance of a full liturgical cycle honoring the diverse feasts of the liturgical year. It is not unusual for JOY to have three or more Divine Liturgies and Vespers in a given week outside of a holy season. Lent is particularly rigorous, with no core offices omitted and services held almost every day. The frequency of liturgical celebration demands challenging compromises: many morning services begin as early as 6:00 a.m. The mission does not typically modify the services so as to shorten their duration; the style of liturgical celebration is fairly crisp, so there is no obvious elongation of a given liturgy. In this vein, JOY fits the profile encountered earlier in ROCOR's Holy Virgin Cathedral (San Francisco), and it seems that the mission happily espouses liturgical maximalism despite the obvious challenges posed to the rector and those who sing and assist during the services.

ANALYSIS OF LITURGY AND ARCHITECTURE IN JOY

The interior iconographic decoration of JOY's worship space coheres with its status as a mission and unveils its evangelistic tone. First, we should note that the architectural scheme for mission churches varies in accordance with the spaces they rent. For communities that rent space for a designated time period on Sunday or on special days, it is not possible to construct a permanent iconostasis: they must set up and tear down, a process the how-tos of which we briefly referenced in the mission planter's kit. JOY's commitment to a full liturgical schedule from the outset of its existence results in the possibility of creating a more permanent worship space. Mission communities that have time constraints in the spaces they rent often have makeshift or portable iconostases, sometimes consisting of two icons placed on stands before an altar.

JOY mitigates its interim status as a mission by committing to a full liturgical schedule, which necessitates a suitable worship space. In this sense, the basic relationship between liturgy and architecture shapes the interior design. The Middle Byzantine architectural synthesis accommodates the liturgical maximalism of the Typikon, so the environment contains a nave, a sanctuary, and a small narthex at the main entrance, along with an area for fellowship.

The interior decoration and arrangement of the worship space does not include any innovations: this would be impossible given the tight general constraints of the small space. The practice of placing the icons in any available space is one of efficiency. Limited financial resources prohibit robust investment in a sophisticated iconographic program (since large donations would be designated for a building), so the mission readily receives donations of icons and relics as gifts for the parish. The eclectic gathering and arrangement of these artifacts might be superficially construed as haphazard, but it conforms to the purpose of mission. The relics and saints represent the broad spectrums of Christian history and location, so the arrangement of holy objects in the church's interior fuses past, present, and future, and most important, provides an opportunity for visitors to find themselves at home. The mission's use of English in liturgy and the absence of an ethnic majority among the people open the possibility for an organic local Orthodoxy to emerge. The diverse arrangement of relics and icons suggests that the small mission is capable of being a microcosm of global Orthodoxy, an evangelistic notion that coheres conveniently with Los Angeles as a multiethnic city. A predetermined iconographic design might define the profile of the parish's identity too narrowly, so the assorted gathering of saints within the church leaves the vision of what the parish might become quite open. The primary identifying marker is that the mission hopes that the parish would consist of saintly people committed to living holy lives like the saints they venerate.

Despite the limitations of the property, JOY capitalizes on its location in America's second largest urban area to bring liturgy into the public square. The mission's location on Sepulveda Boulevard positions the community in the midst of the sea of urban people. While the property itself presents limited opportunities for public outreach, JOY draws from its early history on the Venice Strand and brings liturgy into the public square on the Theophany feast celebrated on January 19 (according to the old-style Julian calendar). The community led by the rector celebrates the blessing of Theophany waters in the Pacific Ocean, with Father Tomasi going into the ocean for the blessing. The public liturgy of blessing the Pacific waters again evokes the memory of stational liturgy discussed by John Baldovin (see chapter 1).[25] As with St. Vladimir's Seminary's liturgical practices outlined in chapter 6, JOY does not promote a consistent stational liturgy. But the small community's venture to the Pacific for the water blessing expresses the same principle of bringing the liturgy from the church to the public. In this instance, JOY's venture to the Pacific draws from the mission's history and functions as a evangelistic tool for the mission to extend liturgy outside its constrained architectural context and to the general public.

This brief exploration of liturgy and architecture at JOY in Culver City yields limited information on the rationale for design because a mission community is in an interim status. The underlying assumption for a mission community is that it will eventually become a permanently established parish, which entails limitations in the architectural design and liturgical planning. JOY has committed to liturgical maximalism, gathering for the divine offices and Eucharistic liturgies as often as possible, and has created a gathering space suitable for that basic purpose. Thus, the relationship between liturgy and architecture is essentially fixed by external limitations: the kind of church JOY might construct in the future, with sufficient growth and funding to procure and sustain a permanent building, is unknown.

Despite the uncertain future, it is crucial to pay attention to the lessons from this particular mission experience. JOY was established as a mission in 2000, so it already has a sixteen-year history (as of this writing). For those who identify JOY as their parish home, sixteen years is a substantial portion of their life. The mission is not a new enterprise and the cycle of services and community life has already contributed to the formation of the community. JOY represents a real possibility for all Orthodox mission communities in America: the interim status may be, in reality, permanent, as long as a critical mass of people continues to gather for worship over an extended period of time. The prospect of mission permanence cuts against the grain of conventional Orthodox thinking on missions reviewed at the beginning of this chapter, which foresees the process of mission planting as populating the American landscape with permanent and healthy parish communities that will presumably own their own property. However, demographic realities impact attempts at planting missions. In best-case scenarios, missions grow more or less in accordance with expectations and build enough momentum while accumulating financial resources to invest in property and build. Some missions are unable to generate sufficient momentum and must close, whereas others plateau and continue to meet without garnering adequate resources to build and become permanently established. As of this writing, JOY is one of many missions healthy enough to continue to meet and gather in community without taking the final step to permanence: they are semi-permanent communities in the liminal status between mission and parish.

The existence of such communities is an important feature of American Orthodoxy. American Orthodoxy purposefully self-identifies as mission-oriented given its establishment by missionaries in the late eighteenth century, and planting missions has been a priority among many Orthodox from the final quarter of the twentieth century. Ideally, one could refer to a range of numbers of people whose lives included a substantial attachment to a mission community—a worthy topic for a doctoral dissertation—and anecdotally, I can claim with a reasonable amount of certitude that a critical mass of Orthodox Christians in America has worshiped in a mission community at minimum, with a sizable number of people having devoted some time to a mission community.

This reflection leads to the hypothesis that the existence of missions, some of which are essentially permanent, manifests the decreasing importance of exterior architecture. One can divide a large room into the appropriate partitions for Byzantine worship, as a makeshift or portable iconostasis permits the creation of a worship space with a nave and a sanctuary since two tables create a prothesis and altar. Besides the vessels and antimension needed for the Byzantine liturgy, the only other requirement for a mission is some kind of iconographic arrangement. Exterior decoration can be minimal, with a sign identifying the mission community, perhaps decorated by a modest icon or three-barred cross. Missions speak to the flexibility of Byzantine architecture; it is truly reducible to the construction of a makeshift wall, the arrangement of a few tables, and decoration of some icons to make it suitable for worship, as a lowest common denominator.

The same principle of flexibility applies to the celebration of the Byzantine liturgy. In comparing missions, one would likely find a wide variety of liturgical styles, and JOY's example of liturgical maximalism is helpful as it demonstrates the possibility of observing a reasonably full Byzantine ordo in a large room. Missions complete the process of dissipation in the symbiosis of liturgy and architecture that Vasileios Marinis identifies in the Middle Byzantine period.[26] The difference in this instance is that architecture has become the inferior partner in the relationship. The perception of the Byzantine liturgy is that it is largely unchangeable and that communities have a responsibility to observe it to the greatest possible degree. To put it bluntly, in most cases, observing a minimal liturgical cycle is undesirable and inappropriate unless absolutely demanded by the community's conditions of assembly (time constraints caused by rental limitations). As long as the community can meet to liturgize, any space will suffice, assuming it has two tables, icons, incense, antimension, and the appropriate vessels for the Eucharistic liturgy. Architectural beauty is an ideal communities should strive to realize, but it is possible to be a liturgical community without it.

This reflection leads to a hypothetical possibility concerning the future of Orthodox missions in America: the parish paradigm is in decline, and more communities will gather to worship without owning permanent property. The potential that this shift may be actualized has real teeth, as evidenced by recent and ongoing work by Michael Plekon.[27] The gradual and steady decline of parish communities in certain regions of America is caused by socioeconomic trends impacting the entire country. These trends are having the most significant impact on parishes in the Northeast and the Midwest, where previously flourishing industries requiring blue-collar laborers (such as automaking, iron, and steel) have evolved to a point where the supply of laborers has outpaced demand. Higher education adjusted to this trend, bringing the children of families in regions with clusters of Orthodox communities to find employment in new industries. Declining communities lacking new people to replace those who move have difficulty financially sustaining their property, which is leading to parish closures and a sharp decline in the overall size of a given diocese.[28] The implications for mission communities are twofold.

First, a dose of religious reality mitigates the enthusiasm that initially fuels the expectation of church growth in a mission setting. While some missions might grow, others will plateau after an initial swelling in size and some will decline. The possibility that the interim status of a mission could become permanent has serious implications for liturgy and architecture. Architectural innovation will be constrained by the limited freedom that comes with designing an interior space with specifications that were not designed for worship. It is possible for liturgy to evolve in a mission setting, but only if communities abandon the perception of liturgy as canonically etched in stone and unchangeable, a popular narrative inconsistent with liturgical history. Second, an obvious consequence of the potential emergence of permanent mission communities is the further detachment of architecture from the liturgy, where symbiosis is severely limited to accommodating basic liturgical requirements and essentially providing a space for the community to gather. That said, permanent mission communities might also provide fertile ground for liturgy and architecture to reciprocally shape one another, creating a new symbiosis for this time and place that accords with the surrounding environment.

CONCLUSION

JOY, the mission parish profiled in this chapter, attempts to create a holy space with a broad representation of intercessors depicted by its icons and relics in a humble environment. For JOY, it is clear that the Church as the body of Christ is what makes the space holy, not the space or its deliberate arrangement, even though JOY has attended to making the best of its space, despite its limitations. A careless review of the space might result in a conclusion of haphazard arrangement that cannot accommodate good liturgy. The parish works very hard at promoting frequent and good liturgy. Besides the quality singing, the people gather frequently, with Orthros, Vespers, and Eucharistic liturgy celebrated multiple times a week. Their space limitations allow their public processions to enter the very public space of Sepulveda Boulevard on Holy Week and Pascha, as they literally circumambulate the entire building complex three times. Perhaps the most indicative aspect of their mission heritage in West Los Angeles is their custom of blessing the waters on Theophany. Parishioners leave their small building and gather at Venice Beach on the Pacific Ocean, with the priest literally entering the sea to bless one of the largest natural sources of water in the world, very much in view of the public.

In conclusion, JOY has adapted to the limitations of its liturgical space with great innovation and has integrated its particular missiological kernel of asking the saints to come to the people into their liturgical iconography. Parishioners' comfort in a small space does not prohibit them from sustaining the mission mindset from their past on the strand; they liturgize in the public view on Sepulveda Boulevard and at Venice Beach. What remains unknown is how their example might contribute to the future trajectory of Orthodox architecture. In many ways, they represent the post-immigration mission mindset of Orthodox America by seeking to give birth to a new community in an urban area with no particular ethnic attachments. However, the formidable economic challenges that constrain them challenge not only the future of Orthodox architecture, but also Orthodoxy in America.

This review of JOY in light of Orthodox missions in America yields a sober picture of the immediate future of liturgy and architecture. First, the general commitment of missions to observing the Orthodox liturgical cycle in its fullness elucidates the perception of liturgy as fixed and unchangeable in Orthodoxy. However one appraises this perception, the possibility of an emerging paradigm shift that would present a critical mass of permanent Orthodox missions that do not own property entails a liturgical adjustment to the new environment. In other words, liturgy has to change in accordance with the life and rhythm of the community, so that the Sabbath is for the people and not the people for the Sabbath. Second, in the case of JOY, we have observed the abandonment of slavishly copying a stereotypical iconographic program on account of the mission's interim status, which excludes the possibility of painting the interior. Instead, JOY has accepted gifts of icons and relics representing global Orthodoxy that corresponds with Los Angeles as a microcosm of the world. In this vein, as a mission, JOY exemplifies Vinogradov's notion of the interior drawing the world into the church, minimizing the need for exterior decoration. This random convergence of factors—economic limitations, the interim status of the community, and rental space—results in the portrayal of a diverse communion of saints that appeals to a broad constituency. Third, the possibility of an emergent permanent mission opens an opportunity for the emergence of a new symbiosis of architecture and liturgy, where the two can reciprocally shape one another in adjusting to the new sociodemographic environments in which local Orthodox assemblies find themselves.

CONCLUSION

In this study, I have surveyed select Orthodox parishes in America and examined the symbiosis of architecture, liturgy, memory, and ecclesial identity in each community. The goal of this study was manifold: to assess the axiom that architectural form follows liturgical function in contemporary American Orthodoxy; to demonstrate that contemporary Orthodox architecture in America is multivalent and communicates ethnic identity and mission along with liturgy; and to ascertain how these parishes might illuminate the future of Orthodox architecture in America.

I commenced by reviewing tradition to illuminate models from the past that might inform the present. In chapter 1, my architectural review showed that liturgy has traditionally exercised primary influence on Byzantine architecture. Constantinople's Hagia Sophia exemplified the liturgy/architecture symbiosis since the Great Church's design facilitated a cathedral liturgy of mobility that encouraged the city to come to the church while sending the church into the city. External events that impacted liturgy also shaped Byzantine architecture. The triumph over iconoclasm resulted in a new monastic hegemony in Byzantium, and icons increasingly adorned the walls and fixtures of the churches. The monastic liturgy was fused with the cathedral, and the monastic dominance was guaranteed by the thirteenth century (when

Constantinople was sacked by Crusaders) and finalized by the fourteenth and fifteenth centuries, with the emergence of Mount Athos as a center of spiritual and liturgical renewal and the empire's defeat by the Ottomans. The monastic influence on the liturgy permeated architecture: the detachment of distinct cathedral elements from the liturgy resulted in smaller churches with basic fixtures, namely, the narthex, the nave, and the sanctuary, with the iconostasis separating the nave from the altar. The peoples of Rus' developed new architectural styles, and some of these were adaptations of earlier Byzantine styles, including that of Kyiv Sophia, but the Middle Byzantine architectural paradigm remained more or less stable.

I offer the following summary of the primary contributions of my study:

1. In some instances, architectural form continues to follow liturgical function, but the emergence of new community priorities is increasingly resulting in the detachment of liturgical function from architectural form.

2. This examination of parishes and their respective architectural styles results in models. These models represent the landscape of Orthodoxy in America, which is a collection of churches with varying ecclesiologies, liturgical styles, and approaches to mission. Three groups define the collections of churches: the immigrant model, the liturgical renewal model, and the American Church model.

3. Despite the diversity separating the parishes of this study, each parish claims to be faithful to tradition, and each community makes a persuasive case.

4. The use of multiple buildings by most communities on their properties manifests a plurality of community rituals. On the surface, this is not unusual since communities have meetings and share fellowship on special occasions, but in some cases the parallel structures are developed for encounters that supersede liturgy, even if involuntarily.

5. The investigation yielded insights on parish notions of liturgy. While each community values liturgy, the following perceptions of liturgy prevail:

    a. Liturgical maximalism entailing daily and rigorous liturgical celebration is ideal, in preparation for the second coming of Christ.

    b. The liturgy does not need to be changed since it was handed down from the previous generation; it is timeless and perfectly suitable for contemporary circumstances.

    c. Liturgical renewal is needed for the Church to be its best self in contemporary America.

6. Varying perceptions of the liturgy in parish life demonstrate that the axiom of architectural form following liturgical function no longer holds, unless parishes begin to express preference for the liturgical renewal model. The perception of the liturgy as fixed and not requiring renewal is one of many factors contributing to the detachment of architectural form from liturgical function.

Above, I mentioned that three models capture the essence of architecture as a multivalent symbol that expresses memory, mission, and ecclesial identity in addition to providing a suitable space for the liturgy. Table C.1 sketches the three models by listing the churches belonging to each group and the chief features of each model.

THE IMMIGRANT MODEL

St. Katherine Ukraine Orthodox Church and Holy Virgin Cathedral are the primary churches of this model, with Annunciation Greek Orthodox Church secondary. Both St. Katherine and Holy Virgin Cathedral have worship edifices that copy models from a mother country, Kyiv Sophia for St. Katherine and Moscow's Dormition Cathedral for Holy Virgin Cathedral. The parish center or community hall is multifunctional for both communities, edifices that privilege cultivation of ethnic identity and host events celebrating one's heritage. Annunciation parish fits this paradigm to a lesser degree because the community retains its heritage of Greek identity and provides abundant space for community gatherings in the massive James W. Pihos Cultural Center next to the church, while the church itself is a modified copy of Hagia Sophia.

    Annunciation differs from the primary models because the community deliberately selected a nontraditional interior style for the sake

Table C.1   Immigrant, Liturgical Renewal, and American Church Models

Immigrant Model	Liturgical Renewal Model	American Church Model
Strict adherence to traditions of mother churches; sustain inherited liturgy with little or no changes, as change is undesirable; development of additional buildings on property; emphasis on the people's memory and cultural sustenance; abundant repositories of émigré history	Engage liturgical history for adapting contemporary liturgical ordo; liturgical renewal primary conduit for ecclesial renewal; design architectural form to accommodate liturgical ordo; liturgical change is necessary for contemporary peoples and times	Emphasize active participation of the laity in the liturgy and community life; loosening of affiliations with mother churches; preservation of ethnic identity not primary; active outreach to and attempt to blend within local neighborhood; architectural innovation encouraged
St. Katherine parish Holy Virgin Cathedral Annunciation parish	Three Hierarchs Chapel Church of the Holy Wisdom St. Matthew parish	St. Matthew parish Three Hierarchs Chapel Church of the Holy Wisdom Annunciation parish JOY mission

of having access to a celebrated architect, which marked the people's arrival on the American scene. The sense of arrival at Annunciation is distinct from the environments prevailing at St. Katherine and Holy Virgin Cathedral. For Annunciation, arrival represents the community's permanent bonds with America; the people honor their Greek heritage, but a perception of America as a temporary respite with the goal of ultimately returning to Greece has disappeared. St. Katherine and Holy Virgin Cathedral continue to provide refuge for immigrants who come from their native countries to the United States. Certainly many of their people have no immediate plans to return to their native homelands, but the motivation to preserve cultural identity and inculcate it into the younger generations is a strong current within the communities, which is represented by the way they use their buildings.

There is diversity within the immigrant church model. For example, Holy Virgin Cathedral adheres to a rubric of liturgical maximalism, whereas St. Katherine observes a less rigorous schedule of liturgical celebrations. Holy Virgin Cathedral has two schools designed to emphasize the retention of cultural and religious identity, whereas St. Katherine has a splendid museum and rents out its facilities to the general public for financial support. Perhaps the most noteworthy common characteristic of both parishes is their resilience in retaining and cultivating the memory of their communities. In both cases, the edifices themselves communicate the people's will to proclaim their victory over the religious oppression of the Soviet Union and its attempt to eradicate the Orthodox Church. St. Katherine and Holy Virgin Cathedral have architectural features that refer to the memory of a recent violent past, as defined by Amy Papalexandrou. At Holy Virgin Cathedral, this memory is cultivated most strikingly by the presence of St. John Maximovich and the community's heritage of honoring Tsar Nicholas II and his family as martyr-saints. For St. Katherine, this memory is communicated by the eclectic interior iconography and the artifacts on display in the museum of the cultural center.

Several churches in this study have deliberately retained the theological typology epitomized by Maximus the Confessor I presented in chapter 1. The presence of domes featuring Christ or the Ancient of Days, apses featuring Mary Theotokos (Platytera) and the Mystical Supper, and arrangements of the communion of saints refer implicitly to Maximus's typology. Despite the continuation of this tradition in its diverse forms in America, this study has demonstrated that the interpretation of these arrangements is not univocal. The eclectic approach to iconography in American Orthodox architecture is increasingly becoming the domain of trained lay amateurs, and the lack of consistency in the arrangements and their meanings in the specific contexts of the parishes in this study renders the future of this typology uncertain.

The churches in this model have a quality we might describe as theological: the symbols adorning the edifices and inscribed on them communicate the people's memory and a rich repository of émigré history. One of the most significant takeaways from the immigrant model, then, is that such churches have the potential to be sources for the study of Orthodox émigré history, and they are also communities to which one might turn in search of models of contemporary sanctity. Ultimately, the community's tireless efforts to adorn and inscribe its liturgical and non-liturgical spaces with its own history is a gift of thanksgiving offered to God, who liberated the people from captivity to the Bolshevik yoke and provided them with refuge in a new land.

As for the future of the immigrant model, one might suspect that it will become passé as the ethnic roots of Orthodox America wither away and the Church becomes increasingly populated by converts. Recent history shows that the passing of the immigrant model will be slow, if it occurs at all, as new waves of immigrants, particularly from the republics of the former Soviet Union, continue to find refuge in Orthodox parishes in America. As long as people belonging to specific ethnic groups cohesively gather to worship in community, they will influence Orthodox American architecture by constructing edifices that communicate their identity and resemble some variant of the structures they remember from their native lands. In this vein, architecture will evolve only inasmuch as it has developed in the countries of origin.

THE LITURGICAL RENEWAL MODEL

This model prioritizes the theological rationale and implementation of liturgical renewal. In this study, the model that best exemplifies liturgical renewal is the Church of the Holy Wisdom at New Skete Monastery. As the community embarked upon developing and cultivating a new liturgical office and ordo corresponding to its reality as a working monastery, it also designed a new temple that was appropriate for the daily patterns of monastic life. New Skete exemplifies the form following function axiom I have explored throughout this study. The monastery's consultations with Juan Mateos and examination of the scholarship of Thomas Mathews, Miguel Arranz, and Robert Taft resulted in an adaptation of an earlier cathedral model of worship. The twentieth-century liturgical movement and reforms of Vatican II inspired the community's freedom to search for an ordo suitable for its life, and the liturgical offices shaped the architectural form. For New Skete, the freedom to choose its own office was essential to its survival as a working community, an instance of local liturgical governance parishes do not enjoy.

New Skete presents a potential model for contemporary liturgical renewal and innovation in architectural design for contemporary Orthodoxy in America. The monastery's adaptation of an extinct cathedral office reinvigorates the functions of ministries, strengthens the universal call to holiness extended to men and women, and broadens the ecclesial perspective by promoting ecumenical hope. In a certain sense, the monastery's decision to adopt a cathedral model for worship is paradoxical, and within this irony lies the power for New Skete to become modular since monasteries have traditionally established liturgical models in the Orthodox Church. A close examination of New Skete's liturgy discloses an energetic capacity for ecclesial renewal through the liturgy. But the appeal of New Skete's liturgy/architecture model begs the question: why has New Skete's influence on liturgy in American Orthodoxy been limited? I reflected on this in chapter 6 and add the following here: the monastery's remote location reduces its ability to create an orbit of influence in American Orthodoxy. When one combines this fact with the vibrant perception of liturgy as unchangeable and canonically finalized that prevails among American Orthodox, one can see why New Skete has not been more influential. The possibility for New Skete's influence to increase in the future remains open, especially if clerical leaders reconsider twentieth-century models of ecclesial renewal and perceptions begin to shift among Orthodox.

Three Hierarchs Chapel at St. Vladimir's Seminary has exercised some influence in American Orthodox architectural styles. As an academic institution serving numerous Orthodox jurisdictions in America, St. Vladimir's created an orbit of influence that had an impact on the Church in America from coast to coast. In chapter 6, I noted that both liturgical renewal and an anticipation of parish life in America are inscribed on the architectural style of Three Hierarchs Chapel. Liturgical renewal at St. Vladimir's was and remains an exercise in discovering and emphasizing aspects of the liturgy within the received tradition that illuminate the laity as a priestly order of the Church. Alexander Schmemann's Eucharistic renewal was the primary way of promoting this initiative, and the architectural style facilitating the merging of clergy and laity at worship within a large nave and providing the people with substantial visual access to the sanctuary was an instance of form following function. Several parishes adopted variants of Vinogradov's Three Hierarchs Chapel, demonstrating a limited diffusion of liturgical and ecclesial renewal within American Orthodoxy. Unlike New Skete, Three Hierarchs Chapel is quite accessible given its proximity to New York City and the stature of St. Vladimir's Seminary as the host of diverse ecclesial and academic gatherings throughout a given year. Three Hierarchs Chapel is thus a solid candidate to serve as a model for American Orthodox architecture for several reasons: it has already been adopted as a model by select parish communities; it promotes liturgical and ecclesial renewal within the received liturgical tradition; the building style is efficient and suitable for contemporary Orthodox demographic trends in America, in which parish size is relatively small; and it promotes a strong sense of fidelity to local and universal tradition—local tradition carries on the precepts of renewal cultivated at St. Vladimir's and universal tradition continues the basic contour of liturgical celebration familiar to Orthodox throughout the world. Fidelity to liturgical tradition and a local architectural style provide enough security for churches to abandon clichés imported from mother countries and build structures that fit the development of a local style.

THE AMERICAN CHURCH MODEL

I have listed five parishes in this emerging model. Essentially, the parishes belonging to this model have constructed edifices that communicate their identity in the particular American context. The American particularity has a complex relationship with Orthodox heritage here, occasionally contradicting it. The best example of the American model is Annunciation Greek Orthodox Church. While the influence of Hagia Sophia is obvious in the building's dome shape, the history of the community and the theater-style interior manifest the adoption of American architectural and ecclesial motifs. As a parish of the Greek archdiocese, Annunciation will always sustain its mission of cultural sustenance in the parish hall, but the construction of a church in the

suburbs by a celebrated American architect is an announcement of ecclesial permanence in America. Most of the attention has focused on
the way the dome resembles a spaceship, but Annunciation's interior is
of greater significance since the liturgical arrangement literally adopts a
predominant motif of American Protestant worship. There is some effort to preserve ethnic identity, but the parish also exercised its freedom to communicate its emerging identity as a distinctly American
community by cutting some ties with its ethnic heritage. I also noted
the participation of laity in the building process at Annunciation and
the gradual development of lay ministry early in the parish's history.
The central feature of Annunciation is the parish's willingness to engage architectural innovation and embrace a new style that conformed
to a type of common core on the American religious scene while retaining enough features of the past to claim a certain degree of fidelity
to tradition.

Another good example of the American Church model is St. Matthew Orthodox Church, which also falls under the liturgical renewal
model. The primary impetus motivating St. Matthew parish was the
desire to build an English-speaking parish that would evangelize the
people who lived in the surrounding community. Furthermore, St. Matthew would distinguish itself from other Orthodox parishes in the area
by eschewing ethnic connections and promoting a strong sense of lay
participation. Elements of liturgical renewal promoted by St. Vladimir's and New Skete are evident in St. Matthew's building: the octagonal motif of the ceiling promotes the church as living in the new time
of the Holy Spirit inaugurated by Pascha and completed in Pentecost,
which is communicated by the iconography at Three Hierarchs Chapel.
The limited iconostasis promoting substantial visual access to the laity
coheres with the themes of both Three Hierarchs Chapel and New
Skete's Church of the Holy Wisdom. St. Matthew's collaborative iconographic program undertaken by the laity reveals a third layer of mission
driving architecture. While the modern movement for lay participation in the liturgy originated in Europe, it found fertile soil in North
America, and it is no accident that the laity as a priestly order has become an architectural feature in Orthodox parishes in America. Annunciation, St. Matthew, St. Vladimir's, and New Skete seem to have

accepted that the emphasis on lay participation would become a permanent fixture on the American Christian landscape. Our examination of Annunciation's church's design, with reference to Jeanne Kilde's studies on paradigm shifts in American religious architecture attributed to a new emphasis on the laity, contributes another dimension to a salient lay-oriented ecclesiology manifested by Orthodox architecture. Our examination of the diverse parishes shows that the architectural features in American Orthodoxy were influenced by the ressourcement theology that restored the priesthood of the laity, but also conveniently and comfortably cohered with the American Christian environment. We conclude that the decision to modify traditional architectural structures to promote lay participation was grounded by an examination of tradition and its acceptance in America.

Joy of All Who Sorrow Orthodox Church (JOY) mission fits this paradigm as well as a mission parish that rents property. Its mission status is naturally suitable for American Orthodoxy since America is not indigenously Orthodox and people plant communities in places where Orthodoxy does not have strong roots. As a mission in an expensive and exceedingly large urban center, JOY shares the mission of being an English-speaking community in West Los Angeles, which distinguishes it from other communities in the general area that have strong ethnic affiliations. This community attempts to adhere to Orthodox tradition as another distinguishing mark that is no less American: the inscription of relics and icons from diverse locations of the Orthodox world on the parish's identity illustrates the community's grounding in universal Orthodoxy. It is unlike other parishes in the region that adhere to churches that have centers in traditionally Orthodox countries. In this vein, JOY refers to the one church marker that unites most Orthodox in the world: the relative uniformity of the Byzantine rite. The community's decision to follow a maximalist liturgical program communicates its self-identity as a church that is able to fulfill the rigorous requirements of the Typikon despite its financial and demographic challenges. JOY is one mission, and no two are alike—its goal is to establish a pattern of frequent liturgical assembly that will draw urban inhabitants into a community that fulfills the Pauline mandate of "praying without ceasing" (1 Thess. 5:17).

CONCLUSION

These three models illustrate diverse patterns that manifest American Orthodox architecture as multivalent. While there is some intersection among the models, particularly between the liturgical renewal and American Church ones, there is no single, dominant architectural pattern shaping the landscape for the foreseeable future. We have examples of churches that adhere to the form-follows-function pattern, but this study has shown that liturgy's influence on architecture has decreased in the American sphere for two reasons: first, a perception of the liturgy as unchangeable or not requiring change generally prevails among the parish faithful; and second, most liturgical renewal has employed fine-tuning within the received tradition as opposed to reconstructing new ordos, New Skete being the lone exception. We have also witnessed parishes designing edifices that promote ethnic identity and memory, as well as theological mission, resulting in slight modifications. In this vein, none of the buildings can be described as a cliché, even if parishes like St. Katherine and Holy Virgin Cathedral patterned their buildings after native models.

The parishes that followed a pattern shaping their new structures introduced innovative changes to the designs, some voluntarily and others by necessity. These changes are actually ongoing and in motion: when pastoral leadership changes or the previous generation of parishioners begins to disappear, the use of all buildings on a property or modest additions to a structure create tangible changes both reflecting and impacting people's experiences in the buildings. The actual impact could be much more substantial than the change: a priest whose vision inspires the architecture will eventually be replaced by someone whose vision of Church differs. For example, the original minimalist approach to iconography in Three Hierarchs Chapel was modified to add icons and expand the sanctuary to adjust to new realities in the midst of community life. The result of architectural and aesthetical development is profound: even if the basic structure remains the same, descriptions and perceptions of experiences in that structure can evolve significantly as the surrounding community changes in motion. This means that not everyone will receive the intended message communicated through the original architectural structure, especially if the symbiosis of ritual and liturgy within that structure evolves through time.

But it is quite normal for such evolution to occur over time. The final question I pose in this study is, what are the implications of this examination for the future of Orthodox architecture in America? The seven communities I profiled here share some commonalities but are also separated by sharp ethnic and theological differences. The diversity is caused by the current plurality of identity within Orthodoxy in America, which falls under ethnic and theological categories. Orthodox architecture is inseparable from the textures of ecclesial identity and memory. I do not foresee an emerging unity that will transcend this plurality, which leads me to predict that architectural forms will experience minor modifications within the three broad models I have defined here. In fact, I think it is entirely likely that plurality in Orthodox identity will increase, which will lead to expanded architectural diversity.

One of the most important patterns noted here is the tendency for Orthodoxy to adopt—sometimes unwittingly—patterns prevalent in American Christian identity. The pattern in the American liturgical scene that will exercise the most influence on Orthodox architectural structures is liturgical plurality. For Orthodox parishes, the common practice of fine-tuning the liturgy within the received tradition will accommodate liturgical plurality without necessitating architectural innovation. The liturgy has become detached from architecture in several of the churches examined in this study: I expect that liturgy's capacity to form architecture will decrease in Orthodox America, with the exception of those parishes that embrace liturgical renewal. The emergence of different kinds of communities communicating particular ecclesiologies, such as the megachurch, will appear on the Orthodox landscape—look for churches to adopt these ecclesiologies from the American Christian landscape and dress them in Orthodox clothing, especially architecture.

Economic challenges and the new demands for energy-efficient buildings will also impact Orthodox architecture. Some churches will consist of modest edifices that are decorated on the interior to distinguish them from mainstream Christianity. Other Orthodox communities will happily blend into the American landscape by purchasing property previously belonging to other churches. One should not be surprised at the appearance of Orthodox communities worshiping in rented theaters or funeral homes, like emergent churches. My review of mission communities in chapter 7 elucidates the emergence of semi-permanent missions, small communities that are unable to achieve parish status but are too advanced to close. The future trajectory of demographic patterns has the capacity to significantly impact American Orthodox architecture. The prevailing architectural models assume a certain level of permanence in community constituencies. But the challenges of the global and local economies will continue to demand mobility among workers, and all parish communities will become increasingly subject to member turnover and attrition. The potential absence of internal community stability might necessitate the construction of buildings with maximal cost-efficiency. The volatility of the real estate market will also prevent some communities from raising sufficient funds to erect and sustain permanent buildings. The existence of semi-permanent missions that do not own their own property, like JOY in Culver City, will add a new and unique dimension to the symbiosis of architecture, liturgy, ecclesial identity, and community memory. One potential positive development from this situation could be an increase in communities celebrating liturgy in the public square. The tradition of blessing the Theophany waters at the Pacific Ocean at JOY and the inconsistent but meaningful public liturgies at St. Matthew and Three Hierarchs Chapel demonstrate the historical resilience of the city coming into the church, only to return to the city. In the future, perhaps Orthodox parishes in America might liturgize in the public square more frequently and not only enter the city, but witness to their confession of faith in its midst.

One final possibility remains, as an alternative to the models studied here: perhaps Orthodox in America will be willing to cross intra-Orthodox ecclesiological, ethnic, and theological boundaries to share resources and collaborate on new models for architecture that anyone could consider home. The first step to walking a common architectural path is for the people to unite and share their resources at all levels of Church life: parochial, diocesan, and regional. If this happens, then it is possible that new branches of an architectural school rooted in tradition and embracing the present and the future might create innovative models demonstrating Orthodoxy as having truly arrived in America. The phenomenon of plurality defining contemporary Orthodoxy in America promotes a sense of local independence that decreases the urgency for the creation of a dialogue on architecture that would include all Orthodox communities. For now, the reader can take refuge in the fact that the current architectural models disclose an incredible ethnic and theological diversity that illustrates the history of Orthodox parishes in America as being in motion.

The local innovation resulting in a mosaic of American Orthodox architecture is also a cause for thanksgiving. One of the remarkable results of this investigation is the innovation one discovers in the architectural environment in each community. There are obvious examples of copying—St. Katherine, Holy Virgin Cathedral, and Annunciation come to mind—but the process of copying is not banal mimesis. In each case, the local community designs its structures so they are not exact copies of their antecedents, but modifications suitable for the living community in the American environment.

Some of our examples yield ironic imperfections: St. Katherine's brilliant exterior overshadows the modest interior; Holy Virgin Cathedral's interior spatial dimensions are disproportionate; and Annunciation's luminous dome has resulted in the need for frequent structural repair. Each community has adjusted to these imperfections in startlingly meaningful gestures: St. Katherine adorned the walls with embroidered icons that narrate the parish's history and represent the ideal of a united Ukraine. Holy Virgin Cathedral has broadened its outreach to innumerable pilgrims who visit the shrine of St. John Maximovich. Annunciation has updated the interior iconography. St. Matthew parish built the church long after it had established St. Matthew House, while St. Vladimir's Seminary and New Skete Monastery constructed new edifices conforming to their respective visions of liturgical and ecclesial renewal. These are modest examples of communities whose lives are not static but in motion, local assemblies that make adjustments on varying scales to minister to their people and those who come to visit them.

The initial acts of building a structure for worship and other edifices for community assembly, followed by ongoing acts of modification and adjustment, are examples of grassroots theology. The building of a church and the subsequent gathering of the assembly is what David Fagerberg terms *theologia prima*, first-level theology where the whole point of having a church building is to encounter God for the privilege of petitioning, thanking, and praising him.[1] Here, I extend the act of theology as going beyond the wonder of erecting a new church building. One might dismiss the significance of the church hall as relegated to the realm of the non-liturgical, but the facilities we have examined in this study convey the wholeness of the community's vitality: the same people of God who gather for the liturgy also come together for various events in the hall. Museums, classrooms, facilities for men and women who cannot care for themselves, halls and cultural centers, and administrative buildings are, in reality, an extension of the church temple. The assemblies that occur in these buildings testify to the wholeness of people's lives.

Members of the community attend liturgy to pray and offer worship, but the fellowship, instruction, and banal business that occurs in the secondary and tertiary buildings on a given property are also theological because they symbolize the vitality of the people of God outside the liturgy.[2] This study has demonstrated that contemporary Orthodox communities have diverse identities that include, but are not limited to, the liturgy. The existence of other buildings on a property has allowed people who would have had no opportunity to come in contact with an Orthodox community the chance to meet them. Secondary and tertiary buildings on property owned by an Orthodox community provide a safe space for ecumenical encounter, even if it is limited to hosting a wedding or a graduation ceremony. They also offer a medium for the diverse dimensions of life within a community. In this vein, they are ideally sacred spaces that derive their central meaning from the Church while providing the local community with the freedom to fully express its identity and the means to sustain itself. Ultimately, all the buildings on a given property exist as living gestures of thanks to God for the privilege of gathering in his name, a source of joy, thanksgiving, hope, and new possibilities for Orthodoxy in America.

Introduction

1. Thomas Mathews, *The Early Churches of Constantinople: Architecture and Liturgy* (University Park: University of Pennsylvania Press, 1971); Cyril Mango, *Byzantine Architecture* (New York: Harry N. Abrams, Inc., 1976); Vasileios Marinis, *Architecture and Ritual in the Churches of Constantinople: Ninth to Fifteenth Centuries* (Cambridge: Cambridge University Press, 2014); Nicholas Patricios, *The Sacred Architecture of Byzantium: Art, Liturgy, and Symbolism in Early Christian Churches* (London: I. B. Tauris, 2014).

2. See Egeria, *Journal de Voyage (Itinéraire)*, ed. and trans. Pierre Maraval, Sources Chrétiennes 296 (Paris: Cerf, 1982).

3. For the Armenian lectionary, see Athanase Renoux, ed., *Le Codex Arménien Jérusalem* 121. I. *Introduction aux origines de la liturgie hiérosolymitaine: Lumières nouvelles*, Patrologia Orientalis 35.1 (Turnhout: Brepols, 1969), and *Le Codex Arménien Jérusalem* 121. II. *Édition Comparée du texte et de deux autres manuscrits*, introduction, textes, traduction et notes par A. Renoux, Patrologia Orientalis 36.2 (Turnhout: Brepols, 1971); for the Georgian lectionary, see Michael Tarchnischvili, ed., *Le grand lectionnaire de l'Église de Jérusalem Ve–VIIIe siècle*, Corpus scriptorum Christianorum Orientalium 189 (Louvain: Secrétariat du Corpus SCO, 1959).

4. John Baldovin, *The Urban Character of Christian Worship: The Origins, Development, and Meaning of Stational Liturgy*, Orientalia Christiana Analecta 228 (Rome: Pontifical Oriental Institute, 1987).

5. Robert F. Taft, *The Byzantine Rite: A Short History* (Collegeville, MN: Liturgical Press, 1992); idem, "The Liturgy of the Great Church: An Initial Synthesis of Structure and Interpretation on the Eve of Iconoclasm," *Dumbarton Oaks Papers* 34–35 (1980–81): 45–75. See also Mango, *Byzantine Architecture*; Mathews, *The Early Churches of Constantinople*.

6. Hans-Joachim Schulz, *The Byzantine Liturgy: Symbolic Structure and Faith Expression*, trans. Matthew J. O'Connell (New York: Pueblo, 1986).

7 . See Robert F. Taft, "Mount Athos: A Late Chapter in the History of the Byzantine Rite," *Dumbarton Oaks Papers* (1988): 179–94.

8. Patricios, *The Sacred Architecture of Byzantium*, 88–244.

CHAPTER ONE   Orthodox Architecture

1. Denis McNamara's informative overview of ecclesial architecture, *How to Read Churches: A Crash Course in Ecclesiastical Architecture* (New York: Rizzoli International Publications, 2011; originally published in Lewes by Ivy Press, 2011), contains many examples of ancient and contemporary Byzantine architecture.

2. Robert F. Taft, *The Liturgy of the Hours in East and West: The Origins of the Divine Office and Its Meaning for Today*, 2nd rev. ed. (Collegeville, MN: Liturgical Press, 1993), 273.

3. Rowland Mainstone, *Hagia Sophia: Architecture, Structure and Liturgy of Justinian's Great Church* (London: Thames and Hudson, 1988); Mathews, *The Early Churches of Constantinople*.

4. Juan Mateos, ed., *Le Typicon de la grande église*, vol. 1, *Le cycle des douze mois*, Orientalia Christiana Analecta 165 (Rome: Pontifical Oriental Institute, 1962); idem, *Le Typicon de la grande église*, vol. 2, *Le cycle des fêtes mobiles*, Orientalia Christiana Analecta 166 (Rome: Pontifical Oriental Institute, 1963); Baldovin, *The Urban Character of Christian Worship*.

5. Mango, *Byzantine Architecture*.

6. Patricios, *The Sacred Architecture of Byzantium*.

7. Marinis, *Architecture and Ritual*.

8. Allan Doig, *Liturgy and Architecture: From the Early Church to the Middle Ages*, Liturgy, Worship and Society Series (Farnham, Surrey, UK: Ashgate, 2008), 68.

9. Ibid., 67.

10. Alexander Grishin, "Eastern Orthodox Iconography and Architecture," in *The Blackwell Companion to Eastern Christianity*, ed. Ken Parry (Malden, MA: Blackwell Publishing, 2007), 371.

11. See Mateos, ed., *Le Typicon de la grande église*, vols. 1 and 2; Mainstone, *Hagia Sophia*; Mathews, *The Early Churches of Constantinople*; Taft, *The Byzantine Rite*; idem, "The Liturgy of the Great Church"; Hugh Wybrew, *The Orthodox Liturgy: The Development of the Eucharistic Liturgy in the Byzantine Rite* (Crestwood, NY: St. Vladimir's Seminary Press, 1990).

12. Robert F. Taft, *A History of the Liturgy of St. John Chrysostom*, vol. 2, *The Great Entrance: A History of the Transfer of Gifts and Other Pre-anaphoral Rites,*

2nd ed., Orientalia Christiana Analecta 200 (Rome: Pontifical Oriental Institute, 1978).

13. Robert F. Taft, William Loerke, and Mark J. Johnson, "Pastophoria," in *The Oxford Dictionary of Byzantium*, ed. Alexander P. Kazhdan (Oxford: Oxford University Press, 1991).

14. For a brief and suitably summarized description of the Great Entrance in Hagia Sophia, see Doig, *Liturgy and Architecture*, 75–76.

15. Richard Krautheimer, *Early Christian and Byzantine Architecture*, 4th ed., rev. Richard Krautheimer and Slobodan Ćurčić (New Haven, CT: Yale University Press, 1986), 206, quoted in Doig, *Liturgy and Architecture*, 68.

16. Quoted in Kallistos Ware, *The Orthodox Church* (London: Penguin, 1963, 1964, 1993 reprint), 264.

17. René Bornert, *Les commentaires byzantins de la Divine Liturgie du VIIe au XVe siècle*, Archives de l'Orient chrétien (Paris: Institut Francais d'études byzantines, 1966), 83–124.

18. *Maximus Confessor, Selected Writings*, trans. George C. Berthold, intro. Jaroslav Pelikan, pref. Irenee-Henri Dalmais (Mahwah, NJ: Paulist Press, 1985), 1–11.

19. For a complete overview of recent debates on the liturgy Maximus knew, see Robert F. Taft, "Is the Liturgy Described in the Mystagogia of Maximus Confessor Byzantine, Palestinian, or Neither?" *Bollettino della badia Greca di Grottaferrata* 7 (2010): 247–95.

20. Bornert, *Les commentaires byzantins*, 123–24.

21. Schulz, *The Byzantine Liturgy*, 58–62.

22. "Having once resided in flesh, the Word consents, by the operation of the Spirit, to reside in temples built by hand, assuring his presence by mystical rites"; anonymous kontakion, quoted in Kathleen McVey, "Spirit Embodied: The Emergence of Symbolic Interpretations of Early Christian and Byzantine Architecture," in *Architecture as Icon: Perception and Representation of Architecture in Byzantine Art*, ed. Slobodan Ćurčić and Evangelia Hadjitryphonos (Princeton, NJ: Princeton University Art Museum, 2010), 56–57.

23. Amy Papalexandrou, "The Memory Culture of Byzantium," in *Companion to Byzantium*, ed. Liz James, Blackwell Companions to the Ancient World Series (Chichester, West Sussex, UK: Wiley-Blackwell, 2010), 113.

24. Ibid.

25. Schulz, *The Byzantine Liturgy*, 58–59.

26. Doig, *Liturgy and Architecture*, 74.

27. Baldovin, *The Urban Character of Christian Worship*, 45–49.

28. Ibid., 48. John Wilkinson, *Egeria's Travels* (Warminster: Aris & Phillips, 1999); Jan Villem Drijvers, *Cyril of Jerusalem: Bishop and City*, Supplements to Vigiliae Christianae (Leiden: Brill, 2004).

29. Baldovin, *The Urban Character of Christian Worship*, 49–54.

30. Ibid., 102–4, and Robert F. Taft, "Historicism Revisited," in *Beyond East and West: Problems in Liturgical Understanding* (Washington, DC: Pastoral Press, 1997), 15–30.

31. Cyril of Jerusalem, *Catéchèses mystagogiques*, ed. and trans. Auguste Piédagnel, Sources Chrétiennes 126 (Paris: Cerf, 1966). See also the English translation *The Works of Cyril of Jerusalem*, trans. Leo P. McCauley and Anthony A. Stevenson (Washington, DC: Catholic University of America Press, 1969–70). For a comprehensive analysis of the authenticity and interpretation of Cyril's mystagogical catecheses, see Donna Hawk-Reinhard, "From Χριστιανοί to Χριστοφόροι: The Role of the Eucharist in Christian Identity Formation according to Cyril of Jerusalem" (PhD diss., St. Louis University, 2011). For an analysis of Cyril's catechetical program, see Nicholas Russo, "The Distribution of Cyril's Baptismal Catecheses and the Shape of the Catechumenate in Mid-Fourth-Century Jerusalem," in *A Living Tradition: On the Intersection of Liturgical History and Pastoral Practice, Essays in Honor of Maxwell E. Johnson*, ed. David Pitt, Stefanos Alexopoulos, and Christian McConnell (Collegeville, MN: Liturgical Press, 2012), 75–102.

32. Baldovin, *The Urban Character of Christian Worship*, 180.

33. Taft, *The Byzantine Rite*, 29–32.

34. Cyril Mango, Alexander Kazhdan, and Anthony Cutler, "Hippodromes," in *The Oxford Dictionary of Byzantium*, ed. Alexander P. Kazhdan (Oxford: Oxford University Press, 1991).

35. Baldovin, *The Urban Character of Christian Worship*, 176.

36. Ibid., 168 and passim.

37. Baldovin traces the origin of the ektene to rogational and supplicatory offices celebrated in Constantinople's liturgy (ibid., 220–25).

38. Helen G. Saradi, "Space in Byzantine Thought," in *Architecture as Icon: Perception and Representation of Architecture in Byzantine Art*, ed. Slobodan Ćurčić and Evangelia Hadjitryphonos (Princeton, NJ: Princeton University Art Museum, 2010), 74–75.

39. Averil Cameron, "The Theotokos in Sixth-Century Constantinople," *Journal of Theological Studies* 24 (1978): 79–108. See also Nicholas Denysenko, "The Soteriological Significance of the Feast of Mary's Birth," *Theological Studies* 68 (2007): 739–60.

40. Saradi, "Space in Byzantine Thought," 83–84.

41. Grishin, "Eastern Orthodox Iconography and Architecture," 373.

42. For a description of the tripartite sanctuary, see Marinis, *Architecture and Ritual*, 30–41. See also Patricios, *The Sacred Architecture of Byzantium*, 383.

43. Grishin, "Eastern Orthodox Iconography and Architecture," 374, and Patricios, *The Sacred Architecture of Byzantium*, 250–63.

44. Schulz, *The Byzantine Liturgy*, 50–59. See also Mango, *Byzantine Architecture*, 196–97.

45. Schulz, *The Byzantine Liturgy*, 59.

46. "The next place of honor in the church is the apse. As terminus of the sanctuary, but closer to the dome than the nave, it calls for an image that stands in special relation to the concrete accomplishment of our redemption here on earth. . . . The incarnation in Mary's maternal womb is represented in the apse, and it is here that the event of redemption, which I rendered liturgically present on the nearby altar, has its start" (Schulz, *The Byzantine Liturgy*, 59). For further explanation of the significance of Mary in the apse, also known as "Platytera ton ouranon," or "she who is wider than the heavens," see Patricios, *The Sacred Architecture of Byzantium*, 257.

47. "Instead of the open marble screen that afforded a view of the apse, a solid wall of icons now stood between the worshipper and the mystery of the Christian service, barely revealing the figure of the Virgin Mary in the semi-dome of the apse. The interior space was thus entirely overrun and obscured by painting" (Mango, *Byzantine Architecture*, 295).

48. Marinis, *Architecture and Ritual*, 43.

49. "Portable icons eventually occupied the templon and the intercolumniations. When this happened has been a matter of debate, with suggestions ranging anywhere from the eleventh century to the post-Byzantine period. The disjointed and at times contradictory nature of the evidence, both textual and material, indicates that the transformation of the templon into the iconostasis was gradual, localized, and became the norm at different times in different places" (Marinis, *Architecture and Ritual*, 45).

50. Schulz, *The Byzantine Liturgy*, 58–59.

51. "In short, the monastery was a miniature, self-enclosed city. In most cases, the monastic complex has disappeared, leaving only the church" (Mango, *Byzantine Architecture*, 198).

52. Schulz, *The Byzantine Liturgy*, 203.

53. Grishin, "Eastern Orthodox Iconography and Architecture," 375.

54. Taft, "The Liturgy in the Mystagogia of Maximus," 292.

55. "Byzantium gave to Russia basically one, all-purpose form of church, namely, the cross-in-square, which could be used in a number of variants. At

its simplest, it had three isles, four piers, and one dome; by fusing the nave with the narthex, a more oblong, six-pier plan could be obtained; or else the core of the church could be surrounded on three sides by an ambulatory, thus producing the effect of a five-aisled church" (Mango, *Byzantine Architecture*, 328–29).

56. Marinis, *Architecture and Ritual*, 115.

57. See, for example, Marinis's reference to a twelfth-century cruciform naos in Chora that replaced an eleventh-century cross-in-square on account of concerns about structural stability (ibid., 115).

58. Grishin, "Eastern Orthodox Iconography and Architecture," 374.

59. "Every single characteristic of the original Constantinopolitan church arrangement changed after Iconoclasm. The most notable among them were the large, single-apse basilical style, with large atrium, narthex, and multiple, monumental entrances on all sides, including the outside entrances to the galleries that surrounded the nave on all but the east or sanctuary side. Inside there was extraordinary openness of design, with no internal divisions, no side-apses, pastophoria, or auxiliary chambers anywhere on the ground floor. . . . The often miniscule post-iconoclastic church turned inward: without atrium or monumental entrances; the altar retreating within the new, triple-apsed, enclosed sanctuary; small enough to be frescoed over every inch of its interior surface; too small to hold galleries, monumental ambo, solea, elevated synthronon; no longer needing a skeuophylakion since gifts are now prepared in a new prothesis or side-apse to the northeast side" (Taft, *The Byzantine Rite*, 61; see also Mango, *Byzantine Architecture*, 249).

60. Taft, *The Byzantine Rite*, 56–60, 78–83.

61. Marinis, *Architecture and Ritual*, 2.

62. This is the practice of most Orthodox Slavs; in many Greek and Antiochian parishes, the Great Entrance is performed around the back of the nave and to the altar via the central aisle.

63. I employ "narthex, nave, sanctuary" throughout this study; note that my description is essentially identical to Marinis's trio of "bema, naos, narthex" in ibid., 114.

64. Andriy Chirovsky, "Towards a Byzantine Liturgical Architecture," *Diakonia* 18 (1983): 203–37.

65. Ibid., 222–23.

66. Ibid.

67. Ibid., 224.

68. "In the earthly liturgy we take part in a foretaste of that heavenly liturgy which is celebrated in the holy city of Jerusalem toward which we journey as pilgrims, where Christ is sitting at the right hand of God, a minister of

the holies and of the true tabernacle; we sing a hymn to the Lord's glory with all the warriors of the heavenly army; venerating the memory of the saints, we hope for some part and fellowship with them; we eagerly await the Saviour, Our Lord Jesus Christ, until He, our life, shall appear and we too will appear with Him in glory." *Sacrosanctum Concilium*, no. 8, http://www.vatican.va/archive /hist_councils/ii_vatican_council/documents/vat-ii_const_19631204_sacro sanctum-concilium_en.html (accessed June 23, 2011).

69. Chirovsky, "Towards a Byzantine Liturgical Architecture," 223.

70. Ibid., 204–5. The bishops updated their teaching on liturgy and architecture with *Built of Living Stones* in 2000. See USCCB, "What Is the Authority of Environment and Art in Catholic Worship?" http://www.usccb.org/liturgy /q&a/environment/environment.shtml (accessed June 3, 2011).

71. USCCB, "Built of Living Stones," http://www.usccb.org/liturgy /livingstonesind.shtml (accessed June 3, 2011).

72. R. Kevin Seasoltz, *Sense of the Sacred: Theological Foundations of Christian Architecture and Art* (New York: Continuum, 2005).

73. Ibid., 345.

74. Ibid., 346.

75. Vincenzo Ruggieri, *Byzantine Religious Architecture (582–867): Its History and Structural Elements*, Orientalia Christiana Analecta 237 (Rome: Pontifical Oriental Institute, 1991).

76. Ibid., 2.

77. Ibid., 135–37.

78. Ibid., 141–68.

79. Jeanne Halgren Kilde, *Sacred Power, Sacred Space: An Introduction to Christian Architecture and Worship* (Oxford: Oxford University Press, 2008).

80. Ibid., 188–89.

81. After acknowledging that the reservation of the sanctuary in Orthodox churches defines clerical power, Kilde asserts that "a significant corporate social power also resides in the congregation that occupies the nave" (ibid., 60).

82. Mathews (*The Early Churches of Constantinople*, 89, 92, 190) and Mainstone (*Hagia Sophia*, 120–24) have identified two baptisteries in Hagia Sophia with some discussion of their function in liturgical celebration.

83. Marinis, *Architecture and Ritual*, 100–111.

84. Olexa Powstenko, *The Cathedral of St. Sophia in Kiev* (New York: The Ukrainian Academy of Arts and Sciences in the United States, 1954), 101–2.

85. Ibid., 23–24.

86. Ibid., 30.

87. Papalexandrou, "The Memory Culture of Byzantium," 113.

88. Sally Gallagher has recently offered an insightful and interdisciplinary presentation on the delicate interplay between sacred space, liturgy, and community identity in three Christian congregations, including one Orthodox parish in America, in "Building Traditions: Comparing Space, Ritual, and Community in Three Congregations," *Review of Religious Research* 47 (2005): 70–85. For a brief and accurate description of Orthodox immigrant parish life, see Thomas E. Fitzgerald, *The Orthodox Church*, Denominations in America 7 (Westport, CT: Greenwood Press, 1995), 76. For an excellent ethnographic study of converts in American Orthodoxy, see Amy Slagle, *The Eastern Church in the Spiritual Marketplace: American Conversions to Orthodox Christianity* (DeKalb: Northern Illinois University Press, 2011).

89. For powerful ethnographic testimonies on the tension between so-called cradles and converts, and ethnic issues in such parishes, see ibid., 124–42.

90. For a sophisticated analysis of the dynamics of émigré architecture and status in the American public sphere, see Joanne Punzo Waghorne, "Spaces for a New Public Presence: The Sri Sivu Vishnu and Murugan Temples in Metropolitan Washington, D.C.," in *American Sanctuary: Understanding Sacred Spaces*, ed. Louis Nelson (Bloomington: Indiana University Press, 2006), 103–27. Waghorne's analysis discloses the relationship between community identity and architecture in motion, as the community's demographic evolves. Her discussion shares important similarities with some examples of this study.

91. Chirovsky, "Towards a Byzantine Liturgical Architecture," 218.

92. For an overview, see Mark Stokoe and Leonid Kishkovsky, *Orthodox Christians in North America: 1794–1994* (n.p.: Orthodox Christian Publication Center, 1995), 99–115. See also a table indicating growth trends in Orthodox America compiled by researcher Alexei Krindatch, "Orthodox Churches in USA: Origins, Growth, Current Trends of Development," http://www.hartfordinstitute.org/research/tab2.pdf (accessed June 17, 2011). See also Anton Vrame, ed., *The Orthodox Parish in America: Faithfulness to the Past and Responsibility for the Future* (Brookline, MA: Holy Cross Orthodox Press, 2003). The Society for Orthodox Christian History in the Americas (SOCHA) maintains a list of quality online sources outlining the history of Orthodoxy in America, which intersects with Orthodoxy's older and contemporary models of mission. See SOCHA, http://orthodoxhistory.org/resources/ (accessed January 27, 2012).

93. Alexander Schmemann, *Introduction to Liturgical Theology*, trans. Asheleigh E. Moorhouse (Crestwood, NY: St. Vladimir's Seminary Press, 1986), 118–19.

94. "The same process began in the Church—only in the opposite direction—when large and more or less costly churches began to appear. Christian worship of the first and second centuries was perforce limited to simplicity and reduced to its most basic and necessary 'lines.' It was devoid of external pomp. A few indispensable actions and ceremonies had to 'express' all its inner movement, its liturgical dynamic. . . . But in the great, magnificent, and indeed solemn basilicas the complication and 'decoration' of worship was inevitable, if only because if it had been celebrated in the old way it simply would not have reached the eyes and ears of those assembled" (ibid., 119).

95. Richard Vosko, "The Language of Liturgical Space: Archetypes and Clichés," *Worship* 86 (2012): 55–59.

96. Ibid., 44–47.

97. Ibid., 58.

98. "During years of assimilation, Jews were apt to build shuls to mimic those in European countries or to replicate even churches and civic buildings in America. Today their concern is to construct places that resonate with their own identity and self esteem in the world today" (ibid., 58).

99. Ibid., 59. A subtext to Vosko's discussion is the current and increasing tension with Roman Catholic communities on ecclesiology, which has recently been played out in the revision of liturgical forms. For a lucid and sober discussion on the implications of antiquarianism in Catholic architecture, see Kevin Seasoltz, "Sacred Space, the Arts, and Theology: Some Light from History," *Worship* 82 (2008): 541–42.

100. See Vosko's report that "the American Institute of Architects (AIA) endeavors to design and construct buildings so they are carbon neutral by the year 2030" (Vosko, "The Language of Liturgical Space," 44). For more on the AIA initiative, see the American Institute of Architects, http://www.aia.org/about/initiatives/AIAB079544 (accessed January 27, 2012).

CHAPTER TWO   St. Katherine Ukrainian Orthodox Church

1. The most recent studies on the autocephalous Church in Ukraine are by Irina Prelovs'ka, esp. *Джерела з історії Української Автокефальної Православної Церкви (1921–1930)—Української Православної Церкви (1930–1939)* (Kyiv: Inst. Ukraïns'koï Archeohrafiï ta Džereloznavstva Im. M. S. Hruševs'koho NAN Ukraïny, 2013). The classical study of the autocephalous Church in Ukraine is by Bohdan Bociurkiw, "The Ukrainian Autocephalous Orthodox Church, 1920–1930: A Case Study in Religious Mod-

ernization," in *Religion and Modernization in the Soviet Union*, ed. Dennis J. Dunn (Boulder, CO: Westview Press, 1977), 310–47. See also Frank E. Sysyn, "The Ukrainian Autocephalous Orthodox Church and the Traditions of the Kyiv Metropolitanate," in *Religion and Nation in Modern Ukraine*, ed. Serhii Plokhy and Frank E. Sysyn (Edmonton: Canadian Institute of Ukrainian Studies, 2003), 23–39, esp. notes 6 and 7. For a recent assessment in Russian, see Metropolitan Feodosij (Protsiuk), *Обособленческие движения в Православной церкви на Украине, 1917–1943* (Moscow: Izdatelstvo Krutitskogo podvorja, 2004). See Dmitry Pospielovsky, *The Russian Church Under the Soviet Regime 1917–1982*, vol. 1 (Crestwood, NY: St. Vladimir's Seminary Press, 1984), 73–76, and also idem, *The Orthodox Church in the History of Russia* (Crestwood, NY: St. Vladimir's Seminary Press, 1998), 211–15. The history of the Ukrainian Autocephalous Orthodox Church is presented in great detail, including several reproductions of official documents, appeals, and letters from individual clergy, in Osyp Zinkewych and Olexander Voronyn, eds., *Мартирологія Українських Церков*, vol. 1 (Baltimore: Smoloskyp Publishers, 1987).

2. See, for example, Pospielovsky, *The Orthodox Church*, 363–71.

3. Українська Православна Церква, http://orthodox.org.ua/ (accessed June 7, 2011).

4. Українська Православна Церква Київський Патріархат, http://www.cerkva.info/ (accessed June 7, 2011).

5. Українська Автокефальна Православна Церква, http://www.uaoc.info/ua/ (accessed June 7, 2011).

6. For the background on the relations between these churches, see Nicholas Denysenko, "Chaos in Ukraine: The Churches and the Search for Leadership," *International Journal for the Study of the Christian Church* 14, no. 3 (2014): 242–59, and idem, "Fractured Orthodoxy in Ukraine and Politics: The Impact of Patriarch Kyrill's 'Russian World,'" *Logos: A Journal of Eastern Christian Studies* 54, nos. 1–2 (2013): 33–68.

7. The Ukrainian Orthodox Church of the USA, http://www.uocofusa.org/ (accessed June 7, 2011).

8. For a historical summary of the UOC/USA, see "An Outline History of the Metropolia Center of the Ukrainian Orthodox Church of the USA," http://www.uocofusa.org/history.html (accessed June 7, 2011). See also Ivan Korowycky, "The Ukrainian Orthodox Church in the United States," in *The Ukrainian Heritage in America*, ed. Walter Dushnyck and Nicholas Chirovsky (New York: Ukrainian Congress Committee of America, 1991), 84–92.

9. Quoted from Leah Cochenet, "St. Katherine's Parish Overcomes Obstacles, Now Open for Services," *Shoreview Press*, August 12, 1997, 15–16.

10. Taken from St. Katherine's monthly bulletin, *The Voice* 36, no. 1 (January–February 1997). The representative from St. George Church "compared Tanasichuk's contribution to the construction of the new church to that made by Hetman Ivan Mazeppa towards the restoration of the Gate Church of the Holy Trinity in Kyiv, Ukraine."

11. Ibid., quoting Tanasichuk.

12. See Nolan Zavoral, "Short on Cash but Long on Optimism, St. Katherine's Struggles to Open," *Minneapolis Star Tribune,* January 4, 1997, B5, B8.

13. Illustrated by a reaction from George Pasichnyk, president of the board at St. Michael parish at the time: "I don't support it because the church belongs to [working-class] people and not millionaires. It's [the donation] very kind of her, but I wish more people were doing it. Is she saying the church is hers or ours?" Quoted in ibid.

14. Clark Morphew, "Bills Keep Church's Doors Closed," *St. Paul Pioneer Press,* January 2, 1997, Metro Section, 1B, 6B.

15. Ibid.

16. "Minutes of the Board of Trustees of Sts. Volodymyr and Ol'ha Ukrainian Orthodox Church and Building Committee of St. Katherine Ukrainian Orthodox Church," October 30, 1996. I am grateful to Maya Gregoret for providing me with a copy of these minutes.

17. From St. Katherine parish archives, courtesy of Maya Gregoret. The loan was secured under the leadership of the parish's primary donor, Vera Tanasichuk, who was elected as president of the church board in 1997.

18. The parish's selection of "Katherine" was also in homage to the memory of Tanasichuk's and Maeser's mother, Katherine Zaslavetz. Cynthia Boyd, "Testament to Tenacious Faith," *St. Paul Pioneer Press,* December 24, 1995, 1B, 5B.

19. Via e-mail exchange with Maya Gregoret, February 8, 2012.

20. Cochenet, "St. Katherine's Parish Overcomes Obstacles," 16.

21. Gregoret, parish archives.

22. Orest Subtelny, *Ukraine: A History* (Toronto: University of Toronto Press, 1989), 195–98.

23. Ibid. See also Powstenko, *The Cathedral of St. Sophia*, 17; James Cracraft, *The Petrine Revolution in Russian Architecture* (Chicago: University of Chicago Press, 1988), 93–96; Ivan Wlasowksy, *Нарис Історії Української Православної Церкви,* vol. 2 (New York: Ukrainian Orthodox Church of the USA, 1956), 280–90.

24. Subtelny, *Ukraine,* 195–96.

25. Cracraft, *The Petrine Revolution,* 93. In his analysis, he largely follows the work of the early twentieth-century scholar Yuri Grabar.

26. Subtelny, *Ukraine,* 195–96.

27. Ibid.

28. UNESCO spearheaded several events marking the millennial anniversary of Kyiv Sophia in 2011. A comprehensive web site, *Національний Заповідник "Софія Київська,"* http://nzsk.org.ua/ukr/default.aspx (accessed January 23, 2012), offers dozens of news reports, articles, virtual tours, and other information promoting the jubilee anniversary of the cathedral, its property, and its significance in Ukrainian history.

29. Cracraft, *The Petrine Revolution*, 94.

30. Powstenko, *The Cathedral of St. Sophia*, 10–11.

31. Ibid., 12.

32. Pospielovsky, *The Orthodox Church*, 211–15, 282–83.

33. Powstenko, *The Cathedral of St. Sophia*, 12.

34. Ibid., 15–17. See also Wlasowsky, *Нарис Історії Української Православної Церкви*, 282.

35. Powstenko, *The Cathedral of St. Sophia*, 17. Additional major restoration occurred in the eighteenth century under the leadership of Metropolitan Raphael Zaborovsky.

36. Ibid., 31–33. Powstenko provides several drawings attempting to reconstruct Sophia's original architectural plan on pages 74–82.

37. "St. Sophia was meant to be the metropolitan church of Russia and was commissioned by the ambitious ruler of a rapidly developing state: consequently it had to be big. Herein lies the explanation of whatever peculiarities St. Sophia possesses. Not only was its Byzantine architect working in an alien milieu with materials that were either improvised or laboriously imported; he was also required to erect a building much bigger than any he had put up at home. The solution he adopted was to multiply rather than to enlarge forms that were familiar to him. He built a dome 25 ¼ feet in diameter . . . about as big as he could on the basis of his experience. Given this dimension, a three-aisled, five-domed church of what must have been normal Constantinopolitan type would not have attained the desired size. So he simply added two more aisles and an extra transverse compartment to the west. Having enlarged the width of the building, he had to heighten it in proportion . . . the form of St. Sophia could have been devised by a Byzantine architect on the basis of dimensions and concepts that were familiar to him, whether or not exactly the same solution had earlier been applied in the capital" (Mango, *Byzantine Architecture*, 327–28).

38. Powstenko, *The Cathedral of St. Sophia*, 17, 143–62. Powstenko presents the details of the nineteenth-century restoration on pages 47–54, with many plates illustrating the architectural plans and artistic renditions of the church building.

39. Ibid., 95–96.

40. Julian K. Jastremsky, "Ukrainian Architecture in America," in *The Ukrainian Heritage in America*, ed. Walter Dushnyck and Nicholas Chirovsky (New York: Ukrainian Congress Committee of America, 1991), 266–87.

41. Ibid., 272.

42. "The education of the young in the Ukrainian language, history, traditions and church precepts as well as providing facilities for church organizations, institutions and church-oriented activities became important factors to be considered, on a local and diocesan level" (ibid., 275).

43. I am grateful to Oleh Gregoret for providing several photos of his drawings for this project in an e-mail exchange on April 18, 2011. I am likewise grateful to Maya Gregoret for sending me several descriptive documents currently being prepared for publication in a special book commemorating the sixtieth anniversary of St. Katherine parish via several e-mail exchanges in 2011–12.

44. Via e-mail exchange with Maya Gregoret, June 16, 2011.

45. A slideshow of the parish celebration, including several photos of the new iconostasis and the church interior, is available at http://www.uocofusa .org/public/sv/gallery.php?ssid=50 (accessed June 9, 2011).

46. See Alan K. Lathrop, *Churches of Minnesota: An Illustrated Guide* (Minneapolis: Regents of the University of Minnesota, 2003), 6–7.

47. See Powstenko, *The Cathedral of St. Sophia*, 95–96, 197.

48. The Typikon is the book that governs the order for celebration of the liturgical year. This description will apply globally to all of the Orthodox parishes covered in this study. For background and current practice among Orthodox, see Vassa Larin, "Feasting and Fasting According to the Byzantine Typikon," *Worship* 83 (2009): 133–48. For the Slavonic text, see Типікон (Moscow: Publishing Council of the Russian Orthodox Church, 2002).

49. *The Lenten Triodion*, trans. Mother Mary and Kallistos Ware (South Canaan, PA: St. Tikhon's Seminary Press, 2002). On the history of the Triodion, see Miguel Arranz, "Les grandes étapes de la liturgie byzantine: Palestine-Byzance-Russie. Essai d'aperçu historique," in *Liturgie de l'église particulière, liturgie de l'église universelle*, Bibliotheca *Ephemerides liturgicae*, subsidia 7 (Rome: Edizioni liturgiche, 1976), 43–72, and M. Momina, "О происхождении греческой Триоди," Палестинський Сборник 28 (1986): 112–20.

50. *The Pentecostarion*, trans. Holy Transfiguration Monastery (Boston: Holy Transfiguration Monastery, 1990); *The Festal Menaion*, trans. Mother Mary and Kallistos Ware (London: Faber and Faber, 1969).

51. For analysis of the frequency of liturgical celebration in American communities, see Nicholas Denysenko, "A Proposal for Renewing Liturgy in the Twenty-First Century," *Studia Liturgica* 40 (2010): 231–59.

52. See, in particular, the recent articles by Peter Galadza, "Schmemann Between Fagerberg and Reality: Towards an Agenda for Byzantine Christian Pastoral Liturgy," *Bolletino della Badia Greca di Grottaferrata* 4 (2007): 7–32, and Nicholas Denysenko, "Towards an Agenda for Byzantine Pastoral Liturgy: A Response to Peter Galadza," *Bolletino della Badia Greca di Grottaferrata* 7 (2010): 45–68.

53. By Philip Shayda, via Maya Gregoret, parish archives.

54. Maya Gregoret, *The Voice* 37, no. 2 (March–April 1997).

55. Via Maya Gregoret, parish archives. Gregoret notes that the parish procured three bids for the icon restoration, ultimately choosing Hordiiv.

56. Via e-mail communication with Wanda Bahmet, August 23, 2011, and Maya Gregoret, January 27, 2012.

57. See "Вишиті ікони Дмитра Блажейовського," http://lemky.com/248-vishiti-ikoni-dmitra-blazhejjovskogo.html (accessed January 27, 2012). Blazhejowsky created several patterns for creating and reproducing icons published in multiple sets, including idem, *Українські Релігійні Вишивки*, 2 vols. (Rome: Nusia, 1979).

58. "Вишиті ікони Дмитра Блажейовського," http://lemky.com/248-vishiti-ikoni-dmitra-blazhejjovskogo.html (accessed January 27, 2012).

59. Ibid.

60. Papalexandrou, "The Memory Culture of Byzantium," 113.

61. Maya Gregoret states that an unknown but substantial number of new immigrants frequent the parish, though they are not official members and do not pay dues (via e-mail exchange, February 8, 2012).

62. "In addition to preserving the Orthodox faith, the parish church was also viewed by the immigrants as an important place where the language of their former homeland was preserved and taught. The religion and language of the Old World were inextricably linked in the minds of the immigrants. It was not uncommon, therefore, that the immigrants sought to organize, from the 1920's onward, afternoon schools to teach their children the language and culture of the old country and to counter the inevitable movement toward acculturation" (Fitzgerald, *The Orthodox Church*, 76). See also Nicholas Denysenko, "A Legacy of Struggle, Suffering, and Hope: Metropolitan Mstyslav Skrypnyk and the Ukrainian Orthodox Church of the USA," *St. Vladimir's Theological Quarterly* 49 (2005): 339–46.

63. Perhaps the most significant symbol of the parish's cultural strategy is the fact that the museum is officially named the Ukrainian Cultural and Educational Center and is a separate organization from the parish and has been officially registered with the state of Minnesota since May 1996.

64. Museum information was graciously provided by Maya Gregoret via e-mail exchange, February 8, 2012.

65. St. Katherine represents a Ukrainian immigrant trend in this regard, as aptly summarized by Jastremsky: "As immigrants, the Ukrainians came from a homeland where every town, village and city had a church. Brought up in a faith and traditions of the church and conscious of their heritage, they have made every effort to continue this in America. In the new homeland, often at great personal sacrifice, they built a church wherever they settled and, almost invariably, it was a church that contained features that identified it as Ukrainian" (Jastremsky, "Ukrainian Architecture in America," 283).

66. Architect Zenon Marzukewich, quoted in Chirovsky, "Towards a Byzantine Liturgical Architecture," 206.

CHAPTER THREE   St. Matthew Orthodox Church

1. Via personal interview with parishioners Anastasia Borichevsky and Susan Petry, April 1, 2012.

2. For a complete listing of parishes in the Archdiocese of DC, see http://wdcoca.org/parish_listings.html (accessed July 12, 2011).

3. Via personal interview with parishioners Anastasia Borichevsky and Susan Petry, April 1, 2012.

4. Currently, V. Rev. Constantine White is the parish's rector. For a list of clergy who have served St. Matthew, see http://www.stmatthewoca.org /about-us/clergy/ (accessed February 20, 2012).

5. I am grateful for copies of plans, photos, and descriptions furnished by Charles Alexander, AIA, via e-mail correspondence on July 1, 2011. Alexander's materials are the basis for much of the description of the architectural plan.

6. Alexander, via e-mail correspondence, July 1, 2011.

7. Charles Alexander, "Procession" and "Orientation" via e-mail correspondence, July 1, 2011.

8. Via e-mail correspondence with Charles Alexander, July 11, 2011.

9. See Slobodan Ćurčić, "Church Plan Types," in *The Oxford Dictionary of Byzantium*, ed. Alexander P. Kazhdan (Oxford: Oxford University Press, 1991).

10. See Anthony Cutler, Alexander Kazhdan, and Alice-Mary Talbot, "Nea Mone," in *The Oxford Dictionary of Byzantium*, ed. Alexander P. Kazhdan (Oxford: Oxford University Press, 1991). See also Anthony Cutler, "Daphni," in *The Oxford Dictionary of Byzantium*, ed. Alexander P. Kazhdan (Oxford: Oxford University Press, 1991).

11. See a photo and an illustration of a splendid octagon in the Baptistery of San Giovanni (eleventh to thirteenth centuries) in Patricios, *The Sacred Architecture of Byzantium*, 300.

12. "The idea is loosely based on the Native American log construction of domed meeting houses further linking the past eastern tradition to a western one" (Alexander in e-mail correspondence, July 1, 2011).

13. Via e-mail exchange with parishioner Anastasia Borichevsky, July 23, 2011.

14. St. Matthew installed royal doors in 2015.

15. Via e-mail exchange with Wayne Hajos, July 3, 2014.

16. "[St. Matthew] wanted a building that spoke to the history of the Church but was also reflective of the unique traits of the parish . . . American but of Russian, Serbian, Greek heritage. In other words something reflective of the here and now but linked to the past as well" (Alexander, via e-mail correspondence, July 1, 2011).

17. In response to a query on promoting sustainability, Alexander remarked that this was not a top priority for St. Matthew, as "churches because of their usage patterns generally do not get the energy savings of a more frequently used building" (e-mail correspondence, July 1, 2011).

18. On the significance of Saturday Vespers in the Byzantine rite, see Miguel Arranz, "N.D. Uspensky: The Office of the All-Night Vigil in the Greek Church and in the Russian Church," trans. Brother Stavros, *St. Vladimir's Orthodox Quarterly* 24 (1980): 83–113, 169–95, and Denysenko, "A Proposal for Renewing Liturgy," 233–36.

19. For the full order of Orthodox Christmas liturgical services, see *The Festal Menaion*, 199–289. For Theophany, see ibid., 295–387.

20. For an overview of the significance of Holy Week and Pascha in the Orthodox liturgical tradition, see Job Getcha, *Le typikon décrypte: Manuel de liturgie byzantine*, pref. Hiéromoine Macaire (Paris: Cerf, 2009), 237–306, and Alkiviadis Calivas, *Great Week and Pascha in the Greek Orthodox Church* (Brookline, MA: Holy Cross Orthodox Press, 1992). On contemporary challenges in the celebration of Holy Week and Pascha, see Pavlos Koumarianos, "Liturgical Problems of Holy Week," *St. Vladimir's Orthodox Quarterly* 46 (2002): 3–21.

21. "A large piece of silk used in the Burial of Christ procession at the Holy Saturday *orthros*, symbolically interpreted as the bier of Christ, was called an *epitaphios*. *Epitaphioi* are usually embroidered either with the image of the Dead Christ or with the Lamentation (*threnos*) and inscriptions. They evolved from Late Byz. aeres, which they resemble in their overall shape and figural decoration, but the texts on the *epitaphioi* derive from Paschal hymns,

especially the *troparion* beginning *Noble Joseph*. The appearance of *epitaphioi* as distinct liturgical cloths coincided with the formalization of the Holy Saturday ritual in the early 14th century" (Anna Gonosová, Alexander Kazhdan, and Elizabeth M. Jeffreys, "Epitaphios," in *The Oxford Dictionary of Byzantium*, ed. Alexander P. Kazhdan [Oxford: Oxford University Press, 1991], 720–22).

22. See Gabriele Bertonière, *The Historical Development of the Easter Vigil and Related Services in the Greek Church*, Orientalia Christiana Analecta 193 (Rome: Pontifical Oriental Institute, 1972).

23. See the web site of New Skete Monastery, http://www.newskete.org /index.html (accessed June 1, 2014).

24. For a description and analysis of the New Skete Vigil, see Nicholas Denysenko, "The Revision of the Vigil Service," *St. Vladimir's Orthodox Quarterly* 51 (2007): 232–51, and Robert F. Taft, "The Byzantine Office in the Prayerbook of New Skete: A Critique," *Orientalia Christiana Periodica* 48 (1982): 336–70.

25. The parish no longer uses the New Skete version of the Vigil, and now celebrates Vespers on Saturday evenings, which conforms to the broader Byzantine Orthodox tradition and has a shorter duration. Its celebration of the New Skete Vigil in the first years of occupying the new church building represents its attempt to promote lay participation.

26. For an overview of Hajos's work, see "Wayne Hajos, Iconographer," http://www.waynehajos.com/home.html (accessed July 20, 2011). Streltsov has worked extensively in Canada and an overview of his studio's work is available at http://www.ikonograph.com/ (accessed July 20, 2011).

27. Via e-mail exchange with Wayne Hajos, July 22, 2011.

28. Via e-mail exchange with Valentin Streltsov, January 25, 2012.

29. Via e-mail exchange with Peter Pearson, January 25, 2012.

30. Via e-mail exchange with Wayne Hajos, July 22, 2011.

31. "Byzantine iconography looks very stern. But in the Russian style, the iconographer puts more of a human, compassionate face." Quoted by Tony Glaros, "Iconographer Paints Holy Images at Orthodox Church of St. Matthew," *Baltimore Sun*, September 22, 2011, http://www.baltimoresun .com/explore/howard/news/community/ph-ho-n-view-icongrapher-0922 -20110922,0,3954720,full.story (accessed January 27, 2012). For a brief description of the Russian iconographic contribution, see Leonid Ouspensky and Vladimir Lossky, *The Meaning of Icons*, 2nd ed., trans. G. E. H. Palmer and E. Kadloubovsky (Crestwood, NY: St. Vladimir's Seminary Press, 1982, 1999 printing), 45–48.

32. Alexander noted that the solid arches on the church exterior maximize the opportunity to fill the interior wall space with new icons (e-mail correspondence, July 1, 2011).

33. Kilde, *Sacred Power, Sacred Space*, 60, 188–89.

34. For a general overview of this theological movement, see Nicholas Denysenko, *Chrismation: A Primer for Catholics* (Collegeville, MN: Liturgical Press, 2014), 96–132.

35. *The Divine Liturgy of Our Father Among the Saints John Chrysostom* (Oxford: Oxford University Press, 1995), 32–33.

36. Chirovsky, "Towards a Byzantine Liturgical Architecture," 224.

37. See the web site for complete details: http://stmatthewfestival.org/ (accessed October 18, 2016).

38. Alexander, via e-mail communication, July 1, 2011.

39. "Church buildings, whether already standing or still in the planning stages, must become more sustainable. We live the Christian faith by example to each other and to the broader community. . . . Saving energy and the responsible stewardship of the earth's resources also lead to good stewardship of parish financial resources"—one of three principles articulated by the Catholic architect Roberto Chiotti in "Worship Space Today: Trends in Modern Architecture," *America Magazine* (May 23, 2011), http://www.americamagazine.org /content/article.cfm?article_id=12874 (accessed July 21, 2011). The Green movement has begun to permeate Orthodox communities in America. In September 2010, St. Vladimir's Seminary in Yonkers, New York, installed solar panels for two buildings as part of its "Go Green" initiative, receiving a grant in the amount of $72,556.50 from the New York State Research and Development Authority. See St. Vladimir's Orthodox Theological Seminary, "Seminary Switches to Solar Energy," http://www.svots.edu/headlines/seminary-switches -solar (accessed July 21, 2011). For more on the green initiative, see St. Vladimir's Theological Seminary, "Go Green Initiative Launched," http://www .svots.edu/content/go-green-initiative-launched (accessed July 21, 2011).

40. I provide an elementary description of New Skete's liturgical reform in chapter 6.

CHAPTER FOUR   Holy Virgin Cathedral

1. Parish information taken primarily from *Joy of All Who Sorrow: The Russian Orthodox Cathedral in San Francisco* (San Francisco: Cathedral Editions, 2002) (also in Russian). Additional information taken from a meeting with

the cathedral's rector, Protopriest Peter Perekrestov, October 4, 2013. I am grateful to Father Perekrestov for his generous sharing of information at this meeting and afterward.

2. The iconostasis in Fulton Street was made of California Redwood that was milled in England. The original architect was a creative artisan named Ilyin.

3. See Catherine Andreyev and Ivan Savicky, *Russia Abroad: Prague and the Russian Diaspora, 1918–1938* (New Haven, CT: Yale University Press, 2004), 174–75.

4. Ibid.

5. See Lydia B. Zaverukha and Nina Bogdan, *Images of America: Russian San Francisco*, foreword Ludmila Ershova (Charleston: Arcadia Publishing, 2010), 96–97. More than four thousand people attended the ceremony. The main cross weighs eight hundred pounds.

6. The Dormition Cathedral of the Kremlin was built in 1475–79 and designed by Aristotele Fioravanti. The design was based on the Dormition Cathedral in Vladimir. This design evolved into a model for Russian Church architecture. See Grishin, "Eastern Orthodox Iconography and Architecture," 385. For the architectural history of this temple in Russian, see S. V. Zagraevsky, *Зодчество Северо-Восточной Руси конца XIII-первой трети XIV века* (Moscow: n.p., 2003), available online at http://www.rusarch.ru/zagraevsky4.htm (accessed November 13, 2013).

7. The cathedral has three choirs: a main choir, a youth choir, and a kliros choir.

8. On the Dormition feast in Eastern Orthodoxy, see Nicholas Denysenko, "Mary's Dormition: Liturgical Cliché, Summer Pascha," *Studia Liturgica* 43, no. 2 (2013): 256–80; Brian Daley, *On the Dormition of Mary: Early Patristic Homilies* (Crestwood, NY: St. Vladimir's Seminary Press, 1998); Stephen Shoemaker, *Ancient Traditions of the Virgin Mary's Dormition and Assumption* (New York: Oxford University Press, 2002); and Kallistos Ware, "'The Final Mystery': The Dormition of the Holy Virgin in Orthodox Worship," in *Mary for Time and Eternity: Essays on Mary and Ecumenism*, ed. William M. McLoughlin and Jill Pinnock, foreword Frances Young, Papers on Mary and Ecumenism at International Congresses of the Ecumenical Society of the Blessed Virgin Mary (Gloucester: Ecumenical Society of the Blessed Virgin Mary, 2007), 219–54.

9. For a brief overview of Archimandrite Kyprian's work at the cathedral, see Zaverukha and Bogdan, *Images of America*, 100–101. See also "The Life of Archimandrite Kyprian (Pyzhov)," Russian Orthodox Church Outside of Russia web site, http://www.synod.com/synod/engdocuments /enart_archimkyprianpyzhov.html (accessed November 8, 2013).

10. A personal anecdote: upon entering Holy Virgin Cathedral during my 2013 visit, I was immediately struck by three things. First, I had expected to sense a strong pull toward the shrine of St. John Maximovich, but this did not happen. Second, I was impressed by the contrast between the vastness of the exterior on the urban landscape and the coziness of the small interior. Third, the iconography left me awestruck: the frescoes were wall-to-wall, and there were so many icons that I initially struggled to focus on one. Usually, when I enter a church, the first thing I notice is the iconostasis, but this was not the case during this visit. The icons communicated salvation history, but I would describe them as offering a profound vision of the cosmos, communicating the story of salvation history through image and word in a manner that binds past, present, and future.

11. See Leonid Ouspensky, *Theology of the Icon*, vol. 2, trans. Anthony Gythiel (Crestwood, NY: St. Vladimir's Seminary Press, 1992), 371–87.

12. See ibid., 385, for references to apologists who favor the depiction of God the Father in icons.

13. The seventy-fifth anniversary commemorative book describes the icon and its history: "A small icon and medallion are embedded in the larger icon. The small icon of the Holy Virgin 'Grace-filled sky' was with the Tsar Martyr Nicholas and his family in Ekaterinburg. It was donated to the Cathedral by the Grand Duke Nikita Romanoff. The medallion contains a piece of the bloodied wall where the Royal martyrs were brutally murdered. Alexander Turgenoff, an officer in General Kolchak's army, accompanied the investigator Sokoloff to the basement of the Ipatieff house and saw first hand the state of the room, where the incredible act of evil took place. Later on in his life, Turgenoff lived in Australia and following his death, the medallion was given to Archbishop Anthony of Western America and San Francisco" (*Joy of All Who Sorrow*, 28).

14. For background on the work of the canonization commission in Moscow, see Archpriest Georgiy Mitrofanov, "Канонизация новомучеников и исповедников российских в Русской Православной Церкви" ("The Canonization of Russian New Martyrs and Confessors in the Russian Orthodox Church"), Moscow Patriarchate web site, http://www.patriarchia.ru/db/text/1295606.html (accessed November 8, 2013). The use of two dates (July 4/17) signifies the thirteen days separating the Gregorian (first date) and Julian (second date) calendars.

15. See Geraldine Fagan, *Believing in Russia: Religious Policy After Communism* (New York: Routledge, 2013), 34.

16. Richard Betts, "From America to Russia: The Myrrh Streaming Icon of Tsar Nicholas II," *Road to Emmaus: A Journal of Orthodox Faith and*

Culture (2000), online version, http://www.roadtoemmaus.net/back_issue
_articles/RTE_01/From_America_to_Russia.pdf (accessed November 15,
2013).

17. Ibid. See also Wendy Slater, "Relics, Remains, and Revisionism:
Narratives of Nicholas II in Contemporary Russia," *Rethinking History: The
Journal of Theory and Practice* 9, no. 1 (2005): 62–64.

18. Betts, "From America to Russia."

19. Slater, "Relics, Remains, and Revisionism," 62–64.

20. Ibid.

21. The lone exception to this cycle is the prohibition of celebrating the
Eucharistic liturgy on Great and Holy Friday in the Orthodox Church.

22. Taken from the informative description of services on the cathedral's web site, "FAQ," Holy Virgin Cathedral, Joy of All Who Sorrow, web
site, http://www.sfsobor.com/index.php?option=com_content&view=article
&id=74&Itemid=82&lang=en (accessed October 23, 2013).

23. For a more complete treatment of liturgy in ROCOR, see chapter 4
of my study *Liturgical Reform After Vatican II: The Impact on Eastern Orthodoxy*
(Minneapolis, MN: Fortress Press, 2015).

24. Michael Pomazansky, *Selected Essays* (Jordanville, NY: Holy Trinity
Press, 1996), 82–102. Pomazansky was critiquing Schmemann's *Introduction to
Liturgical Theology*.

25. Ibid.

26. See Cyril Quatrone, "The Celebrant: Priest or Pastor? An Investigation of the Mystical Prayers of the Holy Apostolic Catholic Orthodox Church,"
taken from Holy Trinity Monastery web site, http://www.jordanville.org
/files/The-Celebrant--Priest-or-Pastor.pdf (accessed October 28, 2013).

27. Ibid.

28. For example, if pilgrims are confused when asked if they have a
spiritual director, the cathedral will encourage them to partake of confession.
The community provides the following guidelines to visitors who would like
to receive communion at the Eucharistic liturgy: "It is the tradition in the
Russian Orthodox Church to have Confession prior to Holy Communion
(1–2 days beforehand). It is expected that all those who wish to receive the
Holy Gifts at our Cathedral adhere to this rule. Don't be surprised if you come
up to the Holy Chalice and the Priest, not recognizing you, asks when you last
had Confession. If the answer to the question of when you last had Confession
isn't recent enough then you should not expect the Priest to allow you to have
Communion (regardless of your spiritual father's blessing)." From "FAQ,"
Holy Virgin Cathedral web site, http://www.sfsobor.com/index.php?option
=com_content&view=article&id=74&Itemid=82&lang=en (accessed

November 4, 2013). For an introduction to the Eastern order of penitents in late antiquity, see Claudia Rapp, "Spiritual Guarantors at Penance, Baptism, and Ordination in Late Antique East," in *A New History of Penance*, ed. Abigail Firey (Leiden: Brill, 2008), 121–48, and James Dallen, *The Reconciling Community: The Rite of Penance* (Collegeville, MN: Liturgical Press, 1991), 44–52. For a comprehensive presentation on the theology of repentance and asceticism in late antiquity, see the recent study by Alexis Torrance, *Repentance in Late Antiquity: Eastern Asceticism and the Framing of the Christian Life c. 400–650 CE* (Oxford: Oxford University Press, 2013).

29. For an overview of govenie, see Theophan the Recluse, *The Path to Salvation: A Manual of Spiritual Transformation*, trans. Seraphim Rose and the St. Herman of Alaska Brotherhood (Platina, CA: St. Herman of Alaska Brotherhood, 1990), 269–73. See also Nadieszda Kizenko, "The Personal Is Liturgical: *Govienie* in Russian Culture," in *On Behalf of All and For All: The Place of Liturgy in Russian Culture*, ed. Ronald Vroon, Jeffrey Riggs, and Sean Griffin, UCLA Slavic Studies (New Series) (Bloomington, IN: Slavica, 2016).

30. St. John's official title is John, Archbishop of Shanghai and San Francisco, the Wonderworker. The principal source is the hagiography in its third edition by Peter Perekrestov, *Владыка Иоанн—Святитель Русского Зарубежья*, 3rd ed., Серия "Жития святых" (Vladyka John—A Saint of the Russian Diaspora) (Moscow: Strentensky Monastery, 2009). A shorter version of the hagiographical narrative appears in Peter Perekrestov, *Man of God: Saint John of Shanghai and San Francisco* (Richfield Springs, NY: Nikodemus Orthodox Publication Society, 1994, 2012 printing). See also *Святитель Іоаннъ (Максимовичъ) и Русская Зарубежная Церковь* (Saint John [Maximovich] and the Russian Church Abroad) (Jordanville, NY: Holy Trinity Monastery, 1996), and *Service and Akathist to Our Father Among the Saints John, Archbishop of Shanghai and San Francisco, The Wonderworker* (San Francisco: Russkiy pastyr, originally published in 2004, 2013 revision).

31. *Святитель Іоаннъ (Максимовичъ) и Русская Зарубежная Церковь*, 11.

32. Ibid.

33. Quoted by Perekrestov in *Man of God*, 65.

34. See Perekrestov, *Владыка Иоанн—Святитель Русского Зарубежья*, 109–14.

35. Ibid., 116–17. Perekrestov also notes that St. John attempted to save those who were unable to depart from Shanghai, especially those who were accused of collaborating with the Japanese (112). See also *Святитель Іоаннъ (Максимовичъ) и Русская Зарубежная Церковь*, 15–16.

36. Perekrestov, *Владыка Иоанн—Святитель Русского Зарубежья*, 119–29.

37. Ibid., 129.

38. Perekrestov, *Man of God*, 63–65.

39. Perekrestov, *Владыка Иоанн—Святитель Русского Зарубежья*, 120–21.

40. Ibid., 223.

41. Perekrestov states that Archbishop Tikhon died during the annual panikhida in memory of Metropolitan Anthony Khrapovitsky, during the singing of the kontakion "With the saints give rest" (ibid., 224).

42. Ibid., 226.

43. See *Святитель Іоаннъ (Максимовичъ) и Русская Зарубежная Церковь*, 17, and Perekrestov, *Владыка Иоанн—Святитель Русского Зарубежья*, 225–27.

44. Perekrestov notes the testimony of Father Peter Lukianov (now bishop of Cleveland), who testified to St. John's attempt to continue to build peace with his opponents in Perekrestov, *Владыка Иоанн—Святитель Русского Зарубежья*, 231.

45. Ibid., 230. See also Perekrestov's citation of Protopresbyter Elias Wen in *Man of God*, 66.

46. Perekrestov, *Владыка Иоанн—Святитель Русского Зарубежья*, 230, and *Святитель Іоаннъ (Максимовичъ) и Русская Зарубежная Церковь*, 17.

47. Perekrestov, *Владыка Иоанн—Святитель Русского Зарубежья*, 239.

48. "No one should leave the Church prematurely, rushing away to eat the meat of animals instead of receiving the most holy body and blood of Christ" ("Concerning the Reception of the Holy Mysteries on Pascha" [n.d.], quoted in Perekrestov, *Man of God*, 233).

49. Ibid., 234.

50. Perekrestov, *Владыка Иоанн—Святитель Русского Зарубежья*, 557–58.

51. Perekrestov, *Man of God*, 30. Archimandrite Ambrose also said that St. John could be equally forgiving and understanding of mistakes.

52. Ibid., 53, quoting E. G. Chertkov.

53. Ibid., 202. He also says, "Such crimes do not remain unpunished. They cry out to heaven and bring God's wrath down upon the earth" (ibid., 203).

54. Ibid., 206–7. Here, St. John is condemning Sergius Bulgakov in particular: he calls sophiology a religious-philosophical trend that is "completely alien to Church teaching."

55. Ibid., 208.

56. Ibid., 204.

57. Ibid., 217–18.

58. Perekrestov stated that Holy Virgin Cathedral is the only parish in the United States to celebrate liturgy daily.

59. For an abbreviated account, see "Report to the Synod of Bishops by the Commission which examined the remains of the Hierarch John of Shanghai and San Francisco," in Perekrestov, *Man of God*, 246–50.

60. For a brief overview of shrines housing saintly relics in the Russian tradition, see "Рака для святых мощей" ("Shrine for Holy Relics"), in *Благоукраситель* no. 39 (published by "Русиздат" Summer 2013), 25–26. Reliquaries originated with the cult of the saints and began to be placed underneath altars in the fourth century. For a survey on reliquaries in the Byzantine tradition, see Anthony Cutler and Margaret E. Frazer, "Reliquary," in *The Oxford Dictionary of Byzantium*, ed. Alexander Kazhdan (Oxford: Oxford University Press, 1991). For further reading, see John Wortley, "Icons and Relics: A Comparison," *Greek, Roman, and Byzantine Studies* 43, no. 2 (2002–3): 161–74.

61. See the seminal study by Robert Greene, *Bodies Like Bright Stars: Saints and Relics in Orthodox Russia* (DeKalb: Northern Illinois University Press, 2010). For shrines comparable to the one of St. John Maximovich, see, for example, the shrine of Saint Simeon at Verkhoturskii Monastery (fig. 2, p. 49) and the shrine of Saint Dimitrii Rostovskii at the Spaso-Iakovlevskii monastery outside Rostov (fig. 3, p. 50).

62. In this section I quote frequently from *Service and Akathist*.

63. *Service and Akathist*, 5.

64. Ibid., 6–7.

65. On this possibility, see St. John's description of Russians who do not attend divine services in Perekrestov, *Man of God*, 209.

66. *Service and Akathist*, 13.

67. Ibid., 16.

68. Ibid., 6.

69. Ibid.

70. Ibid., 16.

71. Ibid., 7.

72. Ibid., 38.

73. Ibid., 23.

74. Ibid., 24–25.

75. Ibid., 37–38.

76. See Peter Brown, *The Cult of the Saints: Its Rise and Function in Latin Christianity* (Chicago: University of Chicago Press, 1982).

77. For a survey of the background, see Pospielovsky, *The Orthodox Church in the History of Russia*, 249–55. For a discussion of the response of the Russian Church abroad, see idem, *The Russian Church*, 255–79. ROCOR

published St. John Maximovich's presentation of the position of his Church in an essay titled "Русская Зарубежная Церковь" ("The Russian Church Abroad") in *Святитель Іоаннъ (Максимовичъ) и Русская Зарубежная Церковь*, 22–39.

78. Greene, *Bodies Like Bright Stars*, 103–6.

79. Ibid., 121.

80. For good examples of this resilience, see ibid., 168 and 195 (summary).

81. Greene states that the exhumation of St. Mitrofan Voronezhskii resulted in the "embarrassment of the clergy" (ibid., 104).

82. Greene, referring to Bishop Alexii of Novgorod's explanations in ibid., 137, 168.

83. See the video by Archpriest Serge Kotar, who explains the experience of uncovering St. John's relics in a first-person narrative in "St. John Maximovich by Fr. Serge Kotar," http://youtu.be/p94cQYHBQJY (accessed November 4, 2013).

84. *Service and Akathist*, 27–28.

85. Sergius Bulgakov offers a helpful insight here: "This entire phenomenology of holy relics is connected (this is the key point!) not with the relics themselves, but with our own state; it belongs to us: we mirror ourselves, we curtain off the other world with ourselves, the veil of Isis is our own materiality, and if we could see and discern in another way, we would see what actually exists, but now we see nothing but our own colored glasses" (idem, *Relics and Miracles: Two Theological Essays*, trans. Boris Jakim [Grand Rapids, MI: Eerdmans, 2011], 35).

86. Papalexandrou, "The Memory Culture of Byzantium," 113.

87. The shrine of St. John stands out as an antithesis to the Soviet creation of a hall of relics at the Narkomzdrav museum in Moscow as chronicled by Greene, *Bodies Like Bright Stars*, 146–52.

88. See Pospielovsky, *The Russian Church*, 272–73, for ROCOR's dismissal of the legitimacy of Moscow's Tomos of autocephaly given to the Orthodox Church in America in 1970.

89. "Act of Canonical Communion," Russian Orthodox Church Outside of Russia web site, http://www.russianorthodoxchurch.ws/synod/eng documents/enmat_akt.html (accessed November 5, 2012).

90. The school has its own Russian-language web site, "Gymnazia," http://www.gymnazia.org/ (accessed October 28, 2013).

91. From The Saint John of San Francisco Orthodox Academy web site, http://www.stjohnsacademysf.org/why-should-i-send-my-children-to-st -john-s (accessed October 28, 2013).

CHAPTER FIVE   Annunciation Greek Orthodox Church

1. I am grateful to the rector of Annunciation parish, Father Angelo Artemis, for the tour of the church and interview on April 10, 2014, in Milwaukee.

2. John Gurda, *New World Odyssey: Annunciation Greek Orthodox Church and Frank Lloyd Wright* (Milwaukee: The Milwaukee Hellenic Company, 1986).

3. Ibid., 24–25.

4. Ibid., 25.

5. Gurda (ibid., 25) quotes parishioner Sofia Shane as saying that "my church was my world, really," with youth regularly gathering on the church steps to sing Greek and American songs and dance.

6. Ibid., 28. Gurda notes the multiethnic dimension of the broader neighborhood since Annunciation was within four blocks of a synagogue, a German Lutheran church, a Welsh Presbyterian congregation, and a Catholic convent.

7. Gurda notes that 30 of the 141 parishes formed in America before 1922 were named "Annunciation," which manifests the fusion of religion and ethnicity in the Greek immigrants (ibid., 24).

8. Ibid., 30. Ironically, this parish still exists and is now also located in Wauwatosa.

9. Ibid., 37–38. Gurda notes that a sense of co-suffering helped to heal general fractures among Greeks in Milwaukee during the Depression.

10. Ibid., 39.

11. Ibid., 25.

12. Ibid., 32.

13. Ibid.

14. Ibid., 38.

15. Ibid., 42–45.

16. Ibid., 49.

17. Ibid., 50–51.

18. Ibid., 52.

19. Ibid., 58.

20. Interview with Father Artemis, April 10, 2014. The feast of the Life-giving Spring of the Theotokos is celebrated on Friday of Bright Week following Pascha. The feast developed in the milieu of the cult of the Theotokos that emerged after the Council of Ephesus in 431 and was based on the legend that Emperor Leo had experienced a miracle in finding fresh water through the intercessions of the Theotokos. For further information, see Virginia M. Kimball, "Liturgical Illuminations: Discovering Received Tradition

in the Eastern Orthros for Feasts of the Theotokos" (STD diss., University of Dayton, 2010), passim, and esp. 446–47. See also Alice-Mary Talbot, "Epigrams of Manuel Philes on the Theotokos tes Peges and Its Art," *Dumbarton Oaks Papers* 48 (1994): 135–65.

21. Gurda, *New World Odyssey*, 57.

22. In Wright's design, the arches were "present in the balcony windows, in the main entrance, in the planting urns, in the details of the visor encircling the dome, and most obviously in the dome itself" (ibid., 61).

23. "The windows create . . . a sort of optical illusion: the heavy dome seems to float on fragile glass balls" (ibid., 81).

24. Gurda notes that congregants noticed this feature from the outset and it received media attention (ibid., 76).

25. Anthony Cutler, "The Tyranny of Hagia Sophia: Notes on Greek Orthodox Church Design in the United States," *Journal of the Society of Architectural Historians* 31 (1972): 42.

26. Interview with Father Artemis, April 10, 2014.

27. Gurda, *New World Odyssey*, 100.

28. Ibid. Gurda notes that Masselink's name was suggested by Wright's wife. He observes that many of the icons bore striking resemblances to people Masselink used as models (ibid., 100).

29. For an explanation of the historical significance of the Platytera icon, see Patricios, *The Sacred Architecture of Byzantium*, 257.

30. Gurda, *New World Odyssey*, 80.

31. Ibid.

32. Interview with Father Artemis, April 10, 2014.

33. Gurda, *New World Odyssey*, 87, 89.

34. One of the crew members described the church as "overdesigned," referring to the sturdiness of the church's shell (ibid., 93).

35. Ibid., 119–20. Annunciation was planning on raising funds for the cultural center but invested the money on renovations to the church instead in 1985.

36. Ibid., 42.

37. Cutler, "The Tyranny of Hagia Sophia," 40. Cutler also profiled Greek Orthodox edifices in Oakland and Atlanta in his assessment.

38. Ibid., 41.

39. Ibid., 48.

40. Ibid., 47, 50.

41. Kostis Kourelis and Vasileios Marinis, "An Immigrant Liturgy: Greek Orthodox Worship and Architecture in America," in *Liturgy in Migra-*

tion: From the Upper Room to Cyberspace, ed. Teresa Berger (Collegeville, MN: Liturgical Press, 2012), 166. Cutler also refers to the church as a "flying saucer" in "The Tyranny of Hagia Sophia," 44.

42. Kourelis and Marinis, "An Immigrant Liturgy," 172.

43. Ibid., 166.

44. Kourelis and Marinis also cover phase 3, which they describe as a self-conscious reaction against the liberties of modernism, a move toward historicism, and a return to canonical Byzantine prototypes. They mention that the Presbyterian model of choice was terminated. They also provide an important reference to a new requirement issued by the Greek Orthodox Archdiocese of America in 2005, called the Uniform Parish Regulation, requiring approval from the local diocesan hierarch for architectural/iconographic projects (ibid., 167). Note that the uniform regulations were updated by the Greek Orthodox Archdiocese in 2007: "Parishes shall maintain the architectural, iconographic and artistic integrity of all Church edifices in accordance with Orthodox tradition." See "Regulations of the Greek Orthodox Archdiocese of America," Greek Orthodox Archdiocese of America web site, http://www .goarch.org/archdiocese/documents/pdf/2007-Regulations-Amended.pdf, section 4 (accessed July 21, 2014).

45. Quoted from Gurda, *New World Odyssey*, 62. See also Cutler, "The Tyranny of Hagia Sophia," 41.

46. Papalexandrou, "The Memory Culture of Byzantium," 113.

47. "The formality was due, in some part, to the distance that the committee members perceived between themselves and their architect. Wright was a legend, a world-famous figure, and no one was about to invite him to a tailgate party before a Braves game" (Gurda, *New World Odyssey*, 84).

48. Ibid., 116–17. Gurda quotes Jim Mahos, the chief critic of the structure in the 1970s and 1980s, as able to "worship in a field on an orange crate" and referring to the church as a "white elephant."

49. Ibid., 108.

50. Iakovos's predecessor, Archbishop Michael, approved the design (ibid., 80).

51. Ibid., 103.

52. Ibid., 104.

53. Ibid., 127.

54. Kourelis and Marinis, "An Immigrant Liturgy," 166.

55. Jeanne Kilde, *When Church Became Theater: The Transformation of Evangelical Architecture and Worship in Nineteenth-Century America* (Oxford: Oxford University Press, 2002), esp. chapter 5.

56. Ibid., 113.

57. "To minimize visual obstructions, load-bearing walls supported ceiling and roof, dispensing with the need for interior columns except the slender iron ones that supported the galleries. Direct sightlines were enhanced by inclined or bowled floors that sloped from the back of the room down to the pulpit stage, and curved pews arranged in semicircular arcs faced the preaching stage, bisected by aisles radiating from the stage like the spokes of a wheel. In many instances, a gallery encircled the audience space, embracing the sanctuary like huge arms. At the front, a preaching stage several feet in length and raised three or four feet above the main floor housed the pulpit, altar, or Communion table, lectern, and chairs. Almost invariably, an elevated choir loft or alcove occupied the rear stage wall, and above it dramatically rose a large case of organ pipes" (ibid., 113).

58. Cutler, "The Tyranny of Hagia Sophia," 50.

59. Ibid., 43.

60. Ibid., 44. Elsewhere, Cutler refers to the nave as a "holy retreat" (47).

61. Kilde, *Sacred Power, Sacred Space*, 60, 188–89.

62. Kourelis and Marinis, "An Immigrant Liturgy," 172.

63. Interview with Father Artemis, April 10, 2014.

64. Cutler, "The Tyranny of Hagia Sophia," 49.

65. Ibid.

66. I have in mind St. John's Abbey's similar circular interior that demands participation. For the background on the construction of the abbey's buildings, see a dated but still relevant article by Marcel Breuer and Hamilton Smith, "The Buildings at St. John's Abbey, Collegeville, Minnesota," *Design Quarterly* 53 (1961): 11. See also Seasoltz, "Sacred Space, the Arts, and Theology," 293–95.

67. Interview with Father Artemis, April 10, 2014.

CHAPTER SIX   St. Vladimir's Seminary and New Skete Monastery

1. On Schmemann's contribution to Eucharistic revival in Orthodoxy, see John Meyendorff, "Postscript: A Life Worth Living," in *Liturgy and Tradition: Theological Reflections of Alexander Schmemann*, ed. Thomas Fisch (Crestwood, NY: St. Vladimir's Seminary Press, 1990), 145–54; Paul Meyendorff, "The Liturgical Path of Orthodoxy in America," *St. Vladimir's Theological Quarterly* 40 (1996): 43–64; idem, "Fr Alexander Schmemann's Liturgical Legacy in America," *St. Vladimir's Theological Quarterly* 53, nos. 2–3 (2009):

319–30; Robert F. Taft, "The Liturgical Enterprise Twenty-five Years after Alexander Schmemann (1921–1983): The Man and His Heritage," *St. Vladimir's Theological Quarterly* 53, nos. 2–3 (2009): 139–77. Also see chapter 3 of my study, *Liturgical Reform After Vatican II.*

2. Via e-mail consultation with Brother Stavros Winner of New Skete, July 5, 2014.

3. Information taken from St. Vladimir's Seminary, *Consecration of the Three Hierarchs Chapel: St. Vladimir's Seminary* (New York: Athens Printing Company, 1983).

4. For a brief overview and video tour of Three Hierarchs Chapel, see "Chapel Tour" narrated by Father Thomas Hopko, dean emeritus of St. Vladimir's Seminary, on St. Vladimir's Orthodox Theological Seminary web site, http://www.svots.edu/community/chapel/video (accessed January 8, 2014).

5. This section is based primarily on a telephone interview conducted with Father Vinogradov on December 19, 2013. I express my sincere gratitude to him for sharing his recollection of the construction of Three Hierarchs Chapel for this chapter.

6. St. Vladimir's also built a new administrative building for faculty offices, classrooms, and the bookstore on the space previously occupied by the old chapel. The construction of the administrative building represented the expansion of the academic community and the need for new spaces. I will not discuss the administrative building here, as the construction of Three Hierarchs Chapel is intertwined with liturgical renewal.

7. "It is as though the building of the new chapel was experienced as truly a common project, a common act of praising God, of proclaiming his will. To all these friends known and unknown, we express not gratitude—for it is for God and not for us that they have shown their love and care—but wishes for God's mercy and help in their life, in their own ascension to the kingdom of God. The second gift, which notably only now we begin to realize, is the feeling, growing into certitude, that by building this bright and shining chapel we have passed an examination, that the stability of the Seminary was tested, and that our inner unity, mutual trust and spirit of common service to God and the Church have been revealed. It took more than forty years to prepare for that examination. These years were very difficult, experienced sometimes as a long peregrination though the desert" (St. Vladimir's Theological Foundation, *14th Annual Orthodox Education Day* [Crestwood, NY: n.p., 1983]).

8. Alexis Vinogradov, "The Architecture of Eastern Orthodox Churches: Contemporary Trends and Possibilities," *Koinonia: The Journal of the Anglican and Eastern Churches Association* 54 (2008): 5.

9. For a brief historical overview and the impact of the OCA's autocephaly on Orthodoxy in America, see Fitzgerald, *The Orthodox Church*, 101–5; Paul Meyendorff, "Fr John Meyendorff and the Autocephaly of the Orthodox Church in America," *St. Vladimir's Theological Quarterly* 56, no. 3 (2012): 335–52; Alexander Schmemann, "Meaningful Storm: Some Reflections on Autocephaly, Tradition and Ecclesiology," *St. Vladimir's Theological Quarterly* 15, nos. 1–2 (1971): 3–27.

10. Notable here is the rejection of an onion dome, which would conform to a Russian model; the pitched roof is prevalent in other Slavic countries.

11. Vinogradov, "The Architecture of Eastern Orthodox Churches," 5.

12. Holy Cross Greek Orthodox School of Theology in Brookline, Massachusetts, near Boston, and Fordham University are the only other Orthodox academic programs in America comparable to St. Vladimir's.

13. See, for example, the seminary's report of the recent concert featuring the music of Estonian composer Arvo Pärt: Deborah Belonick, "Estonian Composer Arvo Pärt Thrills NYC Audience," St. Vladimir's Orthodox Theological Seminary web site, http://www.svots.edu/headlines/estonian -orthodox-composer-arvo-p%C3%A4rt-thrills-new-york-audience (accessed August 4, 2014).

14. Baldovin, *The Urban Character of Christian Worship*.

15. Vinogradov notes that Drillock recommended a minimal narthex so that people, even small children who can be disruptive, would be encouraged to be in church.

16. Per telephone interview with Paul Meyendorff, December 16, 2013.

17. Per Paul Meyendorff, phone interview, December 16, 2013.

18. When I was a student at St. Vladimir's, we referred to this area as the skeuophylakion.

19. Some of this section is based on my own experience as a student at St. Vladimir's from 1997 to 2000. I served the chapel community in two major capacities: I was one of the choir conductors in the rotation from 1997 to 2000; I also served as the chapel ecclesiarch from 1998 to 2000. As ecclesiarch, my duties included creating the orders for each liturgical office, including providing the texts used for the services taken from the Octoechos, Menaion, Triodion, and Pentecostarion, and coaching the choir directors and chanters through the celebration of the divine services.

20. "Orthodox theological education is uniquely and significantly tied to liturgical worship. Seminarians and their families are enriched, challenged, and instructed in Three Hierarchs Chapel, named for Saints Basil the Great, Gregory the Theologian, and John Chrysostom, and consecrated in 1983. Our

academics are inseparable from our daily worship, which provides the context for everything we are doing at the Seminary. This worship is the cornerstone of our spiritual formation" (St. Vladimir's Orthodox Theological Seminary web site, http://www.svots.edu/community/chapel [accessed January 8, 2014]).

21. In the Byzantine rite, the Epistle and Gospel are not taken during the daily offices of Matins and Vespers, but are appointed to the Divine Liturgy. At St. Vladimir's, Father Georges Florovsky inaugurated the practice of adding the readings to the daily offices so that students would hear and rehearse preaching the word of God, a ritual innovation that is still practiced today.

22. The Typikon of the Byzantine rite has a complicated system of ranking feasts. For an explanatory chart of the system of feasts and their ranks in the typikon, see Getcha, *Le typikon décrypté*, 111–12. For great feasts, the seminary typically delays the start of morning classes; for liturgies on the sanctoral cycle, the seminary celebrates an early liturgy.

23. Some students have other parish obligations on Sundays, depending on the needs of their diocesan bishops, so many students do not attend Sunday liturgy.

24. Students are also excused from class for the entirety of Holy Week and Bright Week.

25. See note 1, above.

26. Obviously, not all graduates of St. Vladimir's implemented the liturgical renewal in their pastoral assignments. An assessment of the disparity of liturgical practices and existence of competing liturgical schools in North American Orthodoxy is outside the scope of this study; an ethnographic examination of seminary graduates and their ministries is a worthy candidate for a doctoral dissertation.

27. Kilde, *Sacred Power, Sacred Space*, 188–89.

28. Vinogradov was a consultant for the interior design of St. Mary Magdalene Church in Manhattan, stating that the community desired to be a "faithful expression and sign of Orthodox life and worship—but a life, nonetheless, contextualized in the circumstances of its incarnate historical witness" ("The Architecture of Eastern Orthodox Churches," 3).

29. Vinogradov also designed the interiors, exteriors, and iconostases of no fewer than six churches in the United States and Canada (e-mail exchange on July 3, 2014).

30. On the optimal size of parish communities, Vinogradov says, "Whatever ceremonial and public functions accomplished by the medieval cathedral, it was clearly not a parish church. We will certainly continue the

debate on optimal numbers to form community, but it strikes this author that two hundred households are far less likely to form a cohesive social unity than 75 families" ("The Architecture of Eastern Orthodox Churches," 10).

31. Based on a demographic survey of Orthodox parishes in America by Alexei Krindatch, *The Orthodox Church Today: A National Study of Parishioners and the Realities of Orthodox Parish Life in the USA* (Berkeley, CA: Patriarch Athenagoras Orthodox Institute, 2006), 20, http://www.hartfordinstitute.org/research/OrthChurchFullReport.pdf (accessed July 18, 2014).

32. Monks of New Skete, *In the Spirit of Happiness* (Boston: Little, Brown and Company, 1999), 8–23.

33. Ibid., 9.

34. Ibid.

35. Ibid.

36. Ibid., 8–10.

37. Ibid., 13.

38. Brother Stavros Winner, "Liturgical Renewal: Have We Missed the Boat?" Unpublished essay. Mateos wrote the first volume in the seminal and meticulous history of the liturgy of St. John Chrysostom, succeeded in this endeavor by Robert Taft and Sister Vassa Larin.

39. Brother Stavros Winner, "The Monastery and Applied Liturgical Renewal," in *Worship Traditions and Armenia and the Neighboring Christian East: An International Symposium in Honor of the 40th Anniversary of St. Nersess Armenian Seminary*, ed. Roberta R. Ervine (Crestwood, NY: St. Vladimir's Seminary Press, St. Nersess Armenian Seminary, 2006), 311.

40. Ibid.

41. Ibid.

42. Via e-mail exchange with Brother Stavros Winner, July 5, 2014.

43. Via e-mail exchange with Brother Stavros Winner, July 5, 2014.

44. Note that Maria Skobtsova was canonized by the Ecumenical Patriarchate in 2004, Mother Teresa of Calcutta was canonized by Pope Francis in 2016, and Dorothy Day is currently being considered for canonization.

45. Taken from a conversation with the monks and nuns of New Skete, June 14, 2014.

46. Father Christopher Savage, New Skete's prior, emphasized this ecumenical mission in his remarks on the evening of June 14, 2014.

47. "When the typicon directs, we sing the office of the three antiphons. In good weather, this office is taken outdoors in procession. In such cases, at the end of matins, the clergy go to the temple of the Transfiguration to vest. At the sounding of the bells, they gather at the entrance of the small church, facing the belltower. [If the office of the three antiphons is taken indoors,

then, after vesting in the west sacristy of the new church, they proceed into the nave, to the ambo, where they take their places.]" Monks of New Skete, *The Divine Liturgy* (Cambridge, NY: New Skete, 1987), 72–73, from Divine Liturgy of St. John Chrysostom.

48. See Juan Mateos, *La célébration de la parole dans la liturgie byzantine*, Orientalia Christiana Analecta 121 (Rome: Pontifical Oriental Institute, 1971), 34–71.

49. Taft, "The Liturgy of the Great Church," 50.

50. Mateos, *La célébration*, 143.

51. "O maker and benefactor of all creation, receive your church which approaches you. Bring about all that is best for us, lead us to perfection and make us worthy of your kingdom. By the grace and mercy and love for mankind of your only son, with whom you are bless'd, together with your all-holy, good, and life-giving Spirit: now and forever, and unto ages of ages" (Monks of New Skete, *The Divine Liturgy*, 79, from the Liturgy of St. John Chrysostom). The account of the current practice of singing the office of the antiphons is based on e-mail dialogue with Brother Stavros Winner.

52. "In the center of the nave, there is a permanent ambo.... The liturgy normally begins on the ambo, and the celebration of the word takes place there in its entirety, the altar area being reserved for the celebration of the eucharist" (Monks of New Skete, *The Divine Liturgy*, xix).

53. "Unless specifically indicated, all the prayers . . . are intended to be sung aloud. Those prayers, however, which are clearly indicated to be said silently or quietly, are still said in the hearing of all the clergy concelebrating the liturgy. Dialogues between the priests or between the priest and deacon, as well as certain diaconal remarks, are also said within the hearing of all present" (Monks of New Skete, *The Divine Liturgy*, xx–xxi).

54. Before the prayer of accession, "the deacon bows to the main celebrant, ascends the solea, and enters the altar. He unfolds the iliton and the antimension and steps to the side." The prayer of accession occurs here; then, during the singing of the Cherubikon, "the deacon censes the holy table from all four sides, the clergy, and then the people. Going to the chamber of preparation, he censes the oblation and gives the censer back to one of the attendants. Then, taking the discos in his left hand and the chalice in his right, he makes the entrance with the gifts, accompanied by lights and incense, going along the north side of the church and coming up the center of the nave. In the meantime, the clergy remain at their places at the holy table" (Monks of New Skete, *The Divine Liturgy*, 94, 96).

55. See Robert F. Taft, *Through Their Own Eyes: Liturgy as the Byzantines Saw It* (Berkeley, CA: InterOrthodox Press, 2006), 105–8.

CHAPTER SEVEN   Joy of All Who Sorrow Orthodox Church
              (JOY) Mission

1. See the document "Guidelines for Missions," OCA web site, http://oca.org/cdn/PDFs/evangelization/guidelines-for-missions.pdf (accessed June 30, 2014). In the introductory letter by then Metropolitan Theodosius (written in 1989), the Department of Mission's work consisted of assisting "in the establishment of mission parishes by passing on successful approaches to mission development, distributing liturgical items, attending diocesan assemblies and making field trips to learn firsthand the struggles and concerns of peoples involved in missions."

2. "A vital part of the process of evangelization is to have a sanctified people gather together in a common place of worship to hear the Word of God and to partake of the sacrament of his kingdom" (Metropolitan Theodosius, "letter," ibid.).

3. Ibid.

4. Ibid.

5. Ibid.

6. Ibid.

7. OCA Department of Evangelization, "Mission Planter's Resource Kit," OCA web site, http://oca.org/cdn/PDFs/evangelization/2005-Evangelization-Hndbk.pdf (accessed June 30, 2014).

8. Ibid. For a complete description of the activities assigned to each period, see the handbook. What follows here is a summary of the whole process.

9. The context of the handbook suggests that "non-churched" describes an area that does not have an Orthodox Christian presence but could have communities belonging to other Christian churches.

10. The following comments on location are noteworthy: "Orthodoxy tends to be a destination church, not a drive-by, drop-in church. The average person . . . does not drive farther to church than they do to work. Location will influence which socio-economic group is attracted to your church. A bad neighborhood will be a hindrance to those who are concerned about safety" (ibid.).

11. Ibid.

12. 2014 Church Planting Grant Requirements, OCA web site, http://oca.org/cdn/PDFs/evangelization/2013-0808-OCAPlantingGrantDocumentation.pdf (accessed June 30, 2014).

13. See the list of qualifications in ibid. for a complete description.

14. See "Outreach and Evangelism," Greek Orthodox Archdiocese of America web site, http://www.goarch.org/archdiocese/departments/outreach/aboutus (accessed June 30, 2014).

15. "Missions," Antiochian Orthodox Christian Archdiocese of North America web site, http://www.antiochian.org/missions (accessed June 30, 2014).

16. The establishing of missions in the Antiochian Archdiocese coincides with the reception of the Evangelical Orthodox Church into the archdiocese. For the seminal historical analysis of this group of converts into Orthodoxy, see D. Oliver Herbel, *Turning to Tradition: Converts and the Making of an American Orthodox Church* (Oxford: Oxford University Press, 2013), 103–45.

17. The ROCOR now prohibits use of the Western rite, which was originally authorized by Bishop Tikhon (Belavin, later patriarch of Moscow) in the early twentieth century. There is an abundance of literature on the Western rite in Orthodoxy. See Jack Turner, "The Journey Thus Far: A Review of the Literature of Western-Rite Orthodoxy," *St. Vladimir's Theological Quarterly* 53, no. 4 (2009): 477–505; and idem, "Western Rite Orthodoxy as a Liturgical Problem," *Journal of Eastern Christian Studies* 63, nos. 3–4 (2011): 333–52.

18. For example, the handbook recommends Father Seraphim Slobodskoy's *The Law of God* as a text for rehearsing the divine order of services. The handbook concludes the section on reading and serving with this remark: "ultimately, the best training for readers and priests is to do the divine services as frequently as possible." See "Mission Planter's Resource Kit," OCA web site, http://oca.org/cdn/PDFs/evangelization/2005-Evangelization -Hndbk.pdf (accessed June 30, 2014).

19. Ibid.

20. Data taken from Delegate Handbook, Volume 2: Deanery and Parish Reports, Diocese of the West Orthodox Church in America, 2013 Diocesan Assembly, Diocese of the West web site, http://www.dowoca.org/files/assemblies /2013/2013_rep_book_vol_2_Oct_03.pdf (accessed June 26, 2014).

21. Data taken from Delegate Handbook, Volume 3: Department, Institution, and Financial Reports, Diocese of the West Orthodox Church in America, 2013 Diocesan Assembly, Diocese of the West web site, http://www.dowoca .org/files/assemblies/2013/2013_rep_book_vol_3_Oct_03.pdf (accessed June 30, 2014). I have excluded the 100% growth rate recorded by the Santa Barbara mission, which now has six members, with three reported in 2008.

22. Ibid.

23. Permit an anecdote: in November 2010, the rector of JOY asked me to serve as the first deacon to the diocesan bishop. The beginning of the Eucharistic liturgy was delayed by almost thirty minutes because the bishop could not find a convenient parking space and then had to walk a long distance to the church.

24. See Joy of All Who Sorrow Orthodox Church (JOY) mission, web site, "Music," http://joyofallwhosorrow.org/about/music/ (accessed June 23, 2014).

25. See Baldovin, *The Urban Character of Christian Worship*.

26. Marinis, *Architecture and Ritual*, 115.

27. Plekon terms this paradigm shift "The Church Has Left the Building." For his initial assessment of this situation, see his *Saints As They Really Are: Voices of Holiness in Our Time* (Notre Dame, IN: University of Notre Dame Press, 2012), 221–45.

28. For a macro-level view within the OCA, see the minutes from the March meeting of the OCA's Metropolitan Council, which expose problems in parish attrition, clergy assignments, and seminary self-sustenance. The Council's Audit Committee recommended that the Synod of Bishops and the Metropolitan Council perform a study of pastoral needs projected for the next fifteen to twenty years, to collect data on clergy retirement and mortality rates and projected (Church) growth through missions and parish revitalization to forecast seminary needs. The language of growth and revitalization cloaks the problem of attrition. See the full report, "Metropolitan Council Spring 2012: Committees/Department Reports," http://oca.org/cdn/PDFs/metropolitancouncil/2012/spring-metcouncil/spring12committees.pdf (accessed May 16, 2012). For a micro-level view, see "Minutes of the Meeting of the Officers of the Orthodox Church in America with Diocesan Chancellors and Treasurers, January 17–18, 2012," http://oca.org/cdn/PDFs/metropolitancouncil/2012/spring-metcouncil/spring12-mc-other-reports.pdf (accessed May 19, 2012).

Conclusion

1. See David Fagerberg, *Theologia Prima: What Is Liturgical Theology?* 2nd ed. (Chicago: Archdiocese of Chicago, Liturgy Training Publications, 2004).

2. Skeptics will challenge my reflection on the significance of secondary and tertiary structures by stating that they create a false equivalence between the liturgy and the activities that occur in the other buildings. I realize that the relationship between the buildings is disproportionate for many parishes, especially in communities where parents bring their children to Sunday school without attending liturgy. My intent here is to illustrate the potential vitality of contemporary Orthodox Christian life that can be expressed in diverse environments on a given parish's premises; it is not to undermine the centrality and primacy of the liturgy. The pastoral task that emerges from this conundrum is to make the liturgy the heart of a given complex of buildings, a heart that pumps blood and feeds the content of the activities that occur in the other structures.

BIBLIOGRAPHY

Andreyev, Catherine, and Ivan Savicky. *Russia Abroad: Prague and the Russian Diaspora, 1918–1938.* New Haven, CT: Yale University Press, 2004.

Arranz, Miguel. "Les grandes étapes de la liturgie byzantine: Palestine-Byzance-Russie. Essai d'aperçu historique." In *Liturgie de l'église particulière, liturgie de l'église universelle,* Bibliotheca *Ephemerides liturgicae,* subsidia 7, 43–72. Rome: Edizioni liturgiche, 1976.

———. "N.D. Uspensky: The Office of the All-Night Vigil in the Greek Church and in the Russian Church." Translated by Brother Stavros Winner. *St. Vladimir's Theological Quarterly* 24 (1980): 83–113, 169–95.

Baldovin, John. *The Urban Character of Christian Worship: The Origins, Development, and Meaning of Stational Liturgy.* Orientalia Christiana Analecta 228. Rome: Pontifical Oriental Institute, 1987.

Bertonière, Gabriele. *The Historical Development of the Easter Vigil and Related Services in the Greek Church.* Orientalia Christiana Analecta 193. Rome: Pontifical Oriental Institute, 1972.

Blazhejowsky, Dmitry. *Українські Релігійні Вишивки.* 2 vols. Rome: Nusia, 1979.

Bociurkiw, Bohdan. "The Ukrainian Autocephalous Orthodox Church, 1920–1930: A Case Study in Religious Modernization." In *Religion and Modernization in the Soviet Union,* edited by Dennis J. Dunn, 310–47. Boulder, CO: Westview Press, 1977.

Bornert, René. *Les commentaires byzantins de la Divine Liturgie du VIIe au XVe siècle.* Archives de l'Orient chrétien. Paris: Institut Francais d'études byzantines, 1966.

Breuer, Marcel, and Hamilton Smith. "The Buildings at St. John's Abbey, Collegeville, Minnesota." *Design Quarterly* 53 (1961): 1–31.

Brown, Peter. *The Cult of the Saints: Its Rise and Function in Latin Christianity.* Chicago: University of Chicago Press, 1982.

Bulgakov, Sergius. *Relics and Miracles: Two Theological Essays.* Translated by Boris Jakim. Grand Rapids, MI: Eerdmans, 2011.

Calivas, Alkiviadis. *Great Week and Pascha in the Greek Orthodox Church.* Brookline, MA: Holy Cross Orthodox Press, 1992.

Cameron, Averil. "The Theotokos in Sixth-Century Constantinople." *Journal of Theological Studies* 24 (1978): 79–108.

Chirovsky, Andriy. "Towards a Byzantine Liturgical Architecture." *Diakonia* 18 (1983): 203–37.

Cracraft, James. *The Petrine Revolution in Russian Architecture.* Chicago: University of Chicago Press, 1988.

Ćurčić, Slobodan. "Church Plan Types." In *The Oxford Dictionary of Byzantium.* Edited by Alexander Kazhdan. Oxford: Oxford University Press, 1991.

———, and Evangelia Hadjitryphonos, eds. *Architecture as Icon: Perception and Representation of Architecture in Byzantine Art.* Princeton, NJ: Princeton University Art Museum, 2010.

Cutler, Anthony. "Daphni." In *The Oxford Dictionary of Byzantium.* Edited by Alexander Kazhdan. Oxford: Oxford University Press, 1991.

———. "The Tyranny of Hagia Sophia: Notes on Greek Orthodox Church Design in the United States." *Journal of the Society of Architectural Historians* 31 (1972): 38–50.

———, and Margaret E. Frazer. "Reliquary." In *The Oxford Dictionary of Byzantium.* Edited by Alexander Kazhdan. Oxford: Oxford University Press, 1991.

———, Alexander Kazhdan, and Alice-Mary Talbot. "Nea Mone." In *The Oxford Dictionary of Byzantium.* Edited by Alexander Kazhdan. Oxford: Oxford University Press, 1991.

Cyril of Jerusalem. *Catéchèses mystagogiques.* Edited and translated by Auguste Piédagnel. Sources Chrétiennes 126. Paris: Cerf, 1966.

———. *The Works of Cyril of Jerusalem.* Translated by Leo P. McCauley and Anthony A. Stevenson. Washington, DC: Catholic University of America Press, 1969–70.

Daley, Brian. *On the Dormition of Mary: Early Patristic Homilies.* Crestwood, NY: St. Vladimir's Seminary Press, 1998.

Dallen, James. *The Reconciling Community: The Rite of Penance.* Collegeville, MN: Liturgical Press, 1991.

Denysenko, Nicholas. "Chaos in Ukraine: The Churches and the Search for Leadership." *International Journal for the Study of the Christian Church* 14, no. 3 (2014): 242–59.

———. *Chrismation: A Primer for Catholics.* Collegeville, MN: Liturgical Press, 2014.

———. "Fractured Orthodoxy in Ukraine and Politics: The Impact of Patriarch Kyrill's 'Russian World.'" *Logos: A Journal of Eastern Christian Studies* 54, nos. 1–2 (2013): 33–68.

———. "A Legacy of Struggle, Suffering, and Hope: Metropolitan Mstyslav Skrypnyk and the Ukrainian Orthodox Church of the USA." *St. Vladimir's Theological Quarterly* 49 (2005): 335–51.

———. *Liturgical Reform After Vatican II: The Impact on Eastern Orthodoxy.* Minneapolis, MN: Fortress Press, 2015.

———. "Mary's Dormition: Liturgical Cliché, Summer Pascha." *Studia Liturgica* 43, no. 2 (2013): 256–80.

———. "A Proposal for Renewing Liturgy in the Twenty-First Century." *Studia Liturgica* 40 (2010): 231–59.

———. "The Revision of the Vigil Service." *St. Vladimir's Orthodox Quarterly* 51 (2007): 232–51.

———. "The Soteriological Significance of the Feast of Mary's Birth." *Theological Studies* 68 (2007): 739–60.

———. "Towards an Agenda for Byzantine Pastoral Liturgy: A Response to Peter Galadza." *Bolletino della Badia Greca di Grottaferrata* 7 (2010): 45–68.

The Divine Liturgy of Our Father Among the Saints John Chrysostom. Oxford: Oxford University Press, 1995.

Doig, Allan. *Liturgy and Architecture: From the Early Church to the Middle Ages.* Liturgy, Worship and Society Series. Farnham, Surrey, UK: Ashgate, 2008.

Drijvers, Jan Villem. *Cyril of Jerusalem: Bishop and City.* Supplements to Vigiliae Christianae. Leiden: Brill, 2004.

Egeria. *Journal de Voyage (Itinéraire).* Edited and translated by Pierre Maraval. Sources Chrétiennes 296. Paris: Cerf, 1982.

Fagan, Geraldine. *Believing in Russia: Religious Policy After Communism.* New York: Routledge, 2013.

Fagerberg, David. *Theologia Prima: What Is Liturgical Theology?* 2nd ed. Chicago: Archdiocese of Chicago, Liturgy Training Publications, 2004.

The Festal Menaion. Translated by Mother Mary and Kallistos Ware. London: Faber and Faber, 1969.

Fisch, Thomas, ed. *Liturgy and Tradition: Theological Reflections of Alexander Schmemann.* Crestwood, NY: St. Vladimir's Seminary Press, 1990.

Fitzgerald, Thomas E. *The Orthodox Church.* Denominations in America 7. Westport, CT: Greenwood Press, 1995.

Galadza, Peter. "Schmemann Between Fagerberg and Reality: Towards an Agenda for Byzantine Christian Pastoral Liturgy." *Bolletino della Badia Greca di Grottaferrata* 4 (2007): 7–32.

Gallagher, Sally. "Building Traditions: Comparing Space, Ritual, and Community in Three Congregations." *Review of Religious Research* 47 (2005): 70–85.

Getcha, Job. *Le typikon décrypte: Manuel de liturgie byzantine.* Preface by Hieromonk Macaire. Paris: Cerf, 2009.

Gonosová, Anna, Alexander Kazhdan, and Elizabeth Jeffreys. "Epitaphios." In *The Oxford Dictionary of Byzantium.* Edited by Alexander Kazhdan. Oxford: Oxford University Press, 1991.

Greene, Robert. *Bodies Like Bright Stars: Saints and Relics in Orthodox Russia.* DeKalb: Northern Illinois University Press, 2010.

Grishin, Alexander. "Eastern Orthodox Iconography and Architecture." In *The Blackwell Companion to Eastern Christianity,* edited by Ken Parry, 371–87. Malden, MA: Blackwell Publishing, 2007.

Gurda, John. *New World Odyssey: Annunciation Greek Orthodox Church and Frank Lloyd Wright.* Milwaukee: The Milwaukee Hellenic Company, 1986.

Hawk-Reinhard, Donna. "From Χριστιανοί το Χριστοφόροι: The Role of the Eucharist in Christian Identity Formation according to Cyril of Jerusalem." PhD diss., St. Louis University, 2011.

Herbel, Dellas Oliver. *Turning to Tradition: Converts and the Making of an American Orthodox Church.* Oxford: Oxford University Press, 2013.

Irwin, Kevin. *Context and Text: Method in Liturgical Theology.* Collegeville, MN: Liturgical Press, 1994.

Jastremsky, Julian K. "Ukrainian Architecture in America." In *The Ukrainian Heritage in America,* edited by Walter Dushnyck and Nicholas Chirovsky, 266–87. New York: Ukrainian Congress Committee of America, 1991.

Johnson, Mark, Robert Ousterhoput, and Amy Papalexandrou, eds. *Approaches to Byzantine Architecture and Its Decoration: Studies in Honor of Slobodan Ćurčić.* Burlington, VT: Ashgate, 2012.

Joy of All Who Sorrow: The Russian Orthodox Cathedral in San Francisco. San Francisco: Cathedral Editions, 2002. (also in Russian)

Kazhdan, Alexander, ed. *The Oxford Dictionary of Byzantium.* Oxford: Oxford University Press, 1991.

Kilde, Jeanne. "Reading Megachurches: Investigating the Religious and Cultural Work of Church Architecture." In *America Sanctuary: Understanding Sacred Spaces,* edited by Louis Nelson, 225–49. Bloomington: Indiana University Press, 2006.

———. *Sacred Power, Sacred Space: An Introduction to Christian Architecture and Worship.* Oxford: Oxford University Press, 2008.

———. *When Church Became Theater: The Transformation of Evangelical Architecture and Worship in Nineteenth-Century America.* Oxford: Oxford University Press, 2002.

Kimball, Virginia M. "Liturgical Illuminations: Discovering Received Tradition in the Eastern Orthros for Feasts of the Theotokos." STD diss., University of Dayton, 2010.

Kishkovsky, Leonid, and Mark Stokoe. *Orthodox Christians in North America: 1794–1994*. N.p.: Orthodox Christian Publication Center, 1995.

Kizenko, Nadieszda. "The Personal Is Liturgical: *Govienie* in Russian Culture." In *On Behalf of All and For All: The Place of Liturgy in Russian Culture*. Edited by Ronald Vroon, Jeffrey Riggs, and Sean Griffin. UCLA Slavic Studies (New Series). Bloomington, IN: Slavica, 2016.

Korowycky, Ivan. "The Ukrainian Orthodox Church in the United States." In *The Ukrainian Heritage in America*, edited by Walter Dushnyck and Nicholas Chirovsky, 84–92. New York: Ukrainian Congress Committee of America, 1991.

Koumarianos, Pavlos. "Liturgical Problems of Holy Week. " *St. Vladimir's Theological Quarterly* 46 (2002): 3–21.

Kourelis, Kostis, and Vasileios Marinis. "An Immigrant Liturgy: Greek Orthodox Worship and Architecture in America." In *Liturgy in Migration: From the Upper Room to Cyberspace*, edited by Teresa Berger, 155–75. Collegeville, MN: Liturgical Press, 2012.

Krautheimer, Richard. *Early Christian and Byzantine Architecture*. 4th ed. Revised by Richard Krautheimer and Slobodan Ćurčić. New Haven, CT: Yale University Press, 1986.

Krindatch, Alexei. *The Orthodox Church Today: A National Study of Parishioners and the Realities of Orthodox Parish Life in the USA*. Berkeley, CA: Patriarch Athenagoras Orthodox Institute, 2006.

Larin, Vassa. "Feasting and Fasting According to the Byzantine Typikon." *Worship* 83 (2009): 133–48.

Lathrop, Alan K. *Churches of Minnesota: An Illustrated Guide*. Minneapolis, MN: Regents of the University of Minnesota, 2003.

The Lenten Triodion. Translated by Mother Mary and Kallistos Ware. South Canaan, PA: St. Tikhon's Seminary Press, 2002.

Mainstone, Rowland. *Hagia Sophia: Architecture, Structure and Liturgy of Justinian's Great Church*. London: Thames and Hudson, 1988.

Mango, Cyril. *Byzantine Architecture*. New York: Harry N. Abrams, Inc., 1976.

———, Alexander Kazhdan, and Anthony Cutler. "Hippodromes." In *The Oxford Dictionary of Byzantium*. Edited by Alexander Kazhdan. Oxford: Oxford University Press, 1991.

Marinis, Vasileios. *Architecture and Ritual in the Churches of Constantinople: Ninth to Fifteenth Centuries*. Cambridge: Cambridge University Press, 2014.

Mateos, Juan. *La célébration de la parole dans la liturgie byzantine.* Orientalia Christiana Analecta 121. Rome: Pontifical Oriental Institute, 1971.

———, ed. *Le Typicon de la grande église,* vol. 1, *Le cycle des douze mois.* Orientalia Christiana Analecta 165. Rome: Pontifical Oriental Institute, 1962.

———, ed. *Le Typicon de la grande église,* vol. 2, *Le cycle des fêtes mobiles.* Orientalia Christiana Analecta 166. Rome: Pontifical Oriental Institute, 1963.

Mathews, Thomas. *The Early Churches of Constantinople: Architecture and Liturgy.* University Park: University of Pennsylvania Press, 1971.

Maximus Confessor, Selected Writings. Translated by George C. Berthold, introduction by Jaroslav Pelikan, preface by Irenee-Henri Dalmais. Mahwah, NJ: Paulist Press, 1985.

McNamara, Denis R. *Catholic Church Architecture and the Spirit of the Liturgy.* Chicago: Hillenbrand Books, 2009.

———. *How to Read Churches: A Crash Course in Ecclesiastical Architecture.* New York: Rizzoli International Press, 2011. Originally published in Lewes by Ivy Press, 2011.

McVey, Kathleen. "Spirit Embodied: The Emergence of Symbolic Interpretations of Early Christian and Byzantine Architecture." In *Architecture as Icon: Perception and Representation of Architecture in Byzantine Art,* ed. Slobodan Ćurčić and Evangelia Hadjitryphonos, 39–72. Princeton, NJ: Princeton University Art Museum, 2010.

Meyendorff, John. "Postscript: A Life Worth Living." In *Liturgy and Tradition: Theological Reflections of Alexander Schmemann,* edited by Thomas Fisch, 145–54. Crestwood, NY: St. Vladimir's Seminary Press, 1990.

Meyendorff, Paul. "Fr Alexander Schmemann's Liturgical Legacy in America." *St. Vladimir's Theological Quarterly* 53, nos. 2–3 (2009): 319–30.

———. "Fr John Meyendorff and the Autocephaly of the Orthodox Church in America." *St. Vladimir's Theological Quarterly* 56, no. 3 (2012): 335–52.

———. "The Liturgical Path of Orthodoxy in America." *St. Vladimir's Theological Quarterly* 40 (1996): 43–64.

Momina, M. "О происхождении греческой Триоди." *Палестинський Сборник* 28 (1986): 112–20.

Monks of New Skete. *The Divine Liturgy.* Cambridge, NY: New Skete, 1987.

———. *In the Spirit of Happiness.* Boston: Little, Brown and Company, 1999.

Ouspensky, Leonid. *Theology of the Icon.* Vol. 2. Translated by Anthony Gythiel. Crestwood, NY: St. Vladimir's Seminary Press, 1992.

———, and Vladimir Lossky. *The Meaning of Icons.* 2nd ed. Translated by G. E. H. Palmer and E. Kadloubovsky. Crestwood, NY: St. Vladimir's Seminary Press, 1982, 1999 printing.

Papalexandrou, Amy. "The Memory Culture of Byzantium." In *Companion to Byzantium*, edited by Liz James, 108–22. Blackwell Companions to the Ancient World Series. Chichester, West Sussex, UK: Wiley-Blackwell, 2010.

Patricios, Nicholas. *The Sacred Architecture of Byzantium: Art, Liturgy, and Symbolism in Early Christian Churches*. London: I. B. Tauris, 2014.

The Pentecostarion. Translated by Holy Transfiguration Monastery. Boston: Holy Transfiguration Monastery, 1990.

Perekrestov, Peter. *Владыка Иоанн—Святитель Русского Зарубежья*. 3rd ed. "Житиа святых" Series. Moscow: Stretensky Monastery, 2009.

———. *Man of God: Saint John of Shanghai and San Francisco*. Richfield Springs, NY: Nikodemus Orthodox Publication Society, 1994, 2012 printing.

Plekon, Michael. *Saints As They Really Are: Voices of Holiness in Our Time*. Notre Dame, IN: University of Notre Dame Press, 2012.

Pomazansky, Michael. *Selected Essays*. Jordanville, NY: Holy Trinity Monastery, 1996.

Pospielovsky, Dmitry. *The Orthodox Church in the History of Russia*. Crestwood, NY: St. Vladimir's Seminary Press, 1998.

———. *The Russian Church Under the Soviet Regime 1917–1982*. Vol. 1. Crestwood, NY: St. Vladimir's Seminary Press, 1984.

Powstenko, Olexa. *The Cathedral of St. Sophia in Kiev*. New York: The Ukrainian Academy of Arts and Sciences in the United States, 1954.

Prelovs'ka, Irina. *Джерела з історії Української Автокефальної Православної Церкви (1921–1930)—Української Православної Церкви (1930–1939)*. Kyiv: Inst. Українсʹкої Archeohrafiï ta Džereloznavstva Im. M. S. Hruševsʹkoho NAN Ukraïny, 2013.

Protjuk, Metropolitan Feodosij. *Обособленческие движения в Православной церкви на Украине, 1917–1943*. Moscow: Izdatelstvo Krutitskogo podvorja, 2004.

Rapp, Claudia. "Spiritual Guarantors at Penance, Baptism, and Ordination in Late Antique East." In *A New History of Penance*, edited by Abigail Firey, 121–48. Leiden: Brill, 2008.

Renoux, Athanase, ed. *Le Codex Arménien Jérusalem 121. I. Introduction aux origines de la liturgie hiérosolymitaine: Lumières nouvelles*. Patrologia Orientalis 35.1. Turnhout: Brepols, 1969.

———. *Le Codex Arménien Jérusalem 121. II. Édition Comparée du texte et de deux autres manuscrits*, introduction, textes, traduction et notes par A. Renoux. Patrologia Orientalis 36.2. Turnhout: Brepols, 1971.

Ruggieri, Vincenzo. *Byzantine Religious Architecture (582–867): Its History and Structural Elements.* Orientalia Christiana Analecta 237. Rome: Pontifical Oriental Institute, 1991.

Russo, Nicholas. "The Distribution of Cyril's Baptismal Catecheses and the Shape of the Catechumenate in Mid-Fourth-Century Jerusalem." In *A Living Tradition: On the Intersection of Liturgical History and Pastoral Practice, Essays in Honor of Maxwell E. Johnson,* edited by David Pitt, Stefanos Alexopoulos, and Christian McConnell, 75–102. Collegeville, MN: Liturgical Press, 2012.

Saradi, Helen G. "Space in Byzantine Thought." In *Architecture as Icon: Perception and Representation of Architecture in Byzantine Art.* Edited by Slobodan Ćurčić and Evangelia Hadjitryphonos. Princeton, NJ: Princeton University Art Museum, 2010.

Schmemann, Alexander. *Introduction to Liturgical Theology.* Translated by Asheleigh E. Moorhouse. Crestwood, NY: St. Vladimir's Seminary Press, 1986.

———. "Meaningful Storm: Some Reflections on Autocephaly, Tradition and Ecclesiology." *St. Vladimir's Theological Quarterly* 15, nos. 1–2 (1971): 3–27.

Schulz, Hans-Joachim. *The Byzantine Liturgy: Symbolic Structure and Faith Expression.* Translated by Matthew J. O'Connell. New York: Pueblo, 1986.

Seasoltz, Kevin. "Sacred Space, the Arts, and Theology: Some Light from History." *Worship* 82 (2008): 519–42.

———. *Sense of the Sacred: Theological Foundations of Christian Architecture and Art.* New York: Continuum, 2005.

Service and Akathist to Our Father Among the Saints John, Archbishop of Shanghai and San Francisco, The Wonderworker. San Francisco: Russkiy pastyr, originally published in 2004, 2013 revision.

Shoemaker, Stephen. *Ancient Traditions of the Virgin Mary's Dormition and Assumption.* New York: Oxford University Press, 2002.

Slagle, Amy. *The Eastern Church in the Spiritual Marketplace: American Conversions to Orthodox Christianity.* DeKalb: Northern Illinois University Press, 2011.

Slater, Wendy. "Relics, Remains, and Revisionism: Narratives of Nicholas II in Contemporary Russia." *Rethinking History: The Journal of Theory and Practice* 9, no. 1 (2005): 53–70.

St. Vladimir's Seminary. *Consecration of the Three Hierarchs Chapel: St. Vladimir's Seminary.* New York: Athens Printing Company, 1983.

St. Vladimir's Theological Foundation. *14th Annual Orthodox Education Day.* Crestwood, NY: n.p., 1983.

Stokes, Mark, and Leonid Kishkovsky. *Orthodox Christians in North America, 1794–1994*. N.p.: Orthodox Christian Publication Center, 1995.

Subtelny, Orest. *Ukraine: A History*. Toronto: University of Toronto Press, 1989.

Святитель Іоаннъ (Максимовичъ) и Русская Зарубежная Церковь. Jordanville, NY: Holy Trinity Monastery, 1996.

Sysyn, Frank E. "The Ukrainian Autocephalous Orthodox Church and the Traditions of the Kyiv Metropolitanate." In *Religion and Nation in Modern Ukraine*, edited by Serhii Plokhy and Frank E. Sysyn, 23–39. Edmonton: Canadian Institute of Ukrainian Studies, 2003.

Taft, Robert F. *Beyond East and West: Problems in Liturgical Understanding*. 2nd ed. Washington, DC: Pastoral Press, 1997.

———. "The Byzantine Office in the Prayerbook of New Skete: A Critique." *Orientalia Christiana Periodica* 48 (1982): 336–70.

———. *The Byzantine Rite: A Short History*. Collegeville, MN: Liturgical Press, 1992.

———. *A History of the Liturgy of St. John Chrysostom,* vol. 2, *The Great Entrance: A History of the Transfer of Gifts and Other Pre-anaphoral Rites*. 2nd ed. Orientalia Christiana Analecta 200. Rome: Pontifical Oriental Institute, 1978.

———. "Is the Liturgy Described in the Mystagogia of Maximus Confessor Byzantine, Palestinian, or Neither?" *Bollettino della badia Greca di Grottaferrata* 7 (2010): 247–95.

———. "The Liturgical Enterprise Twenty-five Years after Alexander Schmemann (1921–1983): The Man and His Heritage." *St. Vladimir's Theological Quarterly* 53, nos. 2–3 (2009): 139–77.

———. "The Liturgy of the Great Church: An Initial Synthesis of Structure and Interpretation on the Eve of Iconoclasm." *Dumbarton Oaks Papers* 34–35 (1980–81): 45–75.

———. *The Liturgy of the Hours in East and West: The Origins of the Divine Office and Its Meaning for Today*. 2nd rev. ed. Collegeville, MN: Liturgical Press, 1995.

———. "Mount Athos: A Late Chapter in the History of the Byzantine Rite." *Dumbarton Oaks Papers* (1988): 179–94.

———. *Through Their Own Eyes: Liturgy as the Byzantines Saw It*. Berkeley, CA: InterOrthodox Press, 2006.

———, William Loerke, and Mark. J. Johnson. "Pastophoria." In *The Oxford Dictionary of Byzantium*. Edited by Alexander Kazhdan. Oxford: Oxford University Press, 1991.

Talbot, Alice-Mary. "Epigrams of Manuel Philes on the Theotokos tes Peges and Its Art." *Dumbarton Oaks Papers* 48 (1994): 135–65.

Tarchnischvili, Michael, ed. *Le grand lectionnaire de l'Église de Jérusalem Ve–VIIIe siècle*. Corpus scriptorum Christianorum Orientalium 189. Louvain: Secrétariat du Corpus SCO, 1959.

Theophan the Recluse. *The Path to Salvation: A Manual of Spiritual Transformation*. Translated by Seraphim Rose and the St. Herman of Alaska Brotherhood. Platina, CA: St. Herman of Alaska Brotherhood, 1990.

Torrance, Alexis. *Repentance in Late Antiquity: Eastern Asceticism and the Framing of the Christian Life c. 400–650 CE*. Oxford: Oxford University Press, 2013.

Типікон. Moscow: Publishing Council of the Russian Orthodox Church, 2002.

Turner, Jack. "The Journey Thus Far: A Review of the Literature of Western-Rite Orthodoxy." *St. Vladimir's Theological Quarterly* 53, no. 4 (2009): 477–505.

———. "Western Rite Orthodoxy as a Liturgical Problem." *Journal of Eastern Christian Studies* 63, nos. 3–4 (2011): 333–52.

Vinogradov, Alexis. "The Architecture of Eastern Orthodox Churches: Contemporary Trends and Possibilities." *Koinonia: The Journal of the Anglican and Eastern Churches Association* 54 (2008): 1–11.

Vosko, Richard. "The Language of Liturgical Space: Archetypes and Clichés." *Worship* 86 (2012): 55–59.

Vrame, Anton, ed. *The Orthodox Parish in America: Faithfulness to the Past and Responsibility for the Future*. Brookline, MA: Holy Cross Orthodox Press, 2003.

Waghorne, Joanne Punzo. "The Hindu Gods in a Split-Level World: The Sri Siva-Vishnu Temple in Suburban Washington, D.C." In *Gods of the City*, edited by Robert Orsi, 103–30. Bloomington: Indiana University Press, 1999.

———. "Spaces for a New Public Presence: The Sri Sivu Vishnu and Murugan Temples in Metropolitan Washington, D.C." In *American Sanctuary: Understanding Sacred Spaces*, edited by Louis Nelson, 103–27. Bloomington: Indiana University Press, 2006.

Ware, Kallistos. "'The Final Mystery': The Dormition of the Holy Virgin in Orthodox Worship." In *Mary for Time and Eternity: Essays on Mary and Ecumenism*, edited by William M. McLoughlin and Jill Pinnock, foreword by Frances Young, 219–54. Papers on Mary and Ecumenism at International Congresses of the Ecumenical Society of the Blessed Virgin Mary. Gloucester: Ecumenical Society of the Blessed Virgin Mary, 2007.

———. *The Orthodox Church*. London: Penguin, 1963, 1964, 1993 reprint.

Wilkinson, John. *Egeria's Travels*. Warminster: Aris & Phillips, 1999.

Winner, Brother Stavros. "The Monastery and Applied Liturgical Renewal." In *Worship Traditions and Armenia and the Neighboring Christian East: An International Symposium in Honor of the 40th Anniversary of St Nersess Armenian Seminary*, edited by Roberta R. Ervine, 307–24. Crestwood, NY: St. Vladimir's Seminary Press, St. Nersess Armenian Seminary, 2006.

Wlasowsky, Ivan. *Нарис Історії Української Православної Церкви*. Vol. 2. New York: Ukrainian Orthodox Church of the USA, 1956.

Wortley, John. "Icons and Relics: A Comparison." *Greek, Roman, and Byzantine Studies* 43, no. 2 (2002–3): 161–74.

Wybrew, Hugh. *The Orthodox Liturgy: The Development of the Eucharistic Liturgy in the Byzantine Rite*. Crestwood, NY: St. Vladimir's Seminary Press, 1990.

Zagraevsky, S. V. *Зодчество Северо-Восточной Руси конца XIII-первой трети XIV века*. Moscow: n.p., 2003.

Zaverukha, Lydia B., and Nina Bogdan. *Images of America: Russian San Francisco*. Foreword by Ludmila Ershova. Charleston: Arcadia Publishing, 2010.

Zinkewych, Osyp, and Olexander Voronyn, eds. *Мартирологія Українських Церков*. Vol. 1. Baltimore: Smoloskyp Publishers, 1987.

INDEX

NICHOLAS DENYSENKO

is associate professor of theological studies at Loyola
Marymount University.

CPSIA information can be obtained
at www.ICGtesting.com
Printed in the USA
LVOW06*0233050517
533298LV00003B/4/P